St Antony's/Macmillan Series

General Editors: Archie Brown (1978–1985) and Rosemary Thorp
(1985–), both Fellows of St Antony's College, Oxford

Recent titles include:

Gail Lee Bernstein and Haruhiro Fukui (*editors*)
JAPAN AND THE WORLD
Archie Brown (*editor*)
POLITICAL LEADERSHIP IN THE SOVIET UNION
Deborah Fahy Bryceson
FOOD INSECURITY AND THE SOCIAL DIVISION OF LABOUR IN
  TANZANIA, 1919–85
Victor Bulmer-Thomas
STUDIES IN THE ECONOMICS OF CENTRAL AMERICA
Sir Alec Cairncross
PLANNING IN WARTIME: AIRCRAFT PRODUCTION IN BRITAIN,
  GERMANY AND THE USA
Helen Callaway
GENDER, CULTURE AND EMPIRE
David Cleary
ANATOMY OF THE AMAZON GOLD RUSH
Roger Cooter (*editor*)
STUDIES IN THE HISTORY OF ALTERNATIVE MEDICINE
Robert Desjardins
THE SOVIET UNION THROUGH FRENCH EYES
Guido di Tella and Carlos Rodríguez Braun (*editors*)
ARGENTINA, 1946–83: THE ECONOMIC MINISTERS SPEAK
Guido di Tella and D. Cameron Watt (*editors*)
ARGENTINA BETWEEN THE GREAT POWERS, 1939–46
Guido de Tella and Rudiger Dornbusch (*editors*)
POLITICAL ECONOMY OF ARGENTINA, 1946–83
Saul Dubow
RACIAL SEGREGATION AND THE ORIGINS OF APARTHEID IN SOUTH
  AFRICA, 1919–36
Anne Lincoln Fitzpatrick
THE GREAT RUSSIAN FAIR
Heather D. Gibson
THE EUROCURRENCY MARKETS, DOMESTIC FINANCIAL POLICY AND
  INTERNATIONAL INSTABILITY
David Hall-Cathala
THE PEACE MOVEMENT IN ISRAEL, 1967–87
John B. Hattendorf and Robert S. Jordan (*editors*)
MARITIME STRATEGY AND THE BALANCE OF POWER
Linda Hitchcox
VIETNAMESE REFUGEES IN SOUTHEAST ASIAN CAMPS
Derek Hopwood (*editor*)
STUDIES IN ARAB HISTORY

Amitzur Ilan
BERNADOTTE IN PALESTINE, 1948
Hiroshi Ishida
SOCIAL MOBILITY IN CONTEMPORARY JAPAN
J. R. Jennings
SYNDICALISM IN FRANCE
Maria d'Alva G. Kinzo
LEGAL OPPOSITION POLITICS UNDER AUTHORITARIAN RULE IN
  BRAZIL
Bohdan Krawchenko
SOCIAL CHANGE AND NATIONAL CONSCIOUSNESS IN TWENTIETH-
  CENTURY UKRAINE
Robert H. McNeal
STALIN: MAN AND RULER
Iftikhar H. Malik
US-SOUTH ASIAN RELATIONS, 1940–47
Amii Omara-Otunnu
POLITICS AND THE MILITARY IN UGANDA, 1890–1985
Ilan Pappé
BRITAIN AND THE ARAB–ISRAELI CONFLICT, 1948–51
J. L. Porket
WORK, EMPLOYMENT AND UNEMPLOYMENT IN THE SOVIET UNION
Brian Powell
KABUKI IN MODERN JAPAN
Alex Pravda
HOW RULING COMMUNIST PARTIES ARE GOVERNED
Laurie P. Salitan
POLITICS AND NATIONALITY IN CONTEMPORARY SOVIET-JEWISH
  EMIGRATION, 1968–89
H. Gordon Skilling
CZECHOSLOVAKIA, 1918–88 (editor)
SAMIZDAT AND AN INDEPENDENT SOCIETY IN CENTRAL AND
  EASTERN EUROPE
J. A. A. Stockwin, Alan Rix, Aurelia George, James Horne, Daichi Itô,
  Martin Collick
DYNAMIC AND IMMOBILIST POLITICS IN JAPAN
Verena Stolcke
COFFEE PLANTERS, WORKERS AND WIVES
Jane E. Stromseth
THE ORIGINS OF FLEXIBLE RESPONSE
Joseph S. Szyliowicz
POLITICS, TECHNOLOGY AND DEVELOPMENT
Jane Watts
BLACK WRITERS FROM SOUTH AFRICA
Philip J. Williams
THE CATHOLIC CHURCH AND POLITICS IN NICARAGUA AND
  COSTA RICA

Planning in Wartime

Aircraft Production in Britain, Germany and the USA

Sir Alec Cairncross
Supernumerary Fellow, St Antony's College, Oxford
and Chancellor, University of Glasgow

M

MACMILLAN

in association with
ST ANTONY'S COLLEGE
OXFORD

First published 1991

Published by
MACMILLAN ACADEMIC AND PROFESSIONAL LTD
Houndmills, Basingstoke, Hampshire RG21 2XS
and London
Companies and representatives
throughout the world

Printed in Hong Kong

British Library Cataloguing in Publication Data
Cairncross, Sir Alec 1911–
Planning in wartime: aircraft production in Britain,
Germany and the USA – (St Antony's/Macmillan series)
1. Great Britain. Ministry of Aircraft Production.
Policies, history, industrial economics
I. Title II. St Antony's College III. Series
355.6
ISBN 0–333–53840–4

Series Standing Order

If you would like to receive future titles in this series as they are
published, you can make use of our standing order facility. To place a
standing order please contact your bookseller or, in case of difficulty,
write to us at the address below with your name and address and the
name of the series. Please state with which title you wish to begin your
standing order. (If you live outside the United Kingdom we may not
have the rights for your area, in which case we will forward your order
to the publisher concerned.)

Customer Services Department, Macmillan Distribution Ltd
Houndmills, Basingstoke, Hampshire, RG21 2XS, England.

To the memory of
Ely Devons

Contents

List of Tables and Figures

List of Abbreviations

AD	Assistant Director
AMSO	Air Member for Supply and Organisation
ANB	Army and Navy Board
APB	Aircraft Production Board
ARCO	Aircraft Resources Control Office
ASU	Aircraft Scheduling Unit
BMW	Bayerische Motorenwerke
BOAC	British Overseas Airways Corporation
BSC	British Supply Council
CE	Chief Executive
CFE	Contractor furnished equipment
CIGS	Chief of the Imperial General Staff
C-in-C	Commander-in-Chief
CMA	Controller Materials Allocation
CRD	Controller of Research and Development
CSU	Constant speed unit
DDGQP	Deputy Director General of Equipment Production
DDG Stats P	Deputy Director General, Statistics and Planning Programmes
DDRDA	Deputy Director of Research and Development, Aircraft
DGAP	Director General of Aircraft Production
DGAI	Director General of Aeronautical Inspection
DGCA	Director General of Civil Aviation
DGCE	Director General of Communications Equipment
DGE	Director General of Equipment
DGEMP	Director General of Engines and Materials Production
DRM	Director of Repairs and Maintenance
DTD	Director of Technical Development
GFE	Government furnished equipment
ICI	Imperial Chemical Industries
JAC	Joint Aircraft Commission
MAP	Ministry of Aircraft Production
NDAC	National Defence Advisory Committee
OPM	Office of Production Management
POAE	Principal Officer for Aircraft Equipment

RAF	Royal Air Force
R and D	Research and Development
RLM	Reichsluftfahrtministerium
RPO	Resident Production Officer
RTO	Resident Technical Officer
WPB	War Production Board
USSBS	United States Strategic Bombing Survey
VCIGS	Vice-Chief of the Imperial General Staff

Preface

This book began as a personal memoir, based largely on a wartime diary, and was designed to give an account of what it was like to work in a department planning the activities of some two million people. The theme I had in mind was that planning was just as likely to take the form of muddle qualified by organisation as organisation imposing itself on muddle. Too much is written in terms of a never-never land of perfect planning and too little from first-hand knowledge of its endemic limitations and failings.

In refreshing my memory at the Public Record Office I found history beginning to take over the memoir and called a halt before the lasting impressions formed from the inside became swallowed up in a narrative account pieced together from the outside, using surviving documents.

When it came to preparing the sketches I have given of planning in Germany and the United States, there could be no question of drawing on recollections of what it was like inside the planning system. There is an abundance of historical accounts, but few are informed by past participation in the planning process or concentrate on the fundamental problem of coordination. Most historians confine themselves to an account of the expansion of the aircraft industry in wartime and the planning that this involved, without more than a passing reference to the problem of preserving balance between the many thousands of components that go to make an aeroplane.

In the case of Germany I was fortunate enough to come upon a first-class doctoral thesis by Richard Overy to whom I am greatly indebted for permission to draw on and quote from it. While some of his research appears in his books, *Goering* and *The Air War*, the bulk of it remains unpublished in Cambridge University library. Dr Overy has read the section dealing with German aircraft production and I am greatly indebted to him for useful comments and suggestions. In the case of the United States I found some of the most useful material in the Public Record Office in *The British History of the Aircraft Scheduling Unit* and an account by Professor John Jewkes of his impressions of American aircraft planning in two reports written after visits to the United States in 1942 and 1943.

I have been greatly assisted by comments from my former colleagues in the Ministry of Aircraft Production, Professor and Mrs

Tew. Among others who have provided useful information and comments are Mr. A. J. Nicholls, St Antony's College, Oxford; Mr D. J. Wenden, All Souls College, Oxford; Dr W. P. Howlett, London School of Economics; Professor Dr W. Deist and Dr Horst Boog of the Militärgeschichtliches Forschungsamt, Freiburg-im-Breisgau; Professor Dr Reiner Pommerin, University of Erlangen; Mr Gregory Franklin, Office of Air Force History, Department of the Air Force, Washington DC; Mr Walter Salant, Emeritus Fellow, Brookings Institution, Washington DC; and Miss Paula Thornhill, Merton College, Oxford.

I am grateful also for the help of the staff of the Public Record Office, Kew, and Rhodes House Library, Oxford; to Mrs Anne Robinson for her conversion of my scribbles into impeccable typescript, and to Mrs Anne Rafique for the many improvements she made to the text on its way to the printer.

ALEC CAIRNCROSS

Introduction: Planning Aircraft Production

No one has written a history of the Ministry of Aircraft Production (MAP) – at least not a history describing what happened within the organisation. No history is ever likely to be written so long after the event, especially in view of the limited information on matters of policy which survives in the Public Record Office.[1] It is true that the histories of war production by Postan and Scott and Hughes[2] deal at some length with the aircraft industry; but they rarely touch, except in a rather hushed way, on what went on *inside* the Ministry. And yet it is what happened inside the Ministry that is of lasting interest. For MAP was an experiment in the planning of civilian activity on a scale beyond anything attempted at any other time by a British government. At peak nearly two million workers were producing aircraft and other military equipment under the direction of the Ministry. It is this aspect of MAP – *Planning in Practice* as Ely Devons (latterly the chief planner) called it in the title of the book he published in 1950[3] – that makes it worth studying even now.

Devons's book is almost a textbook in industrial organisation, drawing its examples from the manufacture of aircraft. It is un-equalled as an anatomy of planning, whether in a war economy, in a communist economy, or in any giant enterprise such as the Ministry of Aircraft Production, its nominal subject. But it is, quite deliberately, a depersonified account and does not convey, or aim to convey except incidentally, what it was like to work in the department. Indeed it tends, by dwelling on the *rationale* of planning procedures in MAP, to make the planning decisions that were taken correspondingly *rational* when Devons was only too well aware that life in MAP was one long battle with muddle.

The public, after the war, may have regarded MAP as offering striking testimony to the virtues of economic planning; and there were those who worked in the Ministry – but *not* in the Planning Department – who publicly encouraged this belief. It may be useful, even after the lapse of over forty years, to provide some first-hand evidence on what went on in the planning of aircraft production, illustrating the different aspects of the planning process, and doing justice to its shortcomings as well as its successes.

What follows is intended as a supplement to Devons's analysis and
takes the form of a personal account, based on the four years I spent
in MAP beginning in December 1941. I have relied heavily on my
diary but since this is very patchy, with long gaps between entries,
especially in 1943, the account is more a collection of notes than a
continuous narrative.

I have been conscious in writing this account that planning aircraft
production after 1941 was a very different affair from the planning
that went on earlier. That had been mainly concerned with enlarging
the capacity of the aircraft industry, selecting the right models to
produce and gearing production plans to the eventual size and make-
up of the Air Force. By the end of 1941 that stage in planning had
been virtually completed. The frantic efforts of 1940 to boost
production while the Battle of Britain was in progress were a thing of
the past, the dispersal of production to new locations after the
bombing of aircraft factories was largely over and it was possible to
maintain a steadier and more predictable pace. Planning had become
a matter of coordinating production flows so that components of all
kinds would become available for assembly in the right quantities at
the right time, without shortages and bottlenecks, while amendments
to the aircraft programme took account of the supply position of the
main components, and the production of components was adjusted in
the light of these amendments.

Part I

Great Britain

Part I

Great Britain

1 Planning and Coordination

Let me begin by summarising the thesis from which Devons set out. War, he pointed out, is a great centraliser. It is the government that conducts the war, decides what strategy to follow, and determines how the country's resources can best be used if the war is to be won. For this purpose it assumes in total war all necessary powers, taking control over the entire economy and acting as 'the sole consumer of the products of the economic system', even to deciding what should be left for civilian consumption. Civilians are regarded as instruments for carrying on the war rather than as 'individual persons with separate and different objectives of their own'. A war economy is thus in complete antithesis to a decentralised, consumer-driven, peacetime economy in which market forces, expressing the myriad preferences of individual producers and consumers, dominate the pattern of production and consumption, with the government intervening here and there.

But, secondly, the centralisation of decisions cannot be carried to the point at which they are all taken simultaneously by one superman uniting in himself all the powers and responsibilities of government. The faster decisions multiply, the more essential it is to engage in delegation and create a multiplicity of administrative units to match the multiplicity of decisions. Thus instead of a single dictator there is a cabinet of ministers, and under them a large number of departments, which in turn are divided into separate sections made up of smaller sub-sections and sub-sub-sections, each with its own limited field of responsibility. Delegation means the creation of administrative hierarchies in which decisions taken at one level may be reviewed at a higher level and decisions taken in one hierarchy have to be reconciled with decisions taken in another.

Thus there arises, thirdly, the problem of coordination. If decisions cannot be automatically coordinated in the mind of some extraordinary superman, familiar with every circumstance however detailed, they have to be made as consistent as possible by other means. Unfortunately coordination is extremely difficult: different divisions and sub-divisions are liable to go their own way. Those at the periphery act in ignorance or in disregard of what is being decided at

3

the centre while those at the centre plan in ignorance or in disregard of what is going on at the periphery. The problem intensifies the larger the numbers involved and the more varied the circumstances that each confronts. It is magnified still further by human factors that get in the way of united action, by limited information and limited power to assess and assimilate it, and above all by the rapidity of change and the uncertainties that change creates: uncertainties as to what is going on, as to the reactions of others in the hierarchy, and as to the consequences of whatever is done. In a world at war, rapid and unexpected change is the order of the day and there is an inevitable tension between the urge to leave things to the man on the spot, who is better informed and more up-to-date on matters within his immediate view, and insisting on conformity with a general plan that takes account of wider considerations. The further delegation is carried from one motive, the greater the difficulty of coordination from the other. As Devons pointed out in a striking passage worth quoting at length:

> Every attempt at planning reveals these two problems: first, the need to split up the field to be covered so that each administrative unit can deal efficiently with its own sector; and second, the need to secure that the actions of these separate units all fit into the general plan. But the implementation of these principles always leads to a conflict. For the first requires delegation and devolution, so that plans can be manageable and realistic; and the second requires centralization, so that plans can be co-ordinated.
>
> This conflict between devolution and centralization appeared at every stage in the administrative hierarchy. At each level the co-ordinators regarded the plans of the individual sectors as futile and wasteful, because they took no account of what was happening elsewhere; and those in charge of individual sectors regarded the plans of the co-ordinators as theoretical, academic, and unrelated to the real facts of the situation. On the highest level there was a conflict between the central co-ordinators in the Cabinet Office and Ministry of Production and the planners in the individual departments. The supreme co-ordinators struggled for more centralization, the planners in each department for more to be left to their discretion. But inside each department, the planners, who argued for delegation when dealing with the central organs of Government, argued for centralization of decisions inside their own department. And they, in turn, were in conflict with the individual production divisions in each department, who regarded the work of

the central planners in their own departments as unrealistic. The tables were again turned in the relations between the individual production divisions and the firms. For to the firms the officials of MAP, even at the production level, were co-ordinators who knew little of what was really happening inside the factories. And no doubt the same conflict was repeated at various levels inside the individual firm and factory organization.

Given the limitations of the human mind and capacity, this conflict was inevitable, and was the greatest obstacle to efficient aircraft planning. If the inevitablity of this conflict is not recognized, planning becomes even more inefficient than it need be. For in such circumstances those who influence the planning machinery oscillate between a passion for decentralization, as a result of an exaggerated awareness of the inefficiencies of centralization; and a drive towards central co-ordination as a result of a terror of the illogicalities which emerge when important decisions are taken at the periphery. The system then reels between a condition where action, since delegated and decentralized, is speedy but unco-ordinated and therefore often futile, and a condition where action is coordinated, since highly centralized, but for that very reason often slow and unrealistic. The balance between the two is never found, since at each stage the evils of the existing system and the advantages of the alternative always impress most.[1]

These abstract considerations may seem far removed from the practical problems of planning aircraft production. Not so. They were very much in our minds in seeking to establish a division of labour between ourselves as planners and other departments of MAP concerned with the production of aircraft and aircraft components. We had to be quite clear that planning meant coordination and that this in turn involved establishing requirements and marrying them with production possibilities in a series of programmes. If we did our job properly other departments would have less difficulty in helping aircraft firms to meet their programme or could concentrate more successfully on other functions: developing new and better products, creating additional capacity when it was required, issuing contracts, and so on. But if they tried to do our job for us or declined to be coordinated, output would suffer in the ensuing muddle and we should have to give up our attempt at planning.

We had also to recognise our own limitations and not attempt more than we could do. There were some items such as aero-engines and propellers where coordination with the aircraft programme was indispensable and others such as radio where it was much less important. It would be wise, given our limited capabilities, to concentrate on items of the first kind and decline to multiply programmes beyond what we could manage properly.

A month after Stafford Cripps was appointed Minister of Aircraft Production in November 1942 he went round our chart room with John Jewkes and Ely Devons. 'There is no limit, in theory, is there', he asked, 'to central planning?'. It was a view that Cripps continued to hold and that was given frequent expression by others in post-war years. But as the argument above implies, it is profoundly mistaken. It overlooks the influence of ignorance and uncertainty, the inevitability of delegation, and the inescapable imperfections of the coordinating process. The limits to coordination are essentially the limits to centralisation. These limits were all to plain even in wartime. But in peacetime, so long as consumers and producers are free to decide what they want to do and where they want to work, the forces making for decentralisation are far, far stronger. If war centralises, market forces decentralise; and there is no way in which market forces can be superseded without abandoning freedom of choice and assuming dictatorial powers.

2 Planning in MAP

Until May 1940 when Churchill took over the reins of government
there had been no Ministry of Aircraft Production; arrangements for
the production of aircraft were the responsibility of the Air Ministry.
The needs of the army, navy and air force were all catered for by that
department. It is hardly surprising in these circumstances that the
RAF enjoyed priority over the army and navy, or that the dive
bomber and the seaplane were ranked well below the fighter and the
heavy bomber. Churchill, who had been Minister of Munitions in the
First World War, was a firm believer in taking away from Service
departments responsibility for production of the weapons they used
and took steps to put an end to the exercise of this responsibility by
the Air Ministry. He set up a new department, hived off from the Air
Ministry, to put fresh urgency into the production of aircraft.
Beaverbrook, the first Minister of Aircraft Production, was full of
energy for this task and in the critical summer of 1940 output
responded strongly. Production of combat aircraft climbed from 325
a month at the outbreak of war to 1000 a month by July 1940. But as
time went on, the results of Beaverbrook's efforts were less happy. In
the first half of 1941 output was still just over 1000 a month (although
in terms of structure weight there had been some further expansion).
There was too much drive and too little coordination so that
production had become increasingly disorganised.

A PLANNING DEPARTMENT?

Some of the officials in MAP, particularly the Permanent Secretary,
Sir Archibald Rowlands, asked themselves whether the disorganisation could be reduced by setting up a planning department. Under
Beaverbrook there had been no planning department for the simple
reason that he did not believe in planning. Improvisation? – Yes, of
course. Priority? – Yes, provided it was priority for MAP, not the
Ministry of Supply or some other department. But to lay out
production programmes for aircraft and aircraft components covering
the next two years would have seemed to him futile, if not an act of
downright sabotage.[1] For him the only programme was 'all that can
be done'.

It was not until Beaverbrook ceased to be Minister in May 1941 (to be succeeded in fairly rapid succession by Moore-Brabazon, J. J. Llewellyn, and Stafford Cripps) that Rowlands felt able to pursue the idea of a planning department. He invited John Jewkes, then head of the Economic Section of the War Cabinet Offices, to prepare a report on the subject in May 1941 and Jewkes in turn asked Norman Chester and me, as colleagues of his in the Economic Section of the War Cabinet Offices, to lend a hand. Jewkes was no great admirer, then or afterwards, of central planning in principle and none of us had a very clear idea what planning aircraft production would involve in practice. The evidence we heard from those who worked in MAP conveyed little to us of what we later discovered to be the true state of affairs – not that there was any deliberate attempt to withhold information from us – but it was sufficient to convince us that there was a case for planning of some kind.

The upshot was that when he reported in September Jewkes was asked to take on the job of organising a new department of programmes and statistics. It was this department that I joined in December 1941. By that time Professor Jewkes had succeeded, not without difficulty, in building up a small professional staff of about a dozen, all of them with degrees in economics. (Seven of the staff subsequently occupied university chairs in economics.[2]) What he wanted me to do was to take charge of propeller planning. He put it to me that if I could increase the output of aircraft propellers even by one I should be adding an entire new aircraft to the RAF and that alone would make the move (from the Board of Trade) worthwhile. There were, he said, 300 propellerless Wellingtons on the beach at Blackpool and the whole propeller programme was in a frightful mess.

THE HEAVY BOMBER PROGRAMME

I arrived in MAP only a week or so before Pearl Harbor. A major decision to sanction a big increase in the heavy bomber programme was taken on the day after the attack, on 8 December 1941. We were of course enormously heartened by America's entry into the war and still more by Hitler's quite gratuitous declaration of war on America since this made sure of America's participation in the war in Europe. On the other hand, we were by no means happy about the heavy bomber programme since it seemed to us that with America as our ally we ought to change our production programmes quite radically in other directions, leaving the production of heavy bombers largely to the United States and concentrating on landing craft, tanks, fighters and other equipment needed for an invasion of Europe.[3]

It was not, however, our job to decide what kind of aircraft, and how many of each kind, should be manufactured. That was a form of planning that was normally undertaken at a different level, as part of the higher direction of the war. We might from time to time have some influence on such decisions, as explained below (p. 67), but our influence was as producers, not consumers, and could be exerted only when a decision as to what should be made rested heavily on an intimate knowledge of production possibilities.

At the end of 1941 the production of heavy bombers was still quite limited: less than 500 were produced in that year and production had yet to exceed 60 per month. But already the programme envisaged an expansion to over 600 heavy bombers per month by the end of 1943, a figure well above the maximum rate ever reached: only in one month – March 1944 – did output ever exceed 500. Even so, the heavy bomber programme was scheduled to absorb an increasing proportion of the resources at the disposal of MAP and to account eventually for nearly half the total. So long as this was so, the shape of the aircraft programme was set for the rest of the war and only marginal changes were possible after December 1941.

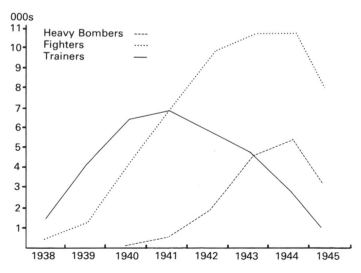

FIGURE 2.1   *Deliveries of heavy bombers, fighters and trainers, 1938–45.*

The planning in which we engaged, therefore, was quite unlike that of pre-war years when the decisions to be taken were dominated by military strategy on the one side and production engineering on the other. There was no question of planning what kind of air force should be created and no question also of planning for the creation of the necessary industrial capacity. We were concerned fundamentally with changes in programmes that were already too ambitious and possessed such a high degree of inertia that change could not be carried very far.

PUTTING THE STATISTICS IN ORDER

The first business of the new branch was to put the statistics in order. This had been our experience in the Economic Section in 1940 when one of the major tasks of the Section had been to produce a series of statistical bulletins, of which the *Monthly Digest of Statistics* is a lineal descendant. Without proper statistical records, production planning would have been a waste of time since it always rests heavily on an analysis of past trends and their projection into the future.[4] But the Ministry, as we discovered, had no adequate system of records either at the centre or in the various production divisions.

Registered files were generally confined to the finance and development branches of the Ministry and recorded the progress of a specific expansion scheme or piece of research. The production divisions kept their own unregistered files but these rarely circulated, communication between one division and another being either verbal, or by loose minute, or by comment on one of the Air Ministry files which occasionally made a fleeting tour of the Department.

Statistical records were in a still more primitive state. It was almost impossible to obtain a comprehensive statement of outstanding contracts at a given date, or to discover what cumulative deliveries of any component had been made up to that date. It was rare to find a production department that had gone to the trouble of keeping running records of deliveries in a form that gave a clear picture of the trend in output. The records of performance were generally supplied by the sales departments of the contractors and were compared, not with targets, but with contracts. There were no statistical bulletins to which it was possible to refer for information as to actual deliveries of aircraft and components. For long stretches of time there was either no aircraft programme, or no aircraft programme to which anyone paid any attention, or the aircraft programme was inaccessible to those who would most have liked to use it. There were no programmes, and never had been, for any aircraft component.

In a ministry of this kind, the atmosphere of rumour and gossip in which decisions were taken can hardly be conveyed. Production directors had no one to whom they could turn for a statement of requirements. They did not know the aircraft programme, the extent to which firms were falling down on their programme, the priorities that should have been observed, the changes in requirements which current development made probable, nor the requirements of the Air Ministry for spares after existing orders had been completed. Ignorance of this kind made it impossible for accurate planning to be undertaken, and snap decisions were the rule. It was frequent for the imminence of a major crisis to be detected only when the crisis had already broken. Each production department, as it took its share of the catastrophes that visited one after another, was constantly struggling to rid itself of a shortage which it had not foreseen, or piling up a surplus which it continued to discount.

Even in such an atmosphere, something might have been done had there been proper coordination, so that all decisions were carefully related to one another and every decision was the recognised responsibility of a specific department. But the decisions taken at one level or in one department often failed to reach the officer whose function it was to implement them or who was most affected by them. It was quite common for the research departments to busy themselves with production problems, for the production departments to lay down the law about requirements, and for the programmes department to usurp the duties of research and development. It was rarely possible to say over any point at issue, with whom it rested to give a final decision, or who should be consulted before a decision was reached, or who should be told the terms of the decision when it was taken. It was futile to expect guidance from higher up since the 'high-ups', who steadily multiplied in number, were uncertain of their functions or had their attention riveted on points of detail, and when they did attempt to lay down a clear line of policy, showed a terrifying partiality for the absurd, the dramatic, and the wasteful. Major decisions of policy, as often as not, were taken, not wilfully or consciously, but unconsciously and by default, by junior officers who were hardly aware that to do nothing was to take a major decision.[5]

One of Jewkes's first acts had been to persuade Ely Devons to join him and take charge of statistics. It was Devons who had been chiefly

responsible for the preparation of the new statistical bulletins issued
by the Economic Section (and later by the Central Statistical Office)
in 1940–41. He now set about collecting material for a similar
statistical digest, with tables showing the output in successive months
of the various aircraft and the main aircraft components by type and
manufacturer. This highly secret information went to not far short of
200 people, to the horrified disapproval of people like Lord Beaverbrook who were more shocked that such secrets should be revealed to
so many people than that anyone should have thought it possible to
plan aircraft production without them.[6] Yet until the statistics had
been assembled and distributed in this way (and not left isolated in
the usual form of incidental statistics known only to a few) there
could be no proper coordination since it was impossible to judge what
was happening and what most needed to be done.

The place of statistics in planning and coordination was not,
however, well understood. Our experience was that colleagues in the
Ministry, from the Chief Executive downwards, tended to regard
statisticians as small fry who might be asked to supply or check a
figure but had no central place in organising the production of
aircraft. We were 'the statistical people', lacking the authority of
members of production departments who were assumed (often quite
wrongly) to be better informed and (often with little more justification) to have the advantage of being technically qualified. It was not
appreciated that coordination is a quite different function from that
of supervising production and rests on a far wider range of information, much of it statistical. As Ely Devons put it, 'statistics is the
language of planning': planning decisions, being essentially choices
between expected outcomes, are almost always quantitative and call
for an intimate knowledge of the magnitudes involved.

The top brass, with few exceptions, had little understanding of
economics or statistics. One had only to listen to them discussing
labour mobility in the closing stages of the war to appreciate how wild
their generalisations could be. They were, of course, used to dealing
with particular figures but not to drawing conclusions from time series
or more complex sets of data, or to generalising by setting the
individual instance against the background of a valid rule. Statistical
tables made little impression on them and their grasp of the elemen-
tary facts of chart construction was fallible in the extreme.

For example, Devons describes the reactions of Sir Charles Bruce
Gardner, Controller of Labour Allocation and Supply, when, on
being shown a chart of structure weight of aircraft per person

employed, he asked to have it copied and enlarged. The source of Sir Charles' fascination was what he took to be a steep upward trend in productivity – a trend which in the enlarged copy, with scales adapted to the size of the chart paper, was much less pronounced. The change in trend produced expressions of bewilderment and consernation, ending with a request for a photographic enlargement of the original so as to preserve the steep upward trend, which Sir Charles evidently thought a truer picture than that shown in the enlargement.[7]

PRODUCTION PROGRAMMES

In parallel with the issue of statistical bulletins we set about preparing a series of production programmes, starting with the 'heavy bomber' aircraft programme of December 1941. Production programmes were such a natural means of organising the activities of the Ministry that it may seem surprising that they were not in use much earlier. There had, of course, always been production programmes for *aircraft*; but apart from the peak rate of output which the Ministry *had* to agree, these had usually been little more than the promises of aircraft manufacturers. What was novel in our approach was the extension of planning to aircraft components, and the effort to ensure consistency between the various programmes instead of leaving things to aircraft manufacturers and their staffs of chasers.

One reason why a more elaborate system of planning had become necessary was that by 1941 MAP was working on a scale far beyond that of pre-war years: at peak it employed nearly two million men. To organise so large a labour force called for a much more systematic form of coordination than in the days in the 1930s when the RAF could keep track of every single aero-engine by sticking coloured pins in a board. In those days it had been enough to plan airframes and work out the capacity needed to meet the expected peak.

The second reason for the absence of production programmes of the kind now thought normal was the need in 1940 to change priorities abruptly as the war changed course. Beaverbrook was no believer in planning (but then, neither was Jewkes) nor in paper work when the house was obviously on fire. He was essentially a privateer who did not in the least mind a little piracy if it served some immediate need at the expense of another department. In his view MAP was entitled to an overriding priority and on the whole he had quite a good eye for priorities. But except in the very short run it is allocation, not priority, that must govern the proper organisation of resources, and Beaverbrook had no intention of abiding by any allocation if he could find a way round it.

The third reason for the lack of production planning was quite simply that British industry had little experience of it. Long after the war there were plenty of British firms that treated production planning in the manner of a small builder who can never stick to the dates he promises: a request for a production schedule is still often met by a vague promise to 'see what can be done'.

Nowadays we associate production programmes with long production runs of standardised goods, often consumer durables, with extensive tooling, line production, and careful design of the product, backed by research and development. All this is relatively new, whether one thinks of production planning or of research and development. Few firms in pre-war days undertook development work on any scale, especially work involving the construction of prototypes, pilot plants, etc. Rolls Royce was one of the few companies that took development seriously and Imperial Chemical Industries another (hence Margaret Gowing's remark that ICI was probably the only British company capable of thinking in the organisational terms required for the production of the atom bomb).

In pre-war Britain the capital goods industries like shipbuilding were geared to the production of one-off items and to development by progressive modification with succeeding orders. Large sections of the consumer goods industries had to meet rapidly varying requirements and were so laid out that there was little economy in long production runs. The way in which the manufacture of standard items in long runs transforms production methods and productivity is familiar from the textbooks but the historical development of production planning for these long runs is a subject that has not been very fully studied.

AIRCRAFT COMPONENTS

The issue of an aircraft programme was followed by the issue of others for engines, propellers, undercarriages, turrets, magnetos, wheels, constant speed units, spinners, bombs, radio valves and radiators. Some components were supplied on embodiment loan, i.e. the government contracted directly with the supplier and took delivery when they were fitted to new aircraft by the airframe manufacturer. Others were ordered by the airframe manufacturer and there was no obligation on the supplier to pay any attention to an official production programme. Nevertheless we were not just asked but harried to produce a programme by manufacturers (e.g. of radiators and jettison tanks) who despaired of establishing in any other way what requirements they ought to be meeting and in what order.

Some of us felt that we should go further in preparing programmes and cover major items like wings. Jewkes (and Devons, who succeeded him early in 1944) took the view that the more programmes we prepared the more we were bound to dilute the effectiveness of our planning.[8] While I was in fundamental agreement with this view, my own experience was that anyone engaged in propeller planning could hardly avoid taking in spinners and constant speed units as well because unless a change in propeller requirements was carried through to the key accessories there could be awkward bottlenecks later in these apparently minor items.

The same was true of engine accessories, especially items like radiators. I rather doubt whether Jewkes would have sanctioned the preparation of a radiator programme. But when presented with a *fait accompli* he did not demur. He also yielded to my insistence on the need for a programme for jettison tanks but this came late in the war – from about the middle of 1943.

AERO-ENGINES

On one central point we were all united. There could be no effective planning of aircraft production unless it was coordinated with the aero-engine programme. The hard core of the problem of coordination lay in the scheduling of engine requirements and this was eventually recognised as the undisputed responsibility of the Programmes Department.

The aero-engine lies at the heart of aircraft design, production and programming. This is partly because of the long interval between the inception of the design of a new engine and its subsequent production in quantity. This makes the aero-engine the most difficult part of an aeroplane to vary quickly in supply and compels an effort to adjust the programme for the aircraft to the engines available or in prospect instead of the other way round.

There is another reason for the primacy of engine planning that

was brought home to me when I visited German aircraft factories in
July 1945. I found then that the German designers were puzzled how
our fighters had always managed to produce the extra power to keep
ahead of theirs. Practically all our fighters had Rolls Royce Merlin
engines and Rolls had found ways of modifying the Merlin on the
production line, with or without a change in Mark number, to yield
more and more engine thrust while their opposite numbers at, say,
BMW (Bayerische Motorenwerke) had relied on discontinuous
changes in specification as one mark of engine replaced another on
the production line. Thus the Germans improved performance in
jumps and as they did not have the benefit of an engine as capable as
the Merlin of further development, any lead they established in one
of those jumps did not last long.

This comparison was a reminder that continuous development on
the British model was only possible if engine accessories kept pace
with increases in engine power. Every improvement in engine design
was liable to require a parallel development of the main engine
accessories and a corresponding upset in their production programmes. The engine was not only the controlling element in the
aircraft programme but kept disturbing the programme for many
other items.

Aircraft development itself is largely a matter of increasing engine
thrust. But with piston engines, increased thrust dictated changes in
other components, not just engine accessories. First there had to be a
propeller capable of taking up the extra power and this usually meant
longer blades. This in turn meant that the aircraft had to stand higher
off the ground so that a new undercarriage might be required. The
extra engine power put a premium on cooling and this meant a new
radiator. The change in propeller carried with it a change in spinner
and constant speed unit. So the very success of manufacturers in their
endless quest for increased engine thrust guaranteed plenty of
headaches for anyone planning aircraft components, especially aero-
engine accessories.

CONTRACTS

The official aircraft and engine programmes served a variety of
purposes. They were, to begin with, the basis on which contracts
were place on the manufacturers. The contracts specified not only the
total quantity on order but the output to be supplied month by month

in accordance with the official programme. This very reasonable procedure was not followed, however, in the case of other components on embodiment loan. Contracts for propellers, for example, were placed on the basis of the number required for installation on new aircraft plus an allowance for spares, without regard to the manufacturers' capacity or production programme (if they had one). This was the source of constant friction and confustion.[9]

THE ROLE OF PRODUCTION PROGRAMMES

The programmes for aircraft and engines also served as a basis for the calculation of labour, material and component requirements and hence for claims in competition with other departments to the limited supply of each of these. Except in respect of labour requirements, our role did not involve pursuit of these claims. We merely observed from the sidelines, mystified, for example, by the wide divergence between the number of workers firms claimed to need and the number they actually recruited. We were, however, conscious that the less realistic the programmes and the bigger the excess over actual performance, the more firms might build up stocks of materials and components that they did not really require. Much the same applied to additions to capacity, which were also justified in terms of the official programme. If production fell short of programme this could be represented as reflecting a shortage of capacity when in fact it had quite other causes.

Production programmes were an attempt to marry in one set of figures demand (or requirements) and supply (or production possibilities) and so accomplish something normally done by the price mechanism. Had everything worked out to perfection the programme would have served many different purposes simultaneously. The aircraft programme, for example, would have indicated both what the Air Ministry wanted by number and type of aircraft and what the aircraft manufacturers thought they would be able to produce. It served as a basis for placing contracts with the firms and for the provisioning of the firms with the materials they required. The programme served also as a measure of achievement month by month since failure to meet the programme normally reflected on the firm's efficiency.

This was the ideal; but things did not work out so satisfactorily. To begin with, the programme was rarely met. It was difficult, therefore, to treat it as firm and base expectations on its achievement *in toto*.

Expectations became shaded and the number of shadow programmes tended to multiply. If departures from programme became too large, the official programme lost all credibility and the end result was as bad as if there were no programme at all. Even before that stage, the various departments responsible for aircraft components would be discounting at varying rates the outputs shown in the programme and using any shortfall as an alibi for their own inadequacies.

Next there was the problem of establishing requirements. This was anything but straightforward. There were many different requirements to be met, many different voices urging them and some voices that remained silent too long or were hard to hear. Above all, requirements were constantly changing because of advances in what was technically possible, or fresh operational experience or changes in the theatre of war or in what appealed to the Air Ministry. We were wrestling all the time with uncertainties on every side. Our information had to be more up-to-date than anybody else's. But it was inevitably incomplete, often suspect, derived perhaps from hearsay and contradicted by others who might or might not be trustworthy. We had to listen carefully to the gossip and sift it for new developments. Not that information was freely yielded: each department liked to keep its secrets since secret information was a prime source of power. There were times when we were driven to think in terms of coordination by spy.

Then there were the uncertainties of the situation. The military balance, the rate and direction of technical development, the availability of men, materials and capacity, were all changing in ways that could not be accurately foreseen and at a pace it was not safe to predict. One day the Spitfire would be on top of enemy fighters; the next we would find that a Spitfire had been shot down by the FW190 and the whole fighter programme would be in doubt; the next again Rolls Royce would mount a new and higher-powered engine – the two-stage Merlin – in the Spitfire by extemporised methods, and its ascendancy over enemy fighters would be restored. Operational research would reveal that the Halifax did not compare with the Lancaster in its ability to deliver bombs and return safely to base. But before we could begin to phase out the Halifax and use the capacity to build Lancaster, we would be invited to re-engine the Halifax with the Hercules VI in place of Merlin engines, so transforming the performance of the Halifax but throwing the aero-engine programme into confusion. Or we might suddenly find, as at the end of 1943, that the Albemarle, then at the very bottom of the Air Ministry's priority list as a light bomber, shot to the top of the priority list as a glider tug.

I cite these examples of the casino-like atmosphere of MAP, not as evidence of the incalculability of requirements and the importance of luck but to demonstrate how, as Per Jacobson, when he was Managing Director of the IMF, used to say, one must always be ready for the unexpected. We were for ever exploring and weighing up contingencies in order to decide where to have a margin in additional stock-building and how large it should be.

TECHNICAL GUIDANCE

But we also needed help in assessing contingencies, particularly those involving changes in technique. How could we hope to know whether liquid-cooled engines held more promise of development than air-cooled? Or what chance there was that the jet engine would supersede both before the war was over? Or at what point a limit would have been reached to the development of the Merlin? Or when a new engine like the Griffon would reach the stage in its development when it would be ready to go into production?

On questions of that kind there was only one way to proceed: find someone of unquestioned standing, with a track record that entitled him to speak, who could take a dispassionate and honest view, and give evidence of consistent good judgement. Such men are rare. We were fortunate in being able to turn to Ernest Hives, of Rolls Royce (later Lord Hives), as an engineer who had both a remarkable flair for business and an extraordinarily accurate judgement of the potentialities for development of the engines his firm was producing. It was Hives who saved Rolls from very heavy losses in the US by winding up in the 1920s a branch of the firm that was trying to pit British one-off craftsmanship against American mass production of motor cars. It was also he who took Rolls into the manufacture of modern aero-engines just when rearmament was about to begin in the 1930s and built up the powerful development team that gave Rolls the edge on German aero-engine firms. We could trust Hives for an honest and competent opinion on the development prospects of the Rolls family of engines and on these difficult technical issues we never found his judgement at fault.

Hives was not of course our only source of technical guidance. We had experienced engineers within the Ministry to whom we could turn, such as Group Captain (later Air Commodore) Banks, Director of Engine Production. Banks, as I later discovered from his auto-biography (*I Kept No Diary*: Airlife Publications, 1978), had led a most adventurous life, commanding a kind of E-boat in the Channel while still in his teens and escaping from the Reds when captured near Odessa a few years later. He gave us strong support and sound advice.

For propellers and accessories I made great use of J. J. Parkes, Val Cleaver and Stephen Appleby, all of de Havilland's. Indeed, what little I understood of the technicalities was learnt almost entirely from Stephen Appleby, who also kept me posted on production difficulties and prospects at de Havilland's. But there were other components for which I can recall no adequate supply of technical comment and no expert whom we could consult with confidence when in difficulties.

TARGET OR 'REALISTIC' PROGRAMMES

In addition to all these difficulties and uncertainties there was the problem of assessing what levels of output could be achieved. Should the aircraft programme rest almost entirely on the estimates and promises of the airframe contractors, as seems to have been the position up to the creation of the planning department, DDG Stats P (Deputy Directorate General of Statistics, Planning and Pro-grammes)?[10] Or should the Ministry impose its own judgement of what was feasible? If so, how was the view of the Production Department to be weighed against that of DDG Stats P? Should the programme set a high target requiring a special effort, and unlikely, in normal circumstances, to be met? Or should it set its face against unrealistic targets and seek to provide as realistic an assessment as possible of the output it was reasonable to expect?

Beaverbrook had believed in setting ambitious targets in order to excite firms to extra effort. But failure to meet programme was disheartening and the programme itself became discredited. There was therefore a natural reaction towards greater realism and setting programmes that, with good management, could reasonably be expected to be fulfilled. This still left a tendency to err on the side of optimism. The outputs shown represented what manufacturers *ought* to be capable of, so that, given that some firms were not efficient, there was nearly always some shortfall in deliveries. One could vote in favour of realism but how was one to tell what was realistic?

It was not possible to rely exclusively on the firms even if they were warned that they would be judged by success or failure in fulfilling their programme. It might be the mark of an efficient firm that it regularly met its programme. But some of the firms were not at all efficient, and fell down again and again when the programme was a deliberately modest one, while most of the others rarely met the programme they had accepted earlier. Even when a new programme was issued in the middle of a month, output could diverge widely from the programme for that month. There was a further difficulty that firms sometimes welcomed a high programme because it helped to ensure an ample supply of materials and components. In doing so they ignored the disadvantage that it showed performance in a poor light and made it difficult ever to argue for extra capacity since a shortfall implied that there was capacity to spare.

Since the programmes provided a measure of requirements for labour, raw materials, equipment, etc. and the authorities allocating each were guided by the programmes, it might be thought that the aircraft firms could count on receiving all they needed and that shortages never occurred. This was far from true. The allocators were well aware of the wide gap in the early years of the war between programme and performance and they were often in no position to supply the full requirements called for by the programme: their own programmes were often underfulfilled. Hence getting enough labour, materials, etc., was a more hit or miss affair than the machinery of programmes seemed to guarantee. There were usually ways of checking who really needed more and who was inflating requirements, so the allocation system was by no means arbitrary; but neither did it prevent genuine shortages.

So far as raw materials were concerned, shortages had largely disappeared by the autumn of 1941 when we began operations and they rarely troubled us afterwards. Shortages of capacity did of course arise but seldom in the last years of the war. Labour, on the other hand, became increasingly hard to find as the needs of the armed forces grew more urgent with the approach of D-Day. The problems of labour supply are discussed later (pp. 70–5) in some detail.

Although it might be difficult to say in advance what was realistic, there were serious dangers in deliberately inflating the programme since there were always some people who took the programme at its face value. The RAF, the Air Ministry and others (including the Prime Minister) might be misled as to prospective deliveries of aircraft and even within MAP it was easy to be taken in by the printed

Planning in Wartime

word (all programmes were printed). The Minister himself was not immune. A good example of the problems posed by 'unrealism' occurred at the end of September 1942 when Colonel J. J. Llewellyn, then Minister of Aircraft Production, had to respond to a 'Clarion Call' for more bombers over the next two and a half months from Sir Archibald Sinclair, the Secretary of State for Air (Churchill wanted 50 squadrons of heavy bombers by the end of the year). In spite of warnings from his officials, Llewellyn promised an all-out effort to increase deliveries of heavy bombers from 521 in the past three months, June to August, to 780 in the next three months, September to November, when, as Sinclair was quick to point out, the amended aircraft programme just issued showed 876 heavy bombers due to be delivered in that later period. To make matters worse, Llewellyn's promises were conditional on the retention in the aircraft industry of skilled fitters lent by the RAF nine months previously for a maximum of six months; and he could give Sinclair no assurance that the aircraft firms employing the fitters had made arrangements to train others to take their place.[11]

It was not possible to hand over the job of drawing up the aircraft programme to technical experts who would work out machine-loadings, man-hour requirements, structure weight and all the other incunabula of the Department of Technical Costings.

There were always those who hankered after a more 'scientific' programme indicating what the labour and equipment in each factory *ought* to be capable of producing and sometimes drawing comparisons with what *could* be done with the same resources (e.g. in America or elsewhere). The day after I joined the Ministry I noted that Bill Smith of Technical Costs:

> is the man really responsible for the aeroplane programmes. For he, as assistant to Sir John Buchanan, tours the factories, calculates the man-hour requirements of each 'plane and notes the 'productive labour' position. It is all the queerest mumbo-jumbo. The man-hour requirements are simply the quotient of output each month (or a moving average of a number of months) divided by the theoretical number of available man-hours of productive labour. This last figure is arrived at by reference to the last known figure for the number of workers, a good deal of introspection, a guess at the trend in employment at the factory, and an allowance for holidays, etc. Bill Smith then carries his estimate forward over the next twelve months or so and this becomes the programme (except,

presumably, for modifications by Buchanan and except for changes in type). Devons came on him the other day trying to push back the Heavy Bomber programme by a month so as to make it square with the November output. Kennard (a colleague in Technical Costs) at one point called out excitedly that he had found some spare labour and Smith calmed him down by asking him to hold it over saying that he was counting on this labour for some deferred bombers. The ultimate result gave totals for March and April considerably above the previous figures put in by Smith, but he wasn't at all disconcerted when Jewkes asked him how, if the factories could produce X before, they were now likely to be able to produce Y.

Had we been concerned only with the aircraft programme and with requirements at peak – as pre-war programmes were – we might have taken more interest in such calculations. We did make use, with due reservations, of estimates of structure weight per man-hour in inter-departmental arguments over man-power requirements.[12] But for programme changes, which were frequent, this approach was of no use at all. The only reliable way to proceed was by extrapolation of past performance. Better results could be obtained by studying the track record of the firms than by listening to their promises or adopting technical assessments of potential output. This was particu-larly true of a change-over from one model of aircraft to another. Most firms took too optimistic a view of the loss involved and were not easily persuaded to modify their estimate.

In assessing what was realistic the Ministry's production depart-ments might be thought to be in the strongest position. In fact this was rarely so. Their concern was largely with current production difficulties and the immediate outlook, or with the need in due course for additional capacity, and they tended in debate to echo the views of the firms. Had requirements and technology never been changed and the supply of components, labour and materials always been abundant they could no doubt have drawn up programmes with some assurance on the basis of peak capacity as estimated for the Supply Board and the date at which capacity operation would be reached. But in fact the two big problems in programming were that things never remained the same for very long and that it was useless to plan aircraft production without regard to the availability of all the things needed for the purpose, especially aero-engines and other compo-nents which were not the business of the (Aircraft) production department. The first problem called for a wide range of up-to-date information and an analysis of past experience of programme changes while the second underlined the need for coordination by a planning department covering the whole range of aircraft components. In other words DDG Stats P was in a much stronger position to set programmes in a rapidly changing situation than any single production department.

CONTROL OVER PROGRAMMES

It must not be supposed that DDG Stats P established control over production programmes without a battle. Those who did not understand the planning process – and that included nearly the whole of MAP – had difficulty in seeing us as more than a kind of publishing house. Each of the production departments began by assuming that it was *their* business to draw up production plans and that while we might help them with incidental information we must not be allowed to deprive them of their functions. It was not easy to get across to them that our role was that of coordinators and that theirs was to ensure that production programmes were met.

In January 1942, for example, members of the engine production section were either against the issue of engine programmes, or against programmes as such, or wanted the engine programme to specify only the total number of Merlin or Hercules engines monthly, without distinction of mark, leaving it to the firms to make use of factory capacity as they thought fit. Some months later, after constant difficulties over the issue of a propeller programme, the Director of Propeller Production insisted that all he needed from us was an aircraft programme and a record of aircraft actually produced. This not only divested us of all responsibility but would have left him free to make his own assessment of the probable output of aircraft (and hence of propeller requirements) when that was not his job. In April he had issued without consultation with us a quite fantastic programme that had to be withdrawn. He then held up for three weeks a programme which I had prepared in consultation with the propeller department and the manufacturers, and then eventually issued it in mutilated form without further consultation. Having begun by writing down drastically the programme for electric propellers because the necessary sets of gears would not be available, he ended by arguing that all incentive to make up to or above programme in the next few months would disappear unless the programme for later months was inflated to remove any danger of lack of work then. Given the difficulties over electric propellers, it would have been more sensible to phase them out, as was agreed later.

I cite these examples to illustrate the incomprehension and irrationality that was common in the lower ranks. But of course the larger difficulty lay with the upper ranks, many of whom were either incompetent or saw things very differently from the way we saw them. In a moment of exasperation Jewkes once remarked, after his first year in MAP, that since the war, aircraft production had been run by 'quack efficiency experts, broken down business men and temperamental Air Marshals'. There was some hyperbole but also some truth in this outburst.

PLANNING AS COORDINATION

What took a long time to sink in was our role as coordinators. One of our main functions was to make sure that the plans of the individual production directorates fitted in with one another. It was not possible to do this by leaving planning to each separate directorate, with the aircraft programme as the only connecting link, since this would be to assume that the limiting factor in production was always airframe capacity and this was usually not so. When programme changes had to be considered, a wide range of alternatives might have to be reviewed, involving choices in the use of components, equipment and raw materials and possible expansions in the capacity to produce them. This review would precede, not follow, any amendment of the aircraft programme. It could not be undertaken by any one production directorate absorbed in its own affairs.

The questions raised did not, as a rule, admit of a straight 'Yes' or 'No' answer such as each directorate might give, since they involved consideration of a complex of complementary or alternative changes in the supply of components affecting several different directorates. The only satisfactory way of proceeding was to turn to someone familiar with the alternatives open to each directorate and invite him to put forward the most significant range of combinations of choices showing what specific additions to the aircraft programme could be made at the expense of specific changes elsewhere. The range covered would not be confined to new production but would be bound to impinge on the supply of spare components and on repairs and maintenance. Somebody had to decide what allowance should be made for spares in the interests of revising component programmes urgently and this was something that no production directorate was willing or able to do.[13]

Our job required us to be *au fait* with what was going on in different parts of the Ministry, with the way opinion on requirements was moving in the Air Ministry, and with much else that might call for a change in programme. It was not just the hard facts about current production and shortages that we needed but indications of what *might* have to be done to meet fresh demands or failures in supply. Information of this kind about what was in contemplation in different places did not flow automatically to any of us and could not be made to flow by official directive. Much of the information was confidential to a very limited group and not readily imparted; the significance of other information might not be realised; above all, thoughtlessness, inertia and lack of imagination reduced the flow of information far more than did outright secretiveness. We had to be constantly on the look-out for significant information that had failed to reach us.

In foraging for information we relied heavily on informal contacts with key officials in other directorates and departments. This might mean cultivating their acquaintance, exchanging gossip and, where possible, combining to promote some agreed line of action. At times, too, we had to indulge in what might be called 'coordination by spy': for example, finding someone disenchanted with their own director-ate and willing to disclose the full story of some event calling for action that had not been taken. Advance information might be got from the Air Ministry in exchange for the latest developments such as impending changes in programme for production reasons. In general what had to be built up was confidence and trust in the way information was used so that its disclosure would not rebound on the person conveying it or on his department. Without a whole network of carefully tended contacts with the production directorates, service departments and firms, our ability to coordinate successfully would have been very much less.[14]

The production programmes that we issued were the main instru-ment of coordination in the department; but coordination was something new and little understood. It was not unnatural that departments accustomed to go their own way should show some resentment at the intrusion of a planning department in what they thought of as their affairs, just as the firms in turn resented the intrusion of MAP in theirs and we ourselves resented the efforts of the Ministry of Production to coordinate the production of armaments of all kinds. The coordinating function conferred power – the power to issue or withhold programmes – and any surrender of power to a planning unit was bound to encounter resistance.

To do our job properly we had to have the latest information, to be made aware of all matters with a bearing on official programmes, and at the very least to be consulted when a change in programme was under consideration. There was, after all, no other point in the Ministry at which proposals for changes in programmes could be reviewed and responded to with promptitude and knowledge of the way in which other programmes would be affected. Yet it constantly happened that nobody took the trouble to tell us, enquiries were routed through other channels without our knowledge, and discussions on programme changes went on elsewhere among officials who made confident mis-statements about matters for which they had no responsibility.

The power enjoyed by DDG Stats P was thus a great deal more limited in practice than its role as coordinator implied. It did not make the final decisions but merely advised those who did. What notice was taken of its advice, either by the Minister, who was concerned only with broad strategic decisions, or by the Chief Executive who had charge of day-to-day management, varied over time. When launched in 1941 the department was the province of a Deputy Director General, not one of the most senior officials, as Jewkes complained in October 1942 when told that his was 'the most pampered directorate in MAP' with 'the plums of the staff'. That was at a time when not one of the staff was at Assistant Secretary level and Jewkes himself was threatening resignation. It remained true throughout the war that we could never count on being told what we needed to know or on being consulted on matters affecting the programmes we issued. We were often not informed of proposed amendments until late in the day after advice had been first sought elsewhere in the Ministry – sometimes in quite inappropriate places.

Few people from the Minister downwards were at all systematic in turning for advice to the official whose job it was to offer it. Minutes wandered all round the department until they reached someone whose responsibility it was to supply an answer or, quite commonly, someone who put boldness before responsibility and supplied an answer in ignorance of the facts. The judgement of DDG Stats P on what additional load a manufacturer could undertake was one among many; and it was only gradually that the Chief Executive came to give weight to the views of Jewkes or, more readily, Devons when he took Jewkes's place at the beginning of 1944.

As time went on, relations with the production departments became increasingly close. They were of course associated with us in drawing up each production programme and guided us, particularly at the beginning, on the scale of output consistent with available capacity. That done, there was plenty of work for them in assisting firms to meet their programme and arranging for further expansions in capacity where this was required. We, for our part, had to keep track of the changes that were in the wind in related programmes (especially the aircraft and engine programmes); the new developments likely to involve the use of improved types of equipment; the pressure on spares and the likely demands of the Air Ministry for more. We had to have the best and most up-to-date information from all quarters, bearing on output and requirements. In short we had to function like a kind of Stock Exchange of the aircraft industry, registering the pressures of supply and demand and issuing market quotations in the form of production programmes.

It would be idle to pretend that this was uniformly successful. Our turret programmes, for example, made little impression on the production department concerned since they preferred to go by what the Air Ministry told them, however often this proved to be based on out-of-date information. They took the view that their obligation was to the RAF and that they could not afford to disregard what the ultimate user said was needed. Similarly, we made no progress with the radio programme because the production department was not interested in educating us in the intricacies of radio valves and because radio requirements were less intimately linked to the aircraft programme itself.

CHANGES IN PROGRAMME

How planning worked was largely a matter, from our point of view, of how changes were made in production programmes. Our starting point had to be the programme as it had taken shape and been modified over the years. We were free to consider further incremental changes, but not some radical re-casting of the entire programme such as had no doubt been possible when rearmament began. The war was already over two years old, production had been greatly expanded and now we were approaching a state of full mobilisation for war in which any expansion in one direction had to be counterbalanced by contraction in another. What we had to engage in was a continuous process of re-planning with narrow limits, not the preparation of a comprehensive new plan.

This did not mean that the output of aircraft stood still, or even that no further increase was planned. The output of combat aircraft at peak in March 1944 was not far short of twice the average monthly output in 1941. All through 1942 more and more aircraft kept being pushed in, and by July the programme showed an extra 300 aircraft scheduled for December 1943. But with the aircraft programme of December 1941 the planning for expansion was largely over. It visualised a rate of production at the end of 1942 of 1865 aircraft a month that had still not been reached at the end of 1943. Indeed what is striking, looking back, is that as early as July 1942 the aircraft programme showed peak rates for heavy bombers, fighters, and all combat aircraft that were insignificantly below the peak rates in any later programme and that were never in fact reached at all. It is true that this is in part a reflection on the optimism of the July 1942 programme, for output eventually fell short of the programme by over 25 per cent; but at least it shows that what was *contemplated* in July 1942 was above – indeed well above – what later was achieved.

How then were changes made? There was no single procedure. The Prime Minister might take the initiative, or the Minister of Production or the Air Minister. Such occasions were rare and examples are discussed later. The Cabinet seems to have discussed the aircraft programme on only two occasions after 1941 and the Defence (Supply) Committee not a great deal oftener. This is apart from those occasions on which Ministers (*not* the Cabinet) agreed on an allocation of labour between the three main departments supplying armaments: the Ministry of Aircraft Production, the Ministry of Supply and the Admiralty.

More commonly, changes were made at the official level: in response to a request from AMSO or some operational department of the Air Ministry; or by MAP themselves, perhaps in recognition of a change in circumstances at the firms (e.g. delay in introducing a new type of aircraft or aero-engine), perhaps to improve the number or capabilities of the aircraft in the programme. Two kinds of pressure to change the programme went on all the time: pressure to produce more aircraft and pressure to incorporate technical improvements on the production line.

Proposals for changes might originate within MAP in many ways.

Sometimes they began with CRD (Controller of Research and Development), sometimes with the Chief Executive, sometimes in one of the production departments, sometimes with DDG Stats P. There might or might not be prior discussion with the Air Ministry or with the firms. In October 1941, shortly after Jewkes arrived in the Ministry, a Planning Committee was set up to consider changes in programme, with the Controller-General in the chair, and about a year later a Planning Sub-Committee was appointed. The division between the two was not altogether clear but the Planning Sub-Committee usually prepared draft amendments to the aircraft programme while the Planning Committee dealt with more general points. Not that all planning decisions were taken in these committees. The Chief Executive might take decisions without a meeting of the Committee, and a new aircraft programme was never submitted to it for approval.

Before illustrating the variety of ways in which programme changes came about, a word must be said about their inconveniences. One obvious drawback was that they made it difficult to use programmes as a measure of performance. Where the changes had their origin in new requirements the revised programme was unlikely to show an unchanged load on the firm making the change and it was not easy to judge what to allow for the burden of the change itself. Where the changes reflected the inability of firms to do what they were asked, there was a reluctance to condone poor performance by adjusting the programme, even if this meant misleading those who took programmes literally. Indeed, if the programme kept being jerked into line with actual performance its usefulness would soon be called in question.

There was a universal tendency to underestimate the cost of programme changes in lost output, or alternatively the gain in output from prolonged operation with an unchanged type of aircraft. Innovation was indispensable to air supremacy. But there could come a point at which the gain in quality was insufficient to counterbalance the loss in volume. Too often only the gain in quality was considered and new items were pushed into the programme without making room for them by adequate cuts elsewhere.

Both of these points were raised by Jewkes soon after he came to MAP. At a meeting of the Planning Committee in April 1942 he pointed out that of the 116 columns in the printed programme corresponding to different marks of aircraft no less than 66 had undergone changes since the issue of the heavy bomber programme four months previously, and a large number of additional columns had been added for new marks and types.[15] In all, 3855 aircraft had been added in four months to a programme for 1942–43 which was supposed to represent the maximum that MAP could achieve. Some of these changes were entirely legitimate: for example, the introduction of additional Hurricanes for Russia. Some reflected difficulties in meeting the engine programme: more Stirling Is had been put in for this reason in place of Stirling IIs; the Sabre engine for the Typhoon was late, the Hercules VI fifty per cent down on programme, the Griffon 61 put into the programme nine to twelve months too early. But there were also changes of mind on the part of the Air Ministry that were difficult to justify. They had asked for 100 more Albemarles, taking no account of the repercussions on other programmes and the loss of production involved. The Air Ministry had first cut their trainer requirements and then, when new Oxford, Anson and Master programmes had been issued, asked to have the original programmes restored.

Jewkes might also have attacked the proliferation of aircraft marks and types. In June 1940 he had already drawn attention to the absence of standardisation of aeroplane types and the consequent multiplicity of different metal sections.[16] There were no less than 42 types of aircraft in production, each requiring up to 200 or 300 different sections. In only seven of the 42 types was reliable information available as to the types of section required, and production was being held up everywhere by a shortage of some type of section while others were frequently in surplus.

The profusion of aircraft types continued, although hardly any introduced after 1940 was of particular value. In November 1943 there were said to be 32 main types of airframe in production[17] and in addition there were many different marks of any one type of aircraft. For example, in 1942 there were at least twelve marks of Spitfire and the multiplication of marks of Mosquito did unmistakable damage to the volume of output. The layman could also be pardoned for doubting whether it was necessary to have such a long list of bombers. The Stirling was reckoned to be about three times as costly, taking account of casualties and labour cost, as the Lancaster. Aircraft like the Buckingham and the Warwick seemed just a mistake.[18]

MINISTERIAL CHANGES IN PROGRAMME

Three examples may be given of programme changes initiated by ministers. The first relates to the heavy bomber programme prepared at the end of 1941 (but before America's entry into the war). A second was made nearly a year later when the new Super-Wellington was under consideration. The third was an attempt in 1944 to begin the rundown in aircraft production before the war with Germany had come to an end.

The Heavy Bomber Programme

The heavy bomber programme was initiated by Churchill personally in September 1941 and approved three months later by the Defence (Supply) Committee on 8 December, the day after Pearl Harbor.

The first move took the form of a letter from Churchill to the Lord President, Sir John Anderson, on 7 September 1941. Churchill expressed concern at the slow expansion of the heavy and medium bomber force and set a target for the size of the force of 4000 aircraft. To meet this target the RAF would need 22 000 bombers between July 1941 and July 1943 whereas what Churchill called 'the forecast' showed a total of only half that number ('the forecast' was apparently 85 per cent of the total in the current aircraft programme). Since 5500 aircraft were due to be delivered to the RAF from the United States over the two-year period, the new target implied an expansion in production in the United Kingdom from 11 000 to 16 500.

After talking to the Minister (Moore-Brabazon) and the Controller General (Sir Charles Craven) Churchill accepted a lower target of 14 500 and directed the Minister to prepare plans for meeting this new requirement. The bomber programme thus enlarged was to enjoy overriding priority before which other projects must give way, even if it were necessary to slow up the Admiralty programme or reduce the flow of armaments to the Army or curtail drastically the building of new factories, for which there was likely to be no manpower to spare anyhow.

A new programme was prepared in MAP after a review of what the aircraft firms could do, possible component shortages, labour requirements, and so on. The programme did not add greatly to the planned production in 1942 (which was already unrealistically high) but added over 50 heavy bombers to the programme for June 1943, with a peak in December 1943 of 625 per month. This might seem a fairly small addition to a programme for about 2000 aircraft a month but, taken in conjunction with the expansion already planned, it represented a doubling of output in terms of structure weight within two years. More labour, materials and capacity would be required. Plans for additional capacity were put in hand and a bid was made for more labour to meet the higher peak. It was on this bid that interdepartmental discussion concentrated.

MAP entered their bid by writing to the Lord President's staff in the Cabinet Office – the Economic Section – on the manpower they claimed to need. Estimates by Technical Costs of the man-hour requirements of each type of aircraft were applied to the programme, before and after amendment to meet the new targets. These appeared to show a manpower requirement at August 1942 of 1 571 000 on the old basis and two million on the new, and an eventual total, including the assembly and repair of American aircraft, of 2 300 000.

Needless to say, employment on MAP work never reached so high a total and neither the precision of the estimate on the old basis nor the imprecision on the new conveys the range of uncertainty in all such calculations. What MAP asked for was 590 000 workers more than in August 1941 (i.e. a total of more than 1.25 million) to meet the old programme at peak and an extra 260 000 for the additions called for in the heavy bomber programme (figures impossible to reconcile with those given above). The total of 850 000 was later reduced to 570 000, to be reached by February 1943 instead of December 1942, but the Ministry of Labour remained unconvinced. Whether by coincidence or not, employment at peak early in 1944 reached 1 820 000 which is exactly 570 000 higher than the August 1941 total (assuming that it is comparable). But there had been many reassessments of labour requirements and changes in programme in the intervening period.[19]

The Super-Wellington

One of the rare occasions when the Cabinet dealt with the aircraft programme was at the end of 1942 when it was necessary to decide what aircraft should succeed the Wellington and Warwick at Vickers. Such decisions were usually taken by the Defence Committee (Supply) with Churchill in the chair.

Vickers themselves wanted to introduce the Super-Wellington, a four-engined bomber then known as the B3/42 and later as the Windsor. This had the support of the Secretary of State for Air, the Air Staff, the Ministry of Production, and all the technical experts. Churchill, however, argued that the Lancaster was a better bet with a proven record and capable of further improvement. On the other hand, workers at Vickers (Supermarine) were familiar with the Wellington geodetic construction but not with that of the Lancaster. The experts also maintained that while the B3/42 would be capable of further improvement, 'there is no likelihood of any further improvement in the Lancaster' (i.e. after the change to the new version with 2-stage Merlin engines).

The matter came before the Cabinet in October 1942 (WM(42) 133, 6 October 1942, in PRO CAB(65) 28) and they invited a report from the Minister of Aircraft Production. Cripps, who was moving to the Ministry in place of Llewellyn, submitted a note on 14 November (WP(42)526 in PRO(66) 32) which was discussed by the Cabinet on 11 December, and he subsequently, at the Cabinet's request, put round a technical note on the merits of the two aircraft. A decision was deferred until March 1943 when it was agreed to go ahead with the B3/42. It was introduced into the aircraft programme starting in October 1944, but in fact none were produced before the end of the war with Germany.

The Cabinet was also asked to approve a changeover from the manufacture of Stirlings to Lancasters at all factories making Stirlings except Short Harland's. MAP was in some difficulty in estimating the loss of heavy bombers involved in this changeover since it was already apparent that the July 1942 programme was hopelessly over-optimistic and the Stirling programme would have to be set back six months. The figures for the loss submitted to the Cabinet were 44 Stirlings in 1943 and 412 in 1944. The Cabinet made no comment on these figures and approved the changeover. But it is unlikely that its approval would ever have been asked if the issue of the Super-Wellington had not been before it at the same time.

Humpty-Dumpty

A third example is the episode I christened 'Humpty-Dumpty'. It is worth discussing at some length.

One of our biggest problems was to scale down aircraft production as the war drew to an end. It seemed wasteful to go on churning out equipment that was unlikely to find a use, especially when there were large stocks that could be drawn down in the concluding months. There was also an increasing shortage of manpower: it had been necessary since 1943 to set limits to what could be employed on arms production in order to release labour for the armed forces. Towards the end of that year the Prime Minister asked departments to consider what relief they could offer to the labour shortage (estimated at 1 million in 1944) if they reduced their requirements to what was needed for the war against Japan but continued to aim at maximum striking effort in 1944. The cuts made in response to the Prime Minister's directive still left the aircraft programme showing an expanding output in 1944 and 1945 although in fact production started to decline from a peak of just under 2100 combat aircraft per month reached in the first half of 1944.

When a fresh allocation of manpower had to be made in the autumn of 1944 the Chancellor of the Exchequer (Sir John Anderson) suggested the use of a similar formula and the Cabinet agreed that it would be safe to work on the assumption that the war with Germany would not continue beyond 30 June 1945.[20] We then drew up what became known as 'the August programme' on this assumption.[21] The August programme (which stretched to December 1946) made substantial cuts in comparison with the outputs scheduled in the previous programme of March 1944; but although output was already on the decline, the programme still showed a continuing if gentle expansion above current levels. This was very evident in the heavy bomber programme which provided for an output of 620 heavy bombers a month in the third quarter of 1946(!) compared with an output of heavy bombers in the third quarter of 1944 averaging only 460.

Just when we were ready to issue the new programme and had asked for Cabinet approval, the Minister of Production had second thoughts and on 4 September urged on the Cabinet a more optimistic view of the ending of hostilities. With the Prime Minister in the chair and the Chiefs of Staff present, it was agreed that 'for the purpose of estimating man-power requirements' it could now be assumed that the war with Germany would not continue beyond 31 December 1944.

It was not at all clear how this decision was to be interpreted. If taken literally it would have meant a drastic reduction in work on aircraft and aircraft components which would not yield finished aircraft by the end of the year. If interpreted differently, it was consistent with carrying on without much immediate reduction and preparing plans for larger cuts to come into effect at the end of 1944. The Ministry of Production wanted action; the Air Ministry insisted that plans would do. The one pointed out that the CIGS (Chief of the Imperial General Staff), asked by Churchill whether he thought the war might be expected to end in 1944, had said he thought so; the other dismissed this as the opinion of a private gentleman, not of the CIGS. We had some sympathy with the Air Ministry, thinking it likely that CIGS was not briefed on the subject but at the same time recognising that he could hardly be expected to ask the Chiefs of Staff every morning when they judged the war was likely to end.

As the debate proceeded, the Air Ministry asked for an insurance in additional aircraft – indeed they wanted more aircraft than were in the August programme. This moved Sir Wilfrid Freeman to ask why we should go to the trouble of getting a Cabinet decision if the Air Ministry was free to ignore it. If everybody added insurances we should be taking June 1945 instead of December 1944 as a date for the ending of the war with Germany.

The matter came before the Cabinet again on 19 September when Churchill was in Quebec and the Chiefs of Staff were also unable to attend. The airborne attack on the Rhine bridges at Arnhem had begun two days previously. Not surprisingly the Vice-Chief of the Imperial General Staff (VCIGS) wanted action on the programme to be suspended for two or three weeks although 'planning' could go ahead. The Secretary of State for Air elaborated the kind of insurance he wanted if the date of 31 December 1944 was still to be accepted. The heavy bomber force would be reduced by 25 per cent by June 1945 if our revised programme was accepted and 800 fighters would be cut out in the first six months of the year. He wanted half the cut in Lancasters and half the cut in fighters to be restored, and the deferment of a proposed switch from Halifax bombers to Halifax transports. Effectively this meant taking 1 April as the date instead of 31 December, releasing only 40 000 workers by the end of 1944 instead of 100 000, and 240 000 in the first quarter of 1945 instead of 300 000.

At first the Cabinet seemed disposed to accept this 'insurance'. But Sinclair, the Air Minister, then overstated his case, launching into a lurid picture of a protracted war in which large forces of Lancasters fought their way through packs of German night fighters and came back in the winter nights with heavy losses. The Cabinet promptly decided that they could forget about an insurance and reaffirmed their earlier decision. Churchill, who had been cabled to, was in some doubt but agreed that while there were likely to be pockets of resistance within Germany after 31 December and the war might drag on for a month or two, the issue would have been settled by the end of the year. This view was endorsed by the Cabinet which did not think that the practical steps proposed would be much affected by the continuation of hostilities for a few months beyond 31 December and asked that their decision be translated into immediate action.

We were pretty sure that the Cabinet had no real understanding of what they were doing and that they couldn't grasp the impact of a cut of £300 million in aircraft orders alone (to say nothing of other munitions) on public opinion. To announce – such things could not be kept quiet – a few days after Arnhem that the war with Germany could be regarded as almost over required some preliminary education of the public to an understanding of what was involved. There was also danger of misunderstanding in America: a drastic cut in the aircraft programme might be misinterpreted there as a way of taking undue advantage of the supplies they were promising us for use against Japan.

In preparing a new programme we underlined heavily that a decision to issue it was irrevocable. We consulted the Ministry of Production, the Board of Trade and the Ministry of Labour about the cuts but they had (literally) nothing to say. On 29 September we issued the new programme and prepared contract and explanatory letters to the firms inviting them to take Joint Production Committees (JPCs) into their confidence. Hardly had we done so than we were asked to withdraw our programmes. The Prime Minister had come back from Quebec in a more cautious mood and was suggesting a later date than 31 December. Things were to be kept 'in abeyance' until he could make up his mind. Since it was impossible to unsay what the new programmes had already told the firms of our intentions, they were asked to disregard the programmes. This meant that we had now no programme at all and were back in the schizophrenic world in which we had one programme (the August programme) that was out-of-date (and known to be so) and another (the September programme) that was to be disregarded (but could not be – least of all by the firms).

The letters to the firms had gone off but not the contract cancellations and the firms had also been warned not to say anything to their JPCs. Freeman was delighted at the tangle, especially once he knew that the programmes had gone out. Reminded of our warnings, he reached for the telephone and rang Sir Robert Sinclair, his opposite number in the Ministry of Production. 'Do you remember a word, Rob', he asked, 'the word irrévocable, or irrevócable if you prefer it that way? Well, we meant it!'

The programme remained in abeyance for a fortnight, of which my chief memory is preparing a minute for Freeman headed 'Humpty-

Dumpty'. Planning aircraft production, I pointed out, was quite unlike planning the production of ammunition where the same item was turned out month after month. It was necessary to decide months in advance which aircraft were to be produced and where, what modifications were necessary and when, what components of all kinds would have to be ready for use at each stage, and so on. The scale and pattern of output were always in flux and could only be reduced to order by comprehensive programmes that could not be suspended one day and reintroduced much later as if all the changes envisaged in the programmes were of no account. A programme with dates left blank for later insertion was not a programme at all.

Cripps circulated a paper making similar points to the Cabinet on 14 October and suggested a compromise.[22] It was impossible to escape from the need to assume some date or other for the ending of the war if only because there was a change in the pattern as well as the volume of requirements in Stage II (i.e. the war against Japan alone). For example, Halifax bombers were no longer required while on the other hand the needs of the Fleet Air Arm would expand. Any delay in operating the September programme would mean a corresponding delay in the re-equipment of the air force for the war in the Far East. Cripps was willing to put back 750 extra medium and heavy bombers and over 500 fighters. There would be no large reduction in the first three months of 1945 compared with the August programme. The changes made were roughly equivalent to assuming that the war with Germany would end about June 1945. This satisfied the Air Ministry who agreed that the programme gave them more in total than they had asked for, and all the heavy bombers.

The acceptance of the modified programme by the Cabinet on 17 October did not get us out of all our difficulties. In mid-November we were still unable to tell sub-contractors of the cut in their programme until the other ministries concerned agreed. Many of the sub-contractors had already completed their contracts and were unable to get any more so it was not just the difficulty of *cutting* contracts that exercised us.

By January the Ministry of Production, always prone to cold feet, decided that the Cabinet must again be consulted. The Prime Minister conveyed to his colleagues on 25 January that the Chiefs of Staff now regarded 30 June 1945 as the earliest and 1 November 1945 as the latest date when the war with Germany was likely to end. (Earlier their dates were 31 January and 30 May.) We had in the meantime settled practically all the details of a new aircraft programme in consultation with the Air Ministry. Apart from adjustments to compensate for delays in some types, this aimed mainly at making cuts from mid-1945 in line with the requirements of a Stage II target force.

Two documents were then prepared by the PS (secretarial) side of MAP which had caught the prevailing chill. I thought at the time that for bad logic and misinformation they could hardly have been surpassed and they seemed calculated to communicate panic to the Cabinet. The first document, submitting the draft programme for Cabinet approval, more or less invited the Cabinet to reject it and made free play with statements for which there was no foundation about the strength of the RAF. The words 'irretrievable', 'colossal', 'formidable', etc. gave an atmosphere of anxiety and bravado calculated to force the Cabinet to abandon the simple-minded view that the war wouldn't last beyond the autumn. It was nowhere suggested that on manpower grounds alone *some* cut in the RAF would eventually be necessary; nor that the Air Ministry felt that they had as many aircraft as they could man without a drastic change in their plans for intake and training. A later secretariat draft contemplated the possibility of maintaining or increasing MAP's labour force in 1945.

It was difficult to understand why the Cabinet should be pressed for a decision confined to aircraft. Other programmes, for example tanks, had already been adjusted on dates later than 30 June. No doubt it was quite proper to give one date to supply departments and another for operations. But at least supply departments should be given consistent instructions. In our view the date should be well ahead and only advanced as confidence grew, never set back. What seemed to be happening was that we were working to a date 9–12 months ahead because this was broadly the period of production and the date was being pushed back in six-monthly doses because nobody wanted smaller ones. In effect we were now being invited to work to 31 December 1945.

If the date was to be as late as that, there were in fact only three programmes (Lancaster, Halifax and York) in need of alteration and, according to our contacts in the Air Ministry, no changes at all if the date was 30 September. All that was needed, therefore, was *either* that everyone should agree to act on the basis of 31 December *without* going to Cabinet *or* that the Cabinet sould be asked to name a date, conscious that no major problem would arise unless the date was later than 31 December. The dates named by the Chiefs of Staff were largely irrelevant to our problems.

Once again there was a delay before we could issue a new programme. The birth-pangs were long and highly vexatious. When we were ready to circulate it and had carefully drilled the Ministry of Production to support a claim for more labour (by now the programme required an extra 100 000 workers by 30 June), Cripps told the Lord President's Committee that he didn't think all the aircraft were needed. It is unlikely that he understood all that this involved. At any rate it was only as a kind of afterthought that he mentioned to the Chief Executive next day that the February programme was not to go out and we were to go back to the October programme. A day later he left for Scotland in apparent unconcern. The Chief Executive (who a fortnight before was still using the draft September programme with some pencil corrections and claimed that it hadn't let him down yet!) fortunately agreed that the October programme could not be issued and that everybody must be made to see that there would be *no* saving in labour if it were: any saving of labour would come from stopping repair work and other changes governed by the date for the ending of the German war. When eventually we put the programme up to the Cabinet it was accepted without a murmur.

Once the February programme was issued we had hoped to see further cuts which would make it possible to forego the extra 100 000 workers. But we soon realised that this could not be done by June if the Air Ministry had first to review their aircraft requirements and we had then to agree with them the cuts that the review permitted. The Air Ministry was bound to take the line that they couldn't cut out more aircraft unless they were given a different date for the ending of the war or could change the size of their target force.

From February onwards until the German surrender there was no set of major changes in programme. Attention was concentrated on other problems. The Prime Minister, it is true, did tell the Manpower Committee on 29 March to make labour allocations on the assumption that the war in Europe would be at an end by 31 May provided there were no unexpected reverses, and confirmed this date on 14 April. But by that time it made little difference what date was given. Comparatively little labour was released in 1945 by MAP before war with Germany ended on 8 May. But in the next eight weeks 45 per cent of MAP's manpower – half a million workers – moved to other work.

The moral I drew from these events was how little those in senior positions understood the nature of a production programme and how impossible it was in a changing situation to suspend it or hold it in abeyance. I also concluded that while it was possible to use allocations of manpower as a way of indicating which programmes to expand or contract and by how much, it was not possible to tie these allocations to some specific contingency such as the ending of hostilities, the chances of which did not remain constant. As the chances varied, so would the appropriate production programmes and with them the labour allocations. But a production programme once changed could not be reinstated, unlike labour allocations which could. The system of labour allocations was appropriate only where they were linked with the issue of fresh programmes at fairly regular intervals.

It was also borne in on me how difficult it is when military victory or defeat is at stake to decide what chances to take. One is used to seeing rapid changes of judgement on the stock exchange and it is hardly surprising if on graver and more uncertain issues opinion changes even faster. But the kind of programme that we issued in February, after Yalta, is not easily reconciled with a rational assessment of the risks. Did it really make sense, for example, to be planning for so many heavy bombers in the autumn of 1945 when there were serious doubts how many we could expect to deploy against Japan? The Americans did not particularly want us there at all and Churchill had had to fight hard at Quebec to be allowed to participate. But that apart, the Air Ministry seemed to be in a state of great confusion and MAP was in deep trouble as well. Even without the advantage of hindsight we need be in no doubt that the cuts in programme in the last stages of the war erred too much on the side of caution.

THE 'HEALTHY' AIRCRAFT PROGRAMME

There was much talk in MAP in the latter days of the war of ensuring the continuation into the peace of a 'healthy' aircraft industry. Looking back, officials did not want to see the industry fade away as it had faded after 1918. But history carried other lessons too. Aircraft in 1918 were very different from aircraft in 1945 and who could say what aircraft would be like in another thirty years? In 1918 aircraft had been made of wood and it had been thought prudent to maintain an ample supply of aeronautical timber in peacetime. But of what use had that proved?

It was perhaps more important to preserve some of the firms making up the industry than to hold a stock of raw materials. But which firms? And how were they to be preserved?

What was at issue was the familiar question: how can a government promote industrial success? There was a limit to what the government could spend on military aircraft. It could pick and choose which firms it most wanted to remain as suppliers but only so long as the number matched what it could afford. The problem was to marry its requirements with civilian needs and export possibilities in such a way as to encourage successful designs. But none of us was likely to be long enough in MAP to have much to do with that problem.

Planning for civil aircraft production after the war raised other problems. In October 1944 we found that programmes were being arranged by DTD (the Director of Technical Development) for Tudor aircraft, a transport that could be used for civil purposes after the war. A. V. Roe were encouraged to think of turning over to the production of Tudors a line that might yet be needed by the RAF for Yorks as paratroop transports. All this was without the aid of a programme, so nobody knew what was wanted. DTD, for example, wanted Tudors within the next few months without knowing whether they had to be pressurised or whether there was a suitable engine.

At the beginning of 1945 there was a debate on whether we ought to programme civil aircraft when A. V. Roe, the only firm concerned, wanted the minimum of interference. As Ely Devons argued, programmes and contracts had to go together: without the backing of a contract programmes were ineffective. We could allow firms a margin of spare capacity for civil aircraft and treat the corresponding labour requirements like those for any other civil product. But as spare capacity fluctuated there were bound to be questions of priority both in the use of this capacity and in the supply of components; and without a programme there could be no guarantee that the right measure of priority would go to RAF requirements and no way of giving priority to civil requirements when we ranked them ahead of what was wanted for the RAF. On the other hand, a programme understood as instructions, like all MAP programmes, meant underwriting the production of civil aircraft.

This worried us until it became clear that there would be no really private sales of large aircraft immediately after the war since all the purchasers, even in Iraq and Argentina, would be government-sponsored joint British agencies. Moreover it looked as if the high cost of building prototypes of large airliners would rule out private ventures and indeed the government was already buying the proto-types. No doubt there would still be a civil market for the smaller machines and these would be made by private arrangement. But all the large aircraft, we thought, would continue to be programmed.

In the case of the Tudor there was, in any event, no great problem because BOAC (British Overseas Airways Corporation) were pre-pared to convert military aircraft for use as passenger-cum-freighters. This information, however, did not for some time reach DDRDA (Deputy Director, R & D, Aircraft) or the manufacturer who was still working on 'interim' and 'final' versions of the York for BOAC when these were no longer needed by them.

When we prepared a draft programme for civil aircraft it did not get very far. The Chief Executive, at Devons's suggestion, asked for it to be sent to Civil Aviation for approval. But first we had to complete a long questionnaire and it took a fortnight for the programme to be sent off. Then we were summoned by DGCA (Director General, Civil Aviation) late in February to a grand meeting 'to consider the programme' i.e. to be asked once again all the questions about requirements that we had already answered. Whether the programme was ever issued I cannot now recall.

3 Organisation

THE PLANNING STAFF

The appointment of a planning staff did not assure it the status and weight which its functions required. Many of its difficulties arose from its subordinate position within the Ministry. Although Jewkes came from a post which later carried the title of Economic Adviser to HMG, he found himself on a par with, or junior to, a number of officials and business men whose capacity to make planning decisions seemed very questionable.

Jewkes, as Director of the Economic Section of the War Cabinet Offices had been on the staff of the Lord President, Sir John Anderson, who was persuaded to lend him for three months from 18 September 1941 'for the specific task of building up an organisation for planning'[1] as I also was 'lent' for three months by the Board of Trade. Neither of us was ever recalled. Jewkes joined as a Deputy Director General under the Controller General (Sir Charles Craven) and his deputy (Sir Alexander Dunbar). He soon found, particularly after Craven's withdrawal, that this was not one of the top posts and eventually, after complaints over his status as 'a junior official' and threats of resignation, he was made a Director General in June 1943. Jewkes was keenly aware that he could not do his job properly without power and place. Lacking a sufficiently exalted position in the MAP hierarchy, he would be denied the central position in the work of the department that planning implied, and bypassed, not informed or consulted, when coordination required access to the latest information and consultation on all proposed changes in programme. In practice those who were sympathetic to the aims of the planning staff did not always bring us in when changes in programmes were under discussion. On more than one occasion there was a showdown with the Chief Executive or the Permanent Secretary, aimed at ensuring recognition of the centrality of planning (and the planning staff) in the organisation of the department. But the motives behind the showdown tended to be misunderstood – 'there is no limit to your ambition' was Rowlands's response to Jewkes's proposal at the end of 1942 to call himself 'Controller of Programmes'.

Under Jewkes there were by October 1942 three Deputy Directors

(Frank Paish, Ely Devons and myself), four Assistant Directors, seven Deputy Assistant Directors, and several other junior members of staff. The total had grown and the personnel had changed over the previous year, nearly all of those who were initially attached to Jewkes having moved elsewhere. In all, the staff numbered 29 by the middle of 1943. The only salary over £1000 a year was that of Jewkes who was paid a salary of £1500. The able young women graduates whom I recruited had to be content with £350.

Ely Devons, beginning as Chief Statistician, became in turn Deputy Director, Director (from June 1943), and on Jewkes's departure Deputy Director General (from 1 February 1944) at the age of 30. He revolutionised the statistical arrangements and in addition took an active interest in programmes from the beginning, becoming increasingly the dominant influence in the directorate-general. Frank Paish and I shared responsibility for programmes, Frank concentrating on aircraft, undercarriages and turrets while I initially took charge of propellers and most other components. The engine programme was prepared first by Eric Bulley with the assistance of Sheila Mobbs and then by Brian Tew but of course others in more senior positions were involved. Marjorie Craigie took over the propeller programme from me when Eric Bulley left to go to the Engine Department. Others in the Directorate were David Champernowne, Walter Hagenbuch, Charles Sharpston and Tony Watson. I brought into the group no less than three women ex-pupils of mine at Glasgow of whom two married colleagues in the Directorate before the end of the war.

We wrote little and spent hardly any time in committee meetings. What we did do was endless arithmetic and endless telephoning. It really *was* like the Stock Exchange. Now and again we tried to rationalise what we were doing. Frank Paish did an anatomy of planning and we mulled it over. I tried to work out a philosophy of embodiment loan (now in PRO AVIA 46/103), i.e. to establish principles by which to decide what items should be supplied at government expense to the aircraft manufacturer and what items should be left to him to procure. But these excursions into theory were rare.

We were a close-knit group, although each of us was very busy with our own affairs. We were all young, high-spirited, and not lacking in a sense of our collective importance. The Ministry was our oyster to which we provided the necessary intellectual grit for the cultivation of those pearls of the higher logic – the production programmes. We could observe other departments with the amused detachment of a visitor to the zoo and report to each other on the latest absurdity. Life was frantic, nonsensical, but above all hilarious. We were endlessly occupied with complex and important issues and yet endlessly entertained by paradoxes and trivialities.

One contribution to our amusement was technical jargon which intrigued, baffled and amused us. We took great pleasure in finding some new term or phrase with which to mystify even the supposed experts. I remember a cable from the United States, the source of a jargon with the special piquancy of a foreign language, in which reference was made to 'cold shuts' in the engine castings – a phrase that seemed made for repetition and appears to be unfamiliar to this day among British metallurgists. Our satisfaction in using cabalistic phrases of this kind derived in part from the tendency of our less expert colleagues to take refuge in jargon whenever we asked awkward questions.

We shared the ICI building next to Lambeth Bridge with the Board of Trade, spending long hours in the office by day and sleeping in the basement when on fire duty. We usually took our lunch in Thames House across Horseferry Road and often dined in the appalling canteen in the basement of the ICI building. We lived for the job and could rarely get away from it except on Sundays when (until I married in 1943) I made a point of cycling out of London or walking in the Chilterns. But there were some who managed to keep a link with peacetime duties. Richard Pares, then in the Board of Trade, could be seen in the evening in the canteen editing the *English Historical Review*. And early in 1943 I found time somehow to complete the last two chapters of my textbook on economics and get it off to the printer.

MINISTERS

At the top of MAP was the Minister who, until the arrival of Cripps, changed every nine months or so – none of the first three ministers lasted more than a year. After Beaverbrook, ministers played a limited part in the running of the department, as was almost inevitable if the Chief Executive was doing his job properly. They had to approve the broad strategic decisions, respond to pressure from the Prime Minister and the Minister of Production, take the fight if necessary to Cabinet (e.g. in defence of an adequate labour allocation), secure the cooperation of the workforce in the aircraft industry and act as spokesmen for the Government in reporting to the public. But they had little to do with the succession of minor crises within the Ministry.

I don't recall that I ever set eyes on a Minister of Aircraft Production in my four years in the department. Jewkes for one thought the less he saw of the Minister the better.[2] There was always a danger that he might try to take decisions that were best left to the management and neglect the political duties he was there to discharge.

Of Beaverbrook and Moore-Brabazon I can say little since the first had gone before I joined the Ministry and the second went before I had completed three months. Llewellyn, of whom I had formed a favourable impression in 1940, proved a disappointment. Soon after he arrived Jewkes called him a bonehead and hardened in this view. He had begun by asking for long hours and weekend attendance on the part of senior officials while himself going off for the weekend, and spent much of his time having the managements of the aircraft firms up for a pep talk. Jewkes rated him below Moore-Brabazon who 'at least understood a fresh point'.

Cripps came to us with a high reputation at a time when he had won powerful backing for criticism of Churchill's leadership. He had earlier rejected appointment as Minister of Supply and at the beginning of October was on the point of resignation. The prospect of such a move created general dismay and a delegation led by Lyttleton went to see Churchill. Two alternatives were put forward: one for Cripps to go as Minister to Washington and be safely out of the way and the other to go to MAP and clear up 'the mess in aircraft production'. He chose the latter and took up office in November 1942.

Jewkes and Devons showed him round our chart-room and were impressed. Devons sized him up as 'too clever to be a minister', too much given to finding out in detail what was going wrong and too little to selecting the right subordinates and trusting to their judgement. Devons was struck by his mechanistic outlook on planning: he seemed to have little or no appreciation of the part played in planning by judgement in the face of uncertainty, nor did he understand the contribution that could be made by skilful management. Cripps was rather disappointed in the chart-room and preferred some charts prepared by Frank Paish which fascinated him because they appeared to show exactly what was holding up the production of each aircraft.

He wanted a Central Operations Room with Colourdex, and operations rooms in each department, so as to allow him to follow a shortage up the trunk and along the branches and twigs. But this was to take a simplistic view of shortages. As each shortage is cured, other shortages are created and output may be little affected. What matters is to foresee what is needed and lay plans in good time rather than to allow bottlenecks to form and concentrate on their removal.

RELATIONS WITH TOP OFFICIALS

Under the Minister, responsibility for production was concentrated first on Sir Charles Craven as Controller-General and, shortly after he resigned in July 1942, on Sir Wilfrid Freeman as Chief Executive. Sir Wilfrid, who had been responsible for development and production in the Air Ministry at the outbreak of war, held office as Chief Executive from October 1942 until January 1945 when his duties, or most of them, passed to Edwin Plowden.

Freeman had by far the strongest personality in the department and could throw his weight around to some purpose, particularly in dealings with the Air Ministry. But he was not a good administrator or production planner and nobody could count on his sustained attention. He was likely to come to us only when at a loss to know whom to consult, or when he wanted to catch out one of the production departments. He never altogether took to Jewkes or fully appreciated what it was that DDGPS sought to do. Jewkes in turn never quite trusted Freeman.

Of the senior civil servants who formed the secretariat and looked after finance and contracts, we thought well of Sir Archibald Rowlands, the Permanent Secretary, and F. W. Smith, an Under-Secretary, but less well of most of the others, including two who were singled out in later years by Robert Hall in his diary as examples of men whose promotion to be Second Secretaries was quite incomprehensible.

On the production side of the Ministry, we owed a great deal to Group Captain (later Air Commodore) Banks who was Director of Engine Production until January 1944 when he moved over to take charge of engine development. Banks understood the need for careful planning of engines and engine accessories and was consistently right in his judgement of development problems, especially in relation to the Sabre.[3] Since he was responsible also for propellers and engine accessories it was fortunate that he was well disposed towards us and exercised a calming influence on the more excitable members of his staff. Banks had the good sense to bring in Brian Davidson in April 1942 as an administrative officer to take charge of plans and programmes in consultation with us. Until his departure to a senior post with the Bristol Aeroplane Company in July 1943 he was a most useful ally in the preparation of programmes for engines, propellers and engine accessories. After his departure we could count on cooperation from his assistant, Eric Bulley, who took his place until he, too, left at the end of 1944.

There were others for whom we had a high regard although our contacts were less frequent: Archie Forbes, Bill Strath, Ronnie Edwards and, in the Materials Production department, Edwin Plowden (the Director General), A. H. Hird and Edward Sara. The rest of the staff were a mixed bunch. Some, on the research and development side, carried on with duties not very different, except in scale and importance, from those of peacetime. The production departments, on the other hand, were manned almost entirely by temporaries with a wide assortment of backgrounds, from taxi-driver and salesman to directors of substantial businesses, with a notable lack of graduates among them. Reporting independently to the Minister were three other officials: a Chief Naval Representative, a Controller of Telecommunications Equipment, and a Controller of Research and Development.[4]

Shortly after I entered the Ministry, Craven went off ill and never returned, so that for the first half of 1942 there was no Controller-General. His Deputy, Sir Alexander Dunbar, was a poor substitute. We had a high regard for Craven, who had courage, common sense and good humour. The fact that his resignation was not accepted until July 1942, long after he had left the Department, was evidence of the Minister's equally high regard and reluctance to see him go. Dunbar, on the other hand, was a ditherer but it was he who was appointed in July 1942 to succeed Craven. He remained as Controller-General for a year, but subordinate after October to Freeman. Other names had been canvassed in April – Freeman himself, Nelson of English Electric, and Rootes, who was already virtually Controller-General of the Ministry of Supply – but no appointment was made. At the time, Jewkes, although anxious for the restoration of 'discipline' in MAP through a fresh appointment, did not take to the suggestion of Freeman whom he dismissed as 'the neurotic type, disposed to self-justification and a trifle querulous'.

In October, when Freeman was about to join the Department – as we understood, *alongside* Dunbar – Jewkes felt increasing frustration over the proposed arrangements and wrote to the Permanent Secretary (Rowlands) to express his disquiet. Sir Charles Bruce Gardner had reappeared as an 'efficiency expert', George Calder was apparently to be brought into the Ministry at a high level to assist Freeman, and there was talk of Ted Wright, the well-known American engineer, being asked to stay on and 'plan' aircraft production. On the other hand, F. W. Smith, one of the few civil servants with the drive and grasp that were needed, was being pushed into the background. In face of the multiplication of top jobs and the lack of understanding in the Ministry of what his own duties involved, Jewkes wanted to strengthen his hand by securing promotion to Director-General – a promotion in which he had expressed no interest when it was suggested in July.

Jewkes was also feeling lukewarm about staying in MAP. He was particularly incensed at Llewellyn's intrusion into organisational and planning affairs that were not his business especially as they only served to make confusion worse confounded. He pointed out that the main things that he had been appointed to do had now been done and that the head of the Programmes Department had a rather different role to play in future. The principal function of MAP was to provide the aircraft industry with a programme and see to it that it was carried out. But a programmes king would inevitably fail if he lacked the necessary standing in his own department and if he had no close contact with the Air Ministry. Jewkes underlined the dangers that would arise if programmes became the plaything of a host of other people, including Lord Cherwell, the Minister of Production (Lyttelton) and the Prime Minister – to say nothing of the increasing number of MAP officials who were taking an interest in agreeing the programme. The letter ended by hinting at resignation if Rowlands thought the suggestions unreasonable.

Rowlands did not take kindly to Jewkes's demands. He sent a noncommittal but essentially negative reply and the matter remained unresolved pending Freeman's arrival a week later. When Jewkes saw the new Chief Executive there was apparent agreement on a number of Jewkes's points. Programme changes should not be made through three layers of officials and there should be a committee to review proposed changes under the Chief Executive. Freeman also agreed that the Minister would have to be advised to confine himself to the proper ministerial functions. Not that that mattered much in the end since Llewellyn lasted only one more month.

Two months later, early in December, there was a fresh crisis. This time Jewkes, bursting for a showdown with Freeman, offered his resignation. He had recently returned from a visit to the United States to find the Chief Executive making no effort to see him, brushing aside suggestions that he should be brought into discussions on the new aircraft programme and, worst of all, making an outrageous attack on DDG Stats P in a document written for the Minister and shown to Jewkes by Rowlands. When he at last saw Freeman he did not mince words. If he was to stay in MAP he must be directly responsible to the Chief Executive and have clear authority over programmes. Planning, he told Freeman, was in greater confusion than at any time in the previous twelve months 'and you're responsible'. Freeman returned soft answers, telling Jewkes that he was in fact responsible to him but admitting, when asked if he had told this to Dunbar, his Deputy and Craven's successor as Controller-General, that he had not. (Exactly the same situation had arisen, as Jewkes discovered, in the case of Air Commodore Banks, who was in charge of engine production). Freeman also let fall that he had been 'looking all over' for a man with an engineering background to take charge of programmes but had been unable to find anybody – this in reply to a suggestion from Jewkes that this might be the right arrangement. Indeed, it was agreed at a meeting with the Minister a day or two later that a production engineer should come and work under Jewkes, but nothing came of this.

These exchanges hardly made for mutual confidence. The real trouble, however, was that neither Freeman nor his deputy could distinguish a planning issue from any other so that Jewkes was not informed of all proposed changes in programme and might even experience efforts to exclude him from meetings called to discuss such changes.

Things dragged on for several months. In February the Chief Executive proposed that we should be called the 'Central Planning, Programming and Statistics Department'. A liaison officer to the department was to be appointed by each of the production departments and it was to be the sole issuing authority for changes in programmes. Three weeks later, in the middle of March, Jewkes responded by submitting draft terms of reference, suggesting that the department should be responsible to the Chief Executive and 'exer-

cise general oversight over programmes, plans and statistics'. At the
end of the month the Chief Executive undertook to speak to the
Minister.[5] Nothing happened. In May Jewkes tried again. This time
he was successful and an office minute on 8 June 1943 announced his
promotion to Director-General, with more specific terms of reference
for his department.

All this manoeuvring seems to have brought promotion but little
else. Before the end of the year Jewkes was becoming increasingly
impatient. Rowlands had left for India, to be Finance Member,
taking F. W. Smith with him, and Jewkes complained that the Chief
Executive had become 'utterly irresponsible' with the removal of
Rowland's restraining hand. Other officials were called in on programme issues instead of DDG Stats P and we were left, once
summoned at the last moment, to clear up the mess. For example,
Jewkes heard only belatedly of a meeting on turrets to which he had
not been invited and which was intended to put everything on a firm
footing. A scheme for re-engining the Sunderland was handled by a
quite inappropriate official who was proposing to make use of surplus
Beaufort engines which we were busy handing back to the United
States. When the Prime Minister asked what relief to labour requirements could be found by reducing requirements for 1945 to those for
the war with Japan, the papers did not at first come to MAP at all
and, when they did, went to Musgrave, a member of the Secretariat.
The Chief Executive was then briefed by Sir John Buchanan for
discussions with the Ministry of Production at the same time as
Jewkes, called in at five minutes' notice, was seeing the Air Ministry
with Musgrave, an under-secretary.

It was incidents like these that finally moved Jewkes to leave MAP
and take up a post at the Ministry of Reconstruction. His departure,
however, was a rather protracted affair and this created difficulties
for Devons who was expected to take over responsibility while
Jewkes was still spending time in MAP and no one had received
official confirmation of the change. It was not until the end of January
that Jewkes was finally transferred on a full-time basis. Until this was
settled there was no office minute and no indication that Devons
should be told things that would normally be communicated to
Jewkes. A further difficulty was that Jewkes was leaving on the
assumption that the rest of us would stay and yet kept pressing us (or
at least Devons and me) to join him in his new department. In mid-
January 1944, for both of us, this looked the most likely outcome.

As he had foreseen, Devons's problems were aggravated by

neglect to inform and consult him. In late February he was complaining that no minutes put up to the Chief Executive ever came straight back from him. He had been deliberately excluded by the CE from a Mosquito meeting on the grounds that he would be wasting his time. Some days later, however, he had it out with the CE, who admitted that he had been 'very naughty' and that as his advisers the planning staff ought to know as much or more than anyone else in the department. In the days that followed, he pushed one thing after another at Devons and made what from our point of view were all the right decisions. Yet a month later he was still asking absentmindedly for Jewkes to be called in on a planning issue and on another occasion wanted to send him to the United States to discuss Packard Merlin engine supplies.

Failure to consult DDG Stats P on proposed changes in programme continued but Devons was able to establish close personal relations with Freeman and ended up as one of his greatest admirers. When he left the Ministry, Freeman offered him a job at Courtauld's which, however, he declined.

Whatever one might think of Freeman he was in a different category from the second rung of officials, for most of whom he had no great use. On one occasion he called in one after another of the experts on fighter aircraft and shrugged his shoulders as each departed, asking Devons what one could expect with such people. A month or two before he left the Ministry I noted in my diary:

> The CE calls a meeting of Director Generals. Who attends? The Director General of Aircraft Production? The CE once remarked in my hearing that he had to see DGAP who would probably tell him everything he already knew. When DGAP looked in on Freeman while he was talking over the new aircraft programme with Devons and offered to join in the discussion if it concerned him, the Chief Executive looked at Devons with a mischievous glint and said 'This wouldn't interest you at all, DGAP. You would just be wasting your time'. The Director General of Communications Equipment? The CE keeps away from radio. DDGQP [the Deputy Director General of Equipment Production]? He talks about nothing but bombs and the CE is tired of bombs – 'Simple things to make: why should we worry about bombs?' DGAI [the Director General of Aeronautical Inspection]? Who wants to consult DGAI on anything important? He can only say that such and such a cut will release so many inspectors. DGRM [Director

General of Repairs and Maintenance]? He might just as well be in another ministry for all he has in common with the production branches. DGEMP (Director General Engines and Materials Production)? But why hold a meeting merely to see Plowden? So for the last six weeks the CE hasn't called any DGs meetings.

It was not with the Chief Executive, however erratic, that we had most difficulty. Nor, after a time, was it with the engine and engine components departments. Within MAP it was mainly with the succession of Directors General of Aircraft Production, of whom the less said the better; and with the Controller of Research and Development (CRD), Air Marshall Linnell, who held office from June 1941 onwards. He was a poor communicator, too aloof from the production departments, and lacking in judgement. Apart from being slow off the mark, he could hardly escape some of the blame when so many of the aircraft reaching the production stage were flops and too many types of aircraft continued to be made. The link between design and production was central to aircraft planning and we needed close relations with R & D. Unfortunately we enjoyed them only at lower levels.

RELATIONS WITH THE AIR MINISTRY

Our difficulties were multiplied by the problem of establishing Air Ministry requirements. There were several different sections of the Air Ministry involved and each often appeared to be ignorant of what the other was proposing. This was particularly true of the Directorate General of Equipment (D of E) in Harrogate. It lay with them to place orders for spares and spare parts but they always seemed to be lagging far behind in their information. Other parts of the Air Ministry were also out of touch with one another and at times in a state of great confusion.

In Whitehall

It would have been easier to establish requirements had we been in closer touch with the Air Ministry and Jewkes pressed to be allowed to establish such contact. The main contact ultimately formed was between Devons and Henry Hindley who came nearest to being our opposite number in the Air Ministry. This was a very helpful contact, particularly in the last year of the war. But what with the physical separation of the two departments and the large number of units within both ministries, there was plenty of room for misunderstanding.

A good example of the confusion within and between the departments is provided by events towards the end of the war when plans had to be made for participation in air attacks against Japan.

In the spring of 1945 requirements for bombers for the Far East were still uncertain. The Lancaster was due to be phased out and replaced by the Lincoln but the Lincoln was several months late and there were technical difficulties affecting the adaptation of both aircraft for use abroad: for example, neither was fully tropicalised. The later the Lincoln became, the more Lancasters had to be produced. This made little difference if the war in Europe continued but when it ended there would be no use for the Lancaster in the Far East without tropicalisation. It would also need to be fitted for refuelling but no provision had been made at the only factory, Austin's, where Lancasters would be supplied (from August) with tropicalised power plants. On the other hand, the parent factory, A. V. Roe in Manchester, *was* providing for refuelling but not tropicalisation. Austin's were being kept in production in case the war in Europe lasted to the end of the year. So aircraft made exclusively for war in Europe (Stage I) would all be fitted with power plants for war with Japan (Stage II) but nothing would be done to equip them for refuelling. At that stage, too, CRD was inviting the Air Ministry to cancel Lincoln refuelling altogether on the grounds that it could only be introduced on aircraft incapable of use overseas because not tropicalised.

The muddle continued. In the middle of March there were still no tropicalised power plants for either aircraft. The Lincoln was now six months late and efforts to use up the surplus Lancasters made instead looked like being frustrated by lack of the only power plants that would make them acceptable.

The muddle in MAP was compounded by confusion within the Air Ministry. Six Lancaster squadrons were to be sent out as Liberator replacements, but beyond that the Chief of the Air Staff wanted Lincolns only. The Director of Operational Requirements, however, insisted on hedging and asked both for 200 Lincolns and 200 Lancasters by 1 September. MAP was led to believe that all 400 aircraft were a definite requirement while another Air Ministry department (OF) had no knowledge of any Lancaster requirement beyond the six squadrons. The Air Ministry by asking for all possible combinations – refuelling *and* saddle tanks on both aircraft – were overloading the manufacturers (A. V. Roe) and making certain that they could not get on fast enough with any of them.

On top of this, Sir Hugh Pugh Lloyd, named as commanding officer for the RAF in the Far East, was dead against refuelling. He did not want to start with the Lincoln, which was not a tried aircraft, but had been overruled. There was still trouble with the ailerons and the cooling – at least as calculated, for there had been no trials. It was very doubtful whether 200 of the new radiator being tested currently would be available by September. As for the Lancaster, one branch of the Air Ministry (OF) assumed that there would be plenty of spare tropicalised radiators while another (DofE), who placed the orders for spares, knew nothing about them and took for granted that all Lancasters would take temperate equipment. In addition, nobody had designed the modifications required in order to fit tropicalised power plants and, as mentioned above, refuelling was going ahead only at the parent factory (A. V. Roe), not at Austin's, where the tropicalised power plants were to be fitted.

A second example of our relations with the Air Ministry was the succession of clarion calls for more aircraft, such as that for heavy bombers which preceded Llewellyn's departure. A clarion call for more fighters was almost an annual affair. The last in the series came at the beginning of February 1945 just as the Russians were about to cross the Oder and had to be held back by Stalin from advancing on Berlin.

'The Air Staff', I noted in my diary, 'are responding to Russia's success by asking for more Hornets, Meteors, Tempests, Spitefuls, and Spitfire 22's although they can't hope for a squadron of the first before August, we're already giving the highest possible priority to the second, we're doubtful about achieving the programme for the third, the fourth is three months late, and the last is bound to go back. Every one of them is in technical trouble – in each case except the Tempest with the tail unit. The net effect of asking for more is to make DGAP's boys come clean on the inevitable set-backs on the last three, and rub in the engine shortage on the second'.

If this reflected on Air Ministry intelligence the rest of my note reflected on Vickers's:

I suggested that we might make up the inevitable loss in Spitefuls with Spitfire XIV's and Major Smith telephoned Elliott at Supermarine's. Today Elliott reported that we could get some 400 extra XIV's but the Spiteful was going back six months. It took half an hour to convince him that he was making the XIV's *by* pushing back the Spitefuls and that it was *Spitefuls* that the Air Staff were asking for.

In Harrogate: Spare Components

There was one branch of the Air Ministry, D of E in Harrogate, with which our relations were often far from happy although they improved and we had many good friends among the squadron leaders. D of E were responsible for ordering spares and spare components, but since requirements of components for new aircraft took priority, the supply available as spares was what was left over after meeting these requirements. Moreover the programme for any component had to be realistic and square with what manufacturers might reasonably be expected to deliver. The result was a constant battle between D of E with its control over orders and MAP with its control over programmes. From our point of view the provisioning of spare components was one long muddle and the source of constant friction from the start.

Matters were not improved by the existence in Harrogate of a branch of MAP, Principal Officer Aircraft Equipment, (POAE) which had responsibility for spare components but based its views on Air Ministry information that was received late and was inevitably out-of-date. We were satisfied that Harrogate methods of estimating spares requirements were hopelessly unreliable while our colleagues in Harrogate put it about that we had a lot to live down. Since there was every prospect that DDG Stats P might end up under the head of the Harrogate branch, there was no love lost between us.

Soon after DDG Stats P was established Devons, as Chief Statistician, paid a visit to Harrogate in order to make arrangements for the supply of information that we needed for planning purposes. He soon ran into difficulty. Instead of a talk with a single senior official in D of E he found himself in a formal meeting confronting three Air Commodores and three Group Captains. His request for regular information on engine stocks touched a sensitive spot and was rejected on grounds which he summarised as follows:

(1) Since requirements are determined by D. of E. and MAP have to accept them, stocks figures have nothing to do with MAP.

(2)   Even if they were the concern of MAP, regular stocks figures
      were not available, and would be very difficult to collect.
(3)   Even if they were available they were out of date, unrepre-
      sentative, inadequate and meaningless.
(4)   Even if they were not statistically inadequate, we should be so
      unfamiliar with them that we would misinterpret them.
(5)   Even if we (Stats P.) didn't misinterpret them others would if
      we circulated them.
(6)   In any case the Production Departments of MAP were getting
      the available figures already and our suggestion that we
      should receive regular figures would make us a bottleneck in
      the transmission of information from D. of E. to MAP.

In reply Devons made an equal number of points, trying to reassure
D of E that the figures would be used sensibly and pointing to the
difficulty of drawing up production programmes without them. While
D of E found production figures and production programmes helpful
in their work, MAP would find data on stocks and requirements
helpful in theirs, even though such data were not their concern.
When he asked how D of E would feel if they were cut off from
production figures there was a storm of protest.[6]

It was in the middle of this exchange that Devons was handed a
copy of the document of agreement on relations between the two
departments and observed that para 16 virtually granted the right of
access to any figures in the possession of the Air Ministry.

It was not only D of E that was reluctant to part with stock figures.
I can recall efforts to obtain figures of stocks from production
departments in MAP in which it was explained to me that since what
was in stock today was liable to pass into use tomorrow and the
figures were constantly changing, one day's figures could be of no
more significance than another's.

D of E were not at all reluctant to supply figures of exports and
imports. But as Devons quickly discovered, the figures were of little
value since they assumed that all imports would go to a maintenance
unit when this plainly did not happen. Imports might go direct to a
firm under contract to assemble or modify them and only reach a
maintenance unit much later, after modification; or they might go to
an aircraft constructor without passing through a maintenance unit at
all. Rotol, for example, had received 359 Wellington IV propellers
from the USA while the maintenance units had received only 32.
Rotol had also received 229 Beaufort IV propellers while the

maintenance units had had 339. In any event, maintenance units recorded only the time when receipt of the item was notified, which might be long after arrival in Britain.

In our experience the system of estimating spares requirements used by the Air Ministry always exaggerated a shortage or a surplus. Their calculations were based on issues from the maintenance units, and there was plenty of room for error in the records of issues. Issues from one unit might be made to another or forwarded to a third before they reached the squadrons and in the process entries might be made more than once. The scarcer any item of equipment became, the more the squadrons were likely to build up stocks or, if they ran out of stock, to seek supplies in a way that gave rise to duplication. Non-recurring requirements for stock were liable to be mixed up with recurrent consumption. Much of what was not to be found in a maintenance unit had probably been mislaid there. The more ribald among us held that stock-taking in the units was carried out by ex-ploughmen and dancers whose arithmetic was poor; and we nourished stories of storemen sitting on crates containing the very items whose existence they denied.

A good illustration of the unreliability of figures of issues was provided in 1942 or 1943 by the case of aircraft wheels. The Air Ministry wanted to place large orders on the basis of issues from maintenance units over the previous year, these figures being taken as a measure of usage. To meet these orders would have meant building two new factories when the strain on manpower was already at peak.

We argued from first principles that there could be no shortage and hence no need for new factories. Wheels were durable items that accumulated in stock once an aircraft had been in service for some time. When aircraft crashed the wheels could be recovered and were rarely if ever written off. Spare wheels should therefore be needed, if at all, only in the early life of the aircraft.

Fortunately it proved unnecessary to engage the Cabinet in speculation on the meaning of Air Ministry statistics. On the morning when the issue was to be discussed, a clerk in Harrogate confessed to an error in the figures and this when corrected was sufficient to deprive the Air Ministry's case of any foundation. We had no more trouble on wheels.[7]

Another example was propellers. I remember discovering early in August 1945 that the Air Ministry wished to place large orders for Hurricane propeller blades. At that time the Hurricane had been out of production for years and the spares requirements were enormous in relation to past experience – the total bill ran to over £2m. I spent a morning with the Air Ministry and found that provisioning for the limited number of Hurricanes due to be sent to the Far East covered every possible contingency. There were spare aircraft in case of damage to the front-line Hurricanes; there were spare propellers in case of damage to the propeller when the Hurricanes landed on the aircraft carriers from which they were to operate; then there were spare blades in case the damage was only to the blades. Damage was thus covered three times over, in spare blades, spare propellers and spare aircraft. The risk of damage was also put very high and no account seemed to be taken of the accumulation of semi-obsolete spares for the Hurricane at home bases. An hour's discussion cut the order by more than half.

These arguments about spares were typical of many. The American practice was to calculate the spares likely to be required over the lifetime of the equipment and plan for the spares to be produced simultaneously with new equipment. The UK divided the responsibility between the two Ministries, one dealing with requirements for new equipment and the other with spares. But for purposes of production planning it was not possible for MAP to wait until the Air Ministry came forward with orders for spares on the basis of experience in use. To do so could mean – and often did – that it was virtually impossible to get the Air Ministry to place orders for equipment that was so new that D. of E. had little or even no knowledge of its intended use, while, on the other hand, large orders tended to be placed for spares after the aircraft needing them had almost disappeared from service. Thus firms which we were urging to introduce new equipment as fast as possible might find themselves held up or planning too modestly for lack of orders or might plead that they had no spare capacity because of large and urgent orders to meet the Air Ministry's supposed operational needs.

Aircraft tyres provide many illustrations of the problems we faced. In September 1944 we were asked to make 2800 spare Wellington tyres per month when provisioning had been at the rate of 1300 per month. Production was boosted to 1800 and preparations were made for a further increase. At that point, in February 1945, we were given revised requirements of 1300 per month – the rate from which we started. The same thing happened with the Stirling. Output was at 399–400 per month when requirements were raised, first to 600 then to 800. Output responded and had reached 550 per month when requirements dropped to 400.

There is of course nothing surprising in a change in requirements in wartime. What is disturbing is the suspicion that it was not requirements that changed but estimates that were plainly mistaken. In the case of Stirling wheels, for example, D of E first requisitioned 8 spare wheels a month, then increased the requirement to 132 and finally cut it to 100. Over a period of six months, 123 spare wheels were delivered to meet what purported to be requirements of 792; but there was no evidence of any shortage. On the Lincoln we were asked for three spare tyres of one kind for each tyre fitted and two spare tyres of another kind for each of that type fitted although it was intended to replace the first kind of tyre by the second. The Spitfire, Spiteful and Seafire took no less than five different kinds of tyre of which the latest was a high pressure tyre, superior to the others, but not included in D of E's requirements. The spare tyres ordered for the Hornet and Meteor – the latest and fastest fighters – were put at only one-third of what was normal for other fighters. On the other hand, a stock of 22 000 Hurricane tyres had been built up, equal to three years' consumption, and the stock of Oxford/Anson tyres was nearly twice as large. And so I could go on. Yet at the end of the war the staff of POAE (which endorsed all these estimates) were doing their best to prevent us from issuing a tyre programme.[8]

Similar problems in securing agreement on requirements arose over modifications of aircraft design or in engine accessories when use overseas was in contemplation. 'Tropicalisation', as it was called, affected radiator, turret and other requirements but the decision to tropicalise often reached us from the Air Ministry in Whitehall long before D of E in Harrogate were informed or had had time to revise their estimates of requirements. Coordination, to be successful, meant that we had to be better informed about what one department of the Air Ministry had in mind than some other departments of the same ministry might prove to be. And, of course, within MAP we had the same problem since the production departments were not always well informed about developments in progress.

An allied problem arose over a proposal in March 1945 to use carburettors from broken-down Merlin engines on new Merlin 24s. To start with, we couldn't break down the engines without the agreement of the engine repair division. If we wanted to cut the programme for new carburettors by the number we hoped to salvage, a whole host of people had to agree. RM5 had to say that they could take off carburettors at the right pace, and RM3 that they could make any necessary repairs. The manufacturers put up a barrage of objections: they hadn't the space, they would need 50 per cent more labour, they threw doubt on the reliability of the carburettors when repaired and warned us that the engine makers (Ford's) would blame any engine defect on the carburettor. POAE, being responsible for spares, although taking no part in initiating the scheme or coordinating it, would have to give it his blessing and issue the necessary instructions to DRM, the director of the repairs and maintenance divisions. The inspectorate would also have to be brought in at headquarters and all the factories affected. Lastly, CRD had to agree that the repaired carburettors would be acceptable.

Dozens of other examples could be given of erratic ordering of spare components. For example, I noted on a single day in February 1945 the following (among other) cases:

Barracuda oil coolers:	The Admiralty wanted to cancel 3000 (of which 1000 under pressure from us) but were too late for the cancellation to take effect.
Warwick oil coolers:	The Air Ministry wanted 2400 when production of the aircraft had almost ceased and 400 spares was all they had had for the 500 aircraft already delivered.
Mosquito fuel coolers:	At the last review, 1674 were cancelled; now 1000 more were wanted.
Lancaster tropicalised radiators and oil coolers:	Only 200 on order as spares behind 5000 power plants.
Lincoln engines:	Air Ministry asking for 130 per cent spares but would be satisfied with 50 per cent without saying why. (Still very high.)

It is easy to point to mistaken estimates of spares – both spare components and spare parts of all kinds. But there were serious difficulties both in assessing requirements and in ensuring that the requirements were met. Firms were usually under pressure to supply new aircraft, and aircraft spares of all kinds tended to take second place. Even if they had set aside an adequate proportion of capacity for the manufacture of spares firms could divert that capacity to relieving shortages on the production line or produce ample spares but of the wrong kind. From 1942 DDG Stats P did its best to keep track of the total volume of spare parts produced by each firm and to find ways of inducing or bullying firms into improving the supply. From about 1943 there is evidence of a marked improvement. But the whole system of provisioning was unsatisfactory. Each manufacturer should have been invited to supply a list of every part, together with the percentage of spares which he thought necessary in each case, and should have been required to produce spare parts to that percentage *pari passu* with the airframe, engine or component to which the part was fitted. There would still have been a need for additional spares when the intensity of use altered substantially or when equipment was used overseas. No system will ever be perfect. But an initial percentage accompanying the finished item is surely the right starting point.[9]

RELATIONS WITH THE MANUFACTURERS

Aircraft

Our contacts with the firms were at first almost exclusively through the production departments. Direct contacts took some time to develop. So far as I can recall we did not often visit any of the aircraft factories but we did see some of the manufacturers at MAP. They included a few prima donnas – usually the entrepreneurs who had survived the lean years between the wars and were now flourishing at the head of large, expanding businesses.

The most conspicuous example was Handley Page who, on the sole occasion when I encountered him, assured me that there was not enough of God in MAP since it was only God who could create order out of such chaos. MAP's opinion of Handley Page was equally derogatory. He was thought to want full charge of the Halifax group so that he could rig it to ensure that the parent factory would always meet its programme. In evidence of this, there was at least one factory that had been taken under Handley Page's wing but was given deficient drawings and very little help. The MAP chairman of the group also maintained that he (Handley Page) was the biggest sinner in the industry as a hoarder of stocks. His stock records were deficient and he could not provide a list of quantities of Halifax parts although he claimed to have them down to the last bolt and nut. When his manager agreed to long runs on some new machines he insisted on short runs, leaving some of the machines idle. Instead of using a standard AGS bolt he designed one that was identical and refused to place an order for the standard bolt until, when forced to do so, he was too late. And so on.

Dobson of A. V. Roe was in the same mould. But when it came to argument with him, and MAP officials (including Freeman) announced in advance that he would be made to toe the line, it was apt to be Dobson who emerged victorious. A good example was a meeting in June 1944 when we wanted to introduce the York transport at Short and Harland's in Belfast (there being nothing else planned for manufacture there). Everybody had been in agreement beforehand that the York could be in production a year ahead of the Lincoln. We were also urging an increase in the Lancaster programme at the expense of the Anson, which Dobson ruled out for a whole variety of reasons, and the Chief Executive was emphatic that he would give Dobson nothing at all in place of the Anson. But by the time Dobson had finished he had not only got away with the assertion that he could provide extra Yorks elsewhere but Short and Harland was to change over to the Lincoln and he was to build more Lancasters as well.

Among the things that struck us in our dealings with the firms were two propositions likely to apply generally. One was that efficiency was highly correlated with ability to stick to a programme. There were no doubt many reasons why firms failed to carry out the programme they had agreed. But the main reason, again and again, was sheer inefficiency. As we maintained all along, the most important ingredient in programme fulfilment was good management. The second proposition was that firms almost invariably underestimated the loss of production in changing over from one model to another. It was on this point, more than any other, that we preferred to use our own judgement based on analysis of past changeovers and the length of time required to reach full-scale production. This proposition applied not only to complete changes in model but to modifications on the production line. Nothing was more destructive of the rhythm of production than interruption of the line to introduce some modification. This was no doubt why the Americans used to turn out aircraft without modification and pass them to a separate factory for all modifications to be carried out as a separate activity. It also helps to explain how Speer managed to increase German aircraft production in the least propitious circumstances of the final year of war.

Engines and Propellers

With the engine and propeller firms our contacts were also mainly in the Ministry. I visited several of the propeller factories and on technical matters to do with propellers profited from exchanges with some of the younger men at de Havilland, especially Stephen Appleby and Val Cleaver. (Rotol's had no similar enthusiasts eager to swap gossip with me.) These exchanges were informative, frank and entertaining but my visits to the firms were not at all to the liking of W. T. O'Dea, who was Director of Propeller Production during my first six months or so. They raised no problems with his successors.

In the case of aero-engines there were regular meetings at MAP with representatives of the firms at which DDG Stats P were represented. The meetings with Rolls Royce were of particular importance, especially after Packard engines started to arrive from the United States. On high level issues the discussions were with the Chairman, Hives. He could be trusted completely in expressing technical judgement, whether on the potentialities of Rolls engines or on the merits of the Packard engines, which he admitted were a better job than the Rolls Merlins of the same vintage. (It was typical of Hives that he was content to drive an Oldsmobile not a Rolls Royce.)

At the start we agreed with him that it was enough to indicate the requirements for engines other than the Merlin XX and ask for these requirements to be met in full, leaving the Merlin XX programme to be adjusted to any surplus or shortage of capacity. The availability of engines later than the Merlin XX conditioned the rate of introduction of new aircraft and the build-up of their manufacture but this did not apply to the Merlin XX itself. With the newer engines we could push ahead with Spitfires that took the two-stage Merlin or the Griffon and provide for the later marks of Mosquito, Barracuda, etc.

The initial formula had a limited life: the engine programme had to specify what outputs we expected of each and every engine. In addition there were all the complexities from late in 1942 of providing for the absorption of an uncertain number of Packard Merlins and for the changeover to two-stage Merlins in Packard's. These were matters which had to be discussed in detail below Hives's level.

When Brian Tew took over the engine programme in 1942 he found no difficulty with the Rolls factories at Glasgow and Manchester. At the Glasgow factory Dr Llewellyn Smith was cooperative and numerate. At the Ford factory in Manchester, Denn was familiar with programmes and as the factory remained on single-stage Merlins throughout, the programme was straightforward. His problem was with Crewe and the parent factory at Derby which made all the latest

Rolls Royce engines and had to introduce a series of modifications on the production line with an inevitable disruption of the published programme. In establishing the programme for these two factories, Tew had to deal with Swift, an engineer who had started as an apprentice with Rolls Royce and worked his way up, was devoted to his job and had a certain shrewdness in practical matters, but was not one of nature's planners and was not well disposed to MAP. Indeed, when Tew took over Swift had just had a flaming row with Banks's deputy, Welman, who had tried to get him sacked over the shortage of an item which turned out to be provided on embodiment loan and was therefore the responsibility of MAP, not of Rolls Royce.

Swift worked with weekly programmes without feeling in any way bound by the monthly programme issued by MAP. He had his own sources of information from the firm's representatives with the airframe contractors and the Squadrons and no doubt felt better able than MAP to judge immediate needs. After a time, however, there was a sudden change and what had previously been confrontation rather than negotiation became continuous dialogue with a regular exchange of information between Swift (or his assistants) and Tew. Tew would be telephoned with news of developments in aircraft production and asked to investigate and report back, as he always did. At the same time he would pass on to Rolls the detailed information lying behind the engine programme so that the programme came to be, as intended, the point of reference from which discussion and action proceeded.[10]

Even so, Rolls were quite capable of sticking by their own counsel if they so chose. In February 1945 Devons kept asking every week why there was no delivery of engines in the Merlin 100 series from Glasgow and kept being told by the Director of Engine Development that he had given instructions that the engines should be delivered without modification. Meanwhile Llewellyn Smith, Rolls's man in charge of the Glasgow factory, was adamant that engines would not be delivered until the modifications were incorporated.

With Bristol, the other main producer of aero-engines, we had no similar problem. Eric Bulley while in DDG Stats P in 1942–43 had been on good terms with Rowbottom and Verdon Smith, representing Bristol, and by the time Tew took over from Bulley in the middle of 1943 he could rely also on contact with Brian Davidson who had just moved to Bristol.

There were always people like the raw materials department who were glad to have a programme and asked no further questions.

There were others who took the programme too literally and expressed consternation when slippage occurred. Others again discounted what was in the programme as they thought fit without any consultation with us. Our own position was that the programme provided a point of reference but that there was always later information, which we did our best to assemble, on the trend in output and prospective new requirements. Tew thought it right to communicate to people like Verdon Smith and Swift something of what was in the wind if they could be trusted not to deviate from the published programme. The programme represented the Minister's instructions and must be obeyed as far as possible. But since everybody knew that ministers changed their mind, it was useful to discuss what changes might occur so that at least contingency plans could be made. This formula appeared sensible; but contingency plans may cost money and impinge on the published programme. It is not easy to operate simultaneously a hard and fast but obsolescent programme and a kind of shadow programme for which there is as yet no official authority.

MAP AND AIRCRAFT REQUIREMENTS

In drawing up the aircraft programme, we were not supposed to give effect to our private views as to what aircraft should or should not be produced. It was for others to state requirements and for us to reconcile their wants with production possibilities. But inevitably we did have views and these were bound to impinge on the aircraft programme. This did not mean that we could challenge specific Air Ministry requirements but that when proposals for changeovers were under discussion, our view of the changes that should be made was bound to be coloured by our assessment of the merits of different aircraft. We had a closer and more continuous view of the options than other people had and, within fairly narrow limits, could select, or at least press for, the changes which in our judgement were in the best interests of the RAF.

In general, however, our views had little influence on the programme-mix. We should certainly have voted for a narrower range of aircraft types. Much of what was produced was, in our view, junk. Some should never have gone into production; some met a requirement more cheaply supplied by another aircraft and merely served to inflate costs by reducing the average length of run and

adding to the overheads of development; some had no other justification than to provide jobs. The department was reluctant to cut out
the junk and switch to better aircraft because of the loss of output in
the changeover and fear of the wrath of the PM (or even the Minister
of Production) when made aware of the dip in production.

Apart from the junk there was the brake on production exercised
by incessant modifications of design. One could not, of course, arrest
changes in design and even to interfere with them was to risk
lowering the performance of the finished aircraft. What made us
uneasy was that there was never any costing of these modifications,
weighing the improvement in quality against the loss in output, which
must have been very considerable.[11]

Similarly there was no attempt in MAP or in the Air Ministry to
frame satisfactory tests of performance in relation to the job the
aircraft was designed to carry out. We only learned how good an
aircraft the Lancaster was compared with the Halifax when figures
were produced showing the losses of aircraft in relation to the
tonnage of bombs dropped; and the research on this came, not from
MAP, but from the PM's section under Lord Cherwell.[12] Not that
tonnage dropped was the ultimate criterion. The Mosquito might well
have exceeded the Lancaster's record in terms of damage done per
man-hour of aircraft construction.

Although our views had no effect on the heavy bomber programme, we thought it a mistake from the day America entered the
war. It made heavy demands on manpower, employing in one way or
another about a million workers, when manpower was *the* limiting
factor in the war effort, so other urgent demands could not be met.
Heavy bombers were used almost exclusively for area bombing and at
night and did not have the decisive effect that was expected on
German war production (as our own experience of German bombing
might well have indicated).[13] Light bombers like the Mosquito, in
which the Air Ministry showed little interest, were far more accurate
and relatively cheap to manufacture. Above all, it would have been
reasonable to rely quite heavily on the Americans who were anxious
to concentrate on bombers and whose Flying Fortresses could make
daylight raids with greater accuracy on selected targets.[14] In any
event, whatever the case for expanding British heavy bomber production in 1942 and 1943, to aim at further expansion not only in the
following year but even in 1945 and 1946 was a mistake.

It was in fighters, not bombers, that the British had an undeniable
advantage. Yet in fighters no effort was made to introduce the

Mustang even when fitted with two-stage Merlin engines although the aircraft was expected in June 1942 to be superior to the FW190 and the Me 109.[15] The subsequent record of the Mustang confirmed its early promise and caused Devons in 1945 to rank our failure to manufacture it as the second biggest mistake in aircraft planning.

Apart from the Mustang (for which there was no programme) and the heavy bombers (where additions to the programme kept being made whatever view we held) there were occasions on which we did have an influence on what went into the programmes. Jewkes was always full of ideas for changes that in his view would offer better value to the Air Force. In March 1942, for example, he wanted to push up the Halifax programme at Handley Page and English Electric, take the Lancaster out of Vickers' Castle Bromwich factory, put in more Griffon Spitfires, convert South Marston to take the Mosquito with two-stage Merlin engines and make more light bombers (preferably Mosquitoes) and turn A. W. Hawksley over from the Albemarle to the Mosquito (we were great supporters of the Mosquito).

Jewkes had no high opinion of the Air Staff. 'We'll win this war with low altitude machines', he said in April 1942. 'How do I know that? Because the Air Staff thinks that we'll win it with high altitude ones!'. While we discounted these flights of fancy, others found them rather disconcerting and they may have been the source of Freeman's uneasiness about Jewkes. Towards the end of 1944, when Freeman expressed more confidence in Devons than in Jewkes, he explained it by saying that he didn't often know what Jewkes was up to and that, whenever Jewkes came back from the United States, he always had some great scheme such as reorganising Fairey or shutting down everything in the United Kingdom.

An outstanding example of our influence on the programme – although not an altogether happy one – was the Lancaster VI (later re-named the Lincoln). In the middle of 1942 it had seemed unlikely that the two-stage Merlin would ever be used in heavy bombers.[16] Meanwhile, however, a flood of single-stage Merlin engines was beginning to arrive from Packard in America, and Ely Devons and Brian Tew (who did the engine planning) concluded that it was time to change over capacity in Britain from single-stage to two-stage engines so as to be ready for the introduction of the latter into the Lancaster, assuming that this would yield the same advantages in the case of bombers as it had done in the case of fighters.

They did not, however, consult Linnell (Controller of Research and Development). When he found out what was proposed he agreed that the idea was a good one but went on to point out that the engine change would require such drastic modifications of the Lancaster that it was virtually a new aircraft, so that a longer warning would have been helpful. The Lincoln did in fact keep being put back (it was already six months late in March 1945) and more Lancasters taking single-stage Merlins had to be fed into the programme. We had to keep balancing the risk of a shortage of single-stage Merlins if the Lincoln continued to be set back and more Lancasters added against a possible surplus of engines for which no use could be found if they were not fitted to Lancasters, the only other application of any importance being the Mosquito. This was not a small matter since with a Lancaster programme of 400 a month in 1945 each month's delay added 1600 (excluding spare engines) to the requirements of single-stage engines. Uncertainty over the engine change in so important an aircraft made it difficult to devise a firm programme for engine production at the three units involved: Rolls Royce (Glasgow), Ford (UK), and Packard (USA). To commit any one of the three to a changeover to two-stage engines in advance of careful assessment of the time required for the introduction of the Lincoln was a serious error.[17]

LABOUR SUPPLY

Officials in MAP were diligent in seeking out alibis and excuses. The Ministry was constantly under attack for not meeting its programme and great ingenuity was shown in meeting these attacks.

One of the Ministry's critics was Beaverbrook. He told the Prime Minister in December 1941 that there was capacity even for the Hennessy programme of October 1940 (see Table 6.2, p. 110) – a larger programme than we had just issued. There was plenty of floorspace, machine tools, extrusion presses, engine capacity, etc., etc. There was nothing wrong with the organisation of his old department. All that was necessary, one might conclude, was to place more orders. This was at a time when output was no more than half the Hennessy programme and the slow upward trend was consistent with nothing better than fulfilment of the (lower) December 1941 programme in two years' time.[18]

From then on, criticism focused on the Heavy Bomber programme. More and more heavy bombers were introduced into the programme but there was always a shortfall. By the middle of 1942 the programme showed a peak of 612 heavy bombers a month by the end of 1943 (output at the end of 1941 had been only 55). In 1943 the programme showed an even higher peak, although only by a very small margin. It was never possible, however, to get output above 520 in April 1944.

We were not surprised that the programme was not met but were not very clear why not. By October 1942 Devons had come to the conclusion that the answer lay in labour supply. Output had been expanding along a logarithmic curve that was now beginning to droop. Yet the programme called for an increase of 100 per cent in structure weight in 1943 compared with one of about 60 per cent achieved in 1942. On this basis Devons argued that it would be only by luck if the output of heavy bombers (which accounted for most of the increase) got to 500 per month by the end of 1943 (and in fact the monthly average in the last quarter of 1943 was still only 427).

The view that it was labour supply that was acting as a brake was highly congenial to the production departments, who embraced it all too eagerly. Manpower requirements had been a bone of contention throughout the war. When in 1941 MAP stated their labour requirements to meet the expanded heavy bomber programme, Bevin and the Ministry of Labour rejected them as excessive, arguing that labour was used inefficiently and pointing out that aircraft firms that were given all the labour they asked for were still unable to meet their programme. A year later, Llewellyn made additional manpower a condition for his promise of an increased output of heavy and medium bombers in response to the Air Minister's 'clarion call'.[19] Shortly afterwards, Freeman pressed on Cripps (without success) the suggestion that the Prime Minister be asked to give bombers priority over all other munitions in their labour requirements.[20] Meanwhile Lyttelton, the Minister of Production, was asking why a labour force of 600 000 in America could produce 3000 aircraft a month while it took 1 400 000 workers in the United Kingdom to produce 2000 aircraft a month.

MAP had in fact been treated very generously in the successive allocations of additional manpower, with an increase of over 300 000 a year at its disposal in 1941–42. Workers were protected from call-up to the armed forces and mechanics in the RAF were withdrawn and lent for a limited period to the aircraft industry. But when the Cabinet came to allocate labour at the end of 1942 it was clear that the limits of available manpower were being reached and MAP's bid for 603 000 workers from the middle of 1942 to the end of 1943 was

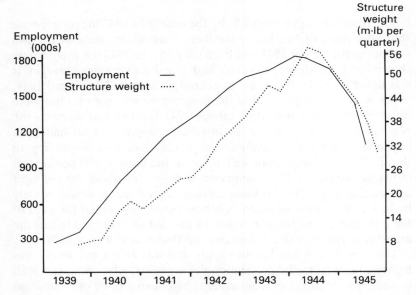

FIGURE 3.1   *Employment on munitions for MAP and structure weight of aircraft delivered, 1939–45. For graph data see Table 6.3, p. 111.*

cut by 100 000. This cut contributed to the downward revision of the aircraft programme to a more 'realistic' level in January 1943.

At the end of 1942 MAP reckoned that, with employment up by 140 000, the allocation entitled them to 360 000 more workers in 1943, or 30 000 a month. The Ministry of Labour denied that there was any such automatic entitlement and a controversy ensued in which Jewkes expressed scepticism of the 'pseudo-scientific methodology' underlying MAP's estimates of labour requirements. These depended on what he described as 'mysticism in the use of statistics of structure weight per head'. The assumed seven per cent increase in this every half-year might double as firms got into their stride: it had risen by 40 per cent or more in the second half of 1942 at English Electric and at A. V. Roe. MAP was already getting the lion's share of any labour that was available, even if it was no more than half its 'requirements'. In any event these 'requirements' included 50–60 000 in the Midlands where there had been no net increase for over six months. It would be much more sensible to move work out of the Midlands than bank on additional labour that simply couldn't be found in that region.

As Jewkes's criticisms implied, the planning of manpower could never be very scientific. Firms gave one figure for labour requirements and returned another for actual recruitment even when they continued to meet their programme. MAP's assessments of what the programme required in manpower took no account of all the other factors that might prevent its achievement – not least, inefficient management and poor utilisation of existing manpower, as Bevin kept insisting. Equally, there could be no exact calculation of labour supply, either in total or by region. Every effort was made, through a system of labour preferences, to give priority to a limited group of factories designated by MAP. But as always happened, the priority list got longer and longer and more and more of the factories on the list moved up to Priority 1.

A further cut of 200 000 was made in July 1943, reducing the allocation of manpower for the year to an extra 160 000 instead of the 360 000 originally asked for. At the end of 1943 came a fresh allocation for 1944 based on Churchill's formula that there should be no further enlargement of the RAF after December 1944. Again MAP's bid was cut, this time by 155 000, and the programme, too, was cut with the intention of reducing manpower by this amount although later calculations suggested that the labour released would not exceed 100 000.[21] A further cut of 112 000 was proposed in July 1944; but by the time this had been translated into the August aircraft programme, the end of the war was in sight and labour requirements were dominated by Cabinet decisions on the date to be assumed for peace in Europe.

My memory of these labour allocations is coloured by recollections of the atmosphere in MAP at the time. A few illustrations may help to convey this.

In October 1942, when Devons was able to produce indications of increasing efficiency in the aircraft industry in the form of a rise in the output of structure weight per head, his figures were at first eagerly seized on to rebut Ministry of Production criticisms based on the disappointing record of output in the previous six months. The Secretariat, however, (in the person of Lindsay Scott, Second Secretary) warned against using the figures for fear that labour would be withdrawn if Bevin got hold of them.

In December 1943 when the Prime Minister had asked for estimates of savings in labour by cutting the 1945 programme, Jewkes estimated that a programme along the lines suggested would save 40 000 workers in 1944 and ultimately 180 000. DGAP (Director

General of Aircraft Production) – at that time Fraser – gave an estimate of 11 250 which the Chief Executive passed on to the Air Ministry. When I suggested that this would dispose the Air Ministry to regard the savings from cuts of junk aircraft as nugatory, Fraser and Buchanan united in asserting that it would dispose the Air Ministry to make bigger cuts; and anyhow their figure was correct. It need hardly be said that neither of these gentlemen would have dreamt of a corresponding expansion in the programme in return for an extra 11 250 workers. Fraser's line was to make cuts and at the same time protest that there was still too little labour to meet the programme so as to have an alibi when the programme was not met.

In February 1944 the Chief Executive found it alarming that the Lancaster programme might continue to be beaten in spite of some loss of labour and feared that at the next labour allocation Bevin would then try to withdraw labour. Freeman went so far as to propose storing Lancasters, presumably to keep deliveries down to the programme level.

In July 1944 Freeman, whose views on labour mobility were no more extravagant than those of many of his colleagues, argued that if an aircraft factory was shut, one-third of its workers would be sure to vanish. Either they would be old men over 60 whom not even Mr Bevin could control, or they would be women who wouldn't go another hundred yards to work, or at least they would never agree to work for Mr Smith because they were devoted to Mr Brown for whom they had worked since infancy. All this was so much propaganda against cuts in manpower for the aircraft industry. Nobody, it was suggested, would succeed in conveying the labour released to the points of scarcity unless these happened to be literally next door.

As the war with Germany drew to an end, we assumed that in cutting the programme we ought to try to release labour in areas of acute labour shortage and delay closure in areas where there was likely to be more difficulty in absorbing the labour released. The Ministry of Labour, Board of Trade and Ministry of Production seemed at first (in September 1944) to have literally no views on the matter, even at a meeting which they had pressed us to hold. Later (in February 1945) their view of the labour situation seemed to be determined by what would get them out of their immediate difficulties, with no really long view of regional policy. Thus Coventry and Scotland came alike to them because both had some unemployment. They did not seem to mind whether Rolls made jets at Wolverhampton or in Glasgow. If Lancasters were to be cut, they preferred that we should make the cut at A. V. Roe in Lancashire rather than at Austin in the Midlands. In the same way they wanted English Electric to release labour from production of the Halifax to meet the needs of Horrocks in Lancashire, and Rootes to carry on at Stoke when they were already well on the way to closure. (These are not the afterthoughts of the 1990s but immediate reactions in February 1945.)

Very often, of course, we had little choice but to close plants in what were areas with doubtful post-war prospects. In this category we included the textile districts in Lancashire and were correspondingly reluctant to begin by closing the de Havilland propeller plant at Lostock or the Bristol engine factory at Accrington rather than make cuts at alternative locations. But closure had to come sooner or later and it was not easy to contrive programmes that allowed even a skeleton production without swelling a surplus that was already unmanageable. Nonetheless there were some who wanted us to carry on production at an aircraft factory like Vickers (Chester) merely to hold the labour for civil work to follow the Lancaster. On this showing we should have had to keep one set of labour figures for aircraft the Air Ministry wanted and another set for aircraft to absorb the unemployed – at that time about 100 000 for the country as a whole.

4 The Engine Programme

As explained earlier, we regarded the engine as the centre-piece of production planning. At first we took it for granted that there could never be too many engines and it was not until late in the war, and once we had confidence that the inflow of Merlin engines from America would continue, that we planned for more than a small decline in production.[1] On the other hand, we had no more use for engines without aircraft than for aircraft without engines. Until at least 1943 we simply regarded it as axiomatic that engines would be the main limiting factor in the output of aircraft.

If we leave aside engines for training aircraft and jet engines, which had only a limited impact on our planning, there were three manufacturers, Rolls Royce, Bristol and Napier. Both Rolls and Bristol by 1942 had one main engine of which they produced over 1000 a month – the liquid-cooled Merlin and the air-cooled Hercules. One mark of these succeeded another until there were, for example, thirty marks of the Merlin in production from Mark XX onwards (including Packard Merlins) and four marks of the Hercules. In addition, both firms had a more powerful engine coming into production at the end of 1942: the Griffon which reached 375 per month in the first half of 1945 and the Centaurus which never averaged more than 150 per month. Napier had one engine only – the Sabre – and in the latter years of the war it, too, was produced at about 150 per month.

Production of aero-engines in total climbed from about 1100 per month in 1939 to a peak of about 5500 a month in the first quarter of 1944 after which there was a steep fall to about 3000 a month in the spring of 1945. Production had been rising fast in 1941 before DDG Stats P was formed and from the spring of 1942 to the autumn of 1943 ran fairly flat. Meanwhile imports, which had been modest in 1941–42 – about 250 per month – began in 1943–44 to approach or exceed 1000 per month and make the spurt in production at the end of 1943 look decidely superfluous.

DEVELOPMENT PROBLEMS

Engine supply was for most of the war a constant anxiety but it was rare for any engine shortage to become acute. The more usual

76

problem was that a new engine or mark of engine took longer to reach series production than was allowed for in the aircraft programme so that arrangements had to be made to prolong some earlier combination of airframe and engine. It was a recognised practice to include a new aero-engine in the programme some months earlier than one could count on delivery. This could be discounted and some allowance made for inevitable delays. On the other hand, it was important to take the earliest possible advantage of a new engine in improving aircraft performance. There was thus a balance of risks which the programme had somehow to resolve and it rested with us to act as insurance brokers, advising on the margins to allow for contingencies on the basis of past experience and what guidance we could obtain.

With the various marks of Merlin the uncertainties of development were nearly always limited. At the other extreme we simply could not attempt to put a date on the availability of jet engines until the war was nearing an end. In between, the Griffon and Centaurus were months late but once in production functioned satisfactorily. The Sabre on the other hand was never really in the clear in the sense that the interval between overhauls remained extremely short.

Apart from changeovers to a new engine, which usually meant a loss of three months or more in production, there was the need to provide for new and additional aircraft and decide how they could best be engined or indeed whether the necessary engines and accessories could be found. On occasion, the insertion of additional aircraft into the programme might require some juggling with the engining of other aircraft in order to release supplies of the engines needed, as when Hercules engines were found for the Albemarle by running the Stirling short of engines. But we did not have to deal, as in the case of engine accessories, with separate orders for spares or have difficulty in raising contracts to back up the production programmes agreed with the firms.

COORDINATION PROBLEMS

We had two main problems. One lay in the very large requirement for the heavy bombers when there was no certainty how long any heavy bomber would continue with the same type of engine. At peak the aircraft programme showed over 600 heavy bombers a month for which it was necessary to provide some 3000 engines a month (including spares). This represented nearly two-thirds of total engine capacity in Britain and nearly all of it was required for two types only, the Lancaster and the Halifax, the Stirling being confined latterly to a single factory. The Lancaster in particular absorbed an enormous proportion of Merlin engines with a monthly requirement at peak of about 2000. It was not possible to assume that the same engine would be specified indefinitely. There had been a Hercules-engined Lancaster although it was phased out and there was every likelihood that the single-stage Merlin in use in 1942–44 would be succeeded by a two-stage Merlin. The Halifax had started with a Merlin engine, changed to a Hercules engine and might change back again to a two-stage Merlin. How could one provide against contingencies on that scale when engine capacity could not be changed over completely from one make of engine to another in less than a couple of years?

The second problem, allied to this, was coordination between supplies from America and domestic production. The problem of coordination arose over all the engines procured from the United States for installation in new British aircraft – e.g. Wright Cyclone 2600A engines for the Stirling II, Pratt and Whitney R 2800 engines for the Warwick, and R 1830 engines for the Beaufort. It arose also in a form of less concern to us in the Air Ministry's requirements for spare engines behind the American aircraft used by the RAF. The numbers involved were large, running into thousands, the supply was uncertain and subject to delay, and the requirements were liable to vary abruptly in spite of fixed contracts. There were also thousands of engines required in Canada and Australia for the Lancaster and Mosquito aeroplanes they were building and more particularly for the Ansons, Harvards and other trainers in use by the RAF in Canada.

Our anxieties were concentrated not so much on these engines as on the American-made Merlins ordered originally in 1940 when Lord Beaverbrook had induced the Packard Motor Company to lay down capacity for the manufacture of 1000 Merlin engines per month against an order for 9000 engines of which 6000 were for the United Kingdom and 3000 for the United States. Delivery began in August 1941 and, after a slow start, built up to 800 a month by the middle of 1942. The story of the Packard Merlins is long and complex and illustrates the difficulties of international coordination in a changing world.[2]

COORDINATION WITH AMERICAN SUPPLIES

There were five different problems all with their own uncertainties.

Problems of Expanding Capacity

The popularity of the Merlin engine, both in the United Kingdom and North America, and the upward trend in aircraft production, led to a steady increase in requirements. No major expansion of engine capacity in the United Kingdom could be faced, so the burden of expansion to meet British requirements fell mainly on Packard and it was necessary to decide the scale of that expansion.

Problems of Allocating Capacity

The decision, however, rested with the United States, not with the United Kingdom, and it was also for the United States to decide how capacity was allocated between the two countries. Under the original agreement two-thirds of the output of the Packard plant was assigned to the United Kingdom and it was generally expected that once the first US contract for 3000 engines was completed the whole output would be made available to the United Kingdom. Fresh contracts were, however, placed by the United States, leaving the basis of allocation in future uncertain.

Problems of Changeover from One Engine Mark to Another

The first Packard Merlins – Merlin 28s – differed from the Merlin 20, the latest type then in production, and in the use of a two-piece cylinder block approximated more closely to the Merlin 22, which did not come into production in Britain until 1942, several months after the arrival of the first Packard engines. The Merlin 28 was later replaced, first by the 38 and then by the 224. These single-stage variants were in their turn replaced by two-stage engines, the Merlin 68 and 300, akin to the British Merlin 61. Each changeover meant some loss of output and each was attended by great uncertainty as to the appropriate timing since this had to match changes in the aircraft programme requiring the installation of the new engines and themselves involving loss of output and uncertainty over the timing.

Problems of Allocation by Aircraft Type

Since the proportion of Packard engines to Rolls Royce engines rose year by year it was necessary to contemplate possible extensions in the range of aircraft types taking the American engine. The only British type actually so fitted apart from a few Spitfires, were the Lancaster and its successor, the Lincoln. Australian and Canadian Mosquitoes and a few Canadian Hurricanes were also fitted with Packard engines but no British-built aircraft of those types, although fitment to the Mosquito (and the Halifax) was considered.

Problems of Engine Accessories

Installation fittings and accessories were required in line with engines. Requirements varied with the aircraft to which these items were fitted and were affected by modifications both to the engines with which they were used and to the accessories themselves. There was thus a problem of coordination between engines and accessories since either was useless without the other.

All of these problems called for the exercise of judgement: in deciding on the eventual level of demand for aero-engines and the proportion that would be for Rolls Royce types; on what output could be expected from British capacity, what share we could assume from Packard, what marginal adjustments we ought to plan for in the British engine programme, and what pressure we should apply for any further expansion at Packard; on the point at which it would be safe to discontinue production of one mark of engine and how much credit to give to the programme for the introduction of its successor. We had also to judge what allowance to make for Canadian requirements in competition with our own, adjust the British aircraft programme to the prospective supply of British and American engines, and coordinate the programmes for engines and engine accessories.

SHARING OUT PACKARD ENGINES

We began pressing for additional capacity (or a larger share of Packard's output) almost as soon as DDG Stats P came into existence. In October 1941, shortly before Pearl Harbor, we learned that existing capacity would provide only 800 engines per month, not the 1000 previously assumed. This news came at a time when we were just about to embark on an expansion in the production of heavy bombers – an expansion almost entirely in Merlin engine types. The Merlin was then the sole type fitted to the Lancaster and Halifax and the sole high performance fighter engine on which we could depend, the Sabre being in serious difficulty and in very limited supply. We were ferrying Hurricanes with borrowed engines, for lack of Merlin XXs and yet at the same time having to introduce a large number of additional Hurricanes into the aircraft programme partly because of a setback in the (Sabre-engined) Typhoon.

A larger share of current Packard output was not acceptable to the United States and would in any event have been of no immediate help since we were not in a position to fit Merlin 28s until the middle of 1942 at the earliest. The Americans had discovered that the Kittyhawk was 35 mph faster with the Merlin fitted than with the Allison engine. While this made them unwilling to part with Merlins it also made them readier to contemplate an expansion in capacity. By April 1942 they had issued instructions to Packards to increase capacity to 1400 per month by September 1943 and General Arnold (of the US Army Air Force) had agreed, 'subject to reconsideration', that the United Kingdom might later have the entire output from the enlarged plant.

This was more than it was thought prudent to assume. The engine programme was amended from showing an importation of 500 engines per month at peak in February 1943 to 600 a month at peak in August 1943. In addition there was an allowance for an increasing requirement for Canadian Mosquitoes and Lancasters that reached 100–150 engines per month. This assessment of prospects may seem unduly cautious, but in the event, arrivals of Packard engines to 30 June 1943 totalled 5693 compared with expectations in March 1942 of 4596 to the same date. Such an outcome, in view of all the uncertainties, does not suggest an excessive margin for contingencies.

What intervened to absorb Packard engines on which we might have counted was the Mustang. In June 1942 we cabled to say that the Mustang equipped with a Merlin engine – especially the two-stage version – was likely to be a quite outstanding fighter. We had in mind the shipment of American airframes modified to allow fitment of a Merlin 61 engine. Instead, the American Air Corps promptly decided to fit 125 Mustangs a month with two-stage Packard Merlins, starting in January 1943, and soon afterwards raised the 125 per month to 300 per month. Although we were prepared to provide 600 British engines and propellers for American Mustang airframes shipped to

Britain in advance of the production of two-stage Packard engines, the Americans preferred to let airframes accumulate and standardise on the two-stage Merlin 68. Regrettably, no Mustangs were assembled in the United Kingdom.

The Mustang programme, and a simultaneous expansion in the programme for Commonweath aircraft – mainly Canadian Mosquitoes – taking Packard engines, forced us to abandon earlier plans to use surplus engines in the Mosquito, Hurricane or Halifax and confine the use of Packard engines to the Lancester III. Whatever the combination of single-stage and two-stage engines supplied, we concluded in July 1942 that we could not afford to let the total from Packard drop below 1100 per month, of which 700 would be for the United Kingdom and 400 for the Commonwealth. We were prepared in September, however, to release for the Mustang rather more than the 300 engines a month that were left, provided we could count on more than 1100 engines per month in 1944. This was on the assumption that Packard would be able to change over to making at least 300 Merlin 68s a month early in 1943 – a very optimistic assumption.

EXPANDING PACKARD

It was common ground that an expansion in capacity was needed. Packard's were instructed in 1942 to plan for a peak output of 2000 engines a month. This was regarded as the limit of possible expansion but MAP pressed for capacity to produce a further 1000–1200 engines per month and at the end of 1942 Jewkes was sent over to negotiate on the various issues involved.[3] The proposal for still more capacity reflected a fear of being caught short of first class fighters (e.g. through destruction of aero-engine capacity) and a desire to leave room for an increase in the production of Mustangs – the one American fighter that we regarded as equal (or superior) to our own. We also revived the proposal to assemble Mustangs in Britain – now suggesting 400 per month – from American components and engines, but the proposal was again abandoned.[4]

Jewkes was successful in persuading the Americans to set on foot an expansion to a peak of 2700 engines a month, to be reached by July 1944. On the other hand, Packard did not expect to exceed 1400 engines per month until the beginning of 1944. Jewkes had also been asked to urge a changeover at Packard to two-stage engines as fast as possible; and in 1943 all two-stage engines were likely to go to the Mustang. The USAAF expected production of the Merlin 68 to begin in January 1943 and reach 600 per month by June (the actual output was 62 and our guess 100). On that basis the most the United Kingdom and Dominions would have received would have been 800 engines a month, 300 fewer than we were counting on. A surplus in 1942 would have been converted into a deficit of 2800 engines by the end of 1943. But with the big expansion in the Lancaster programme discussed by ministers in October 1942 we needed, not 300 fewer but 300 more engines per month.

There was also a danger, which we did not at first appreciate, that if Packard succeeded in changing over quickly to two-stage engines we would run out of single-stage engines for the Lancaster. We had to plead in the middle of 1943 for an additional supply from Packard. Fortunately Packard themselves proposed changes in their programme that extended production of the Merlin 38, which had replaced the Merlin 28 at the 6001st engine, well into 1944.

In the summer of 1943 Jewkes made a further visit to the United States. By this time it had been agreed to expand capacity yet again by bringing in a new firm, Continental, to produce 1350 Packard engines a month in a separate factory. This raised total capacity to over 4000 Merlin engines a month, or about three-quarters of the capacity of the entire British aero-engine industry. But the war was over before Continental had produced their first engine. Jewkes had asked for no more than 700 engines a month, as before, and was satisfied that there would be enough to meet British requirements, particularly if Commonwealth aircraft programmes proved to be too optimistic, as he suspected, and if the USAAF limited their requirements for spare engines, as they agreed to do. The flow of Packard engines to the United Kingdom reached the suggested rate of 700 per month by August 1944, by which time the changeover to two-stage engines was well advanced.

Delay in Fitting Packard Merlins

In the meantime a large stock of Merlin 28s had accumulated in the United Kingdom in 1941–42; 3000 were delivered before the first Lancaster III flew at the end of 1942.[5] These engines had been arriving since September 1941 but it was not until nine months later, in June 1942, that MAP suddenly discovered that they could not be fitted to power plants for lack of certain engine accessories known as

DIS(B) items (mainly pumps and drives) which had not been put on order along with the engines. The discovery came at a time when the programme provided for the installation of 1600 Merlin 28s by the end of 1942. There was no possibility of receiving deliveries in time from the United States but Rolls Royce made a great effort to supply 1000 sets using British components and succeeded in reaching a total of 800 by the end of the year.[6]

The delay in fitting Merlin 28s made it necessary to go on fitting Rolls Royce Merlins until near the end of 1942. That we were able to find engines for the Lancaster in 1942 in spite of these difficulties was attributable to the rapid expansion in production at the new factories making Merlin engines at Ford in Manchester and at Hillingdon in Glasgow. Between the first quarter and the last in 1942 output rose from 1500 per month to nearly 2000. But with the continuing rise in Lancaster production in 1943 it was vital to draw on the supply of American engines from the beginning of the year, and this we were able to do.

For the moment we had a stock of Merlin 28s that could be drawn upon for the Lancaster III in 1943. But the bomber programme was still expanding and there were doubts whether engine capacity was sufficient.[7] The demand for Merlins came from four different countries – the United Kingdom, the United States, Canada and Australia – and five, possibly six, different aircraft – the British Lancaster, the American Mustang, the Canadian Mosquito and Lancaster, the Australian Mosquito and possibly also the British Mustang. The demand was for one-stage and two-stage engines with no certainty as to the date of introduction of the aircraft using the two-stage engine or as to the timetable for the changeover from one engine to the other.

PROBLEMS OF ONE- AND TWO-STAGE MERLINS

At first the pressure was to move over to American Merlin 68s and British Merlin 85s as fast a possible. Rolls Royce had already begun production of two-stage engines at Derby at the end of 1941 but progress thereafter had been disappointingly slow. Arrangements were made to change over part of the capacity at Glasgow to the Merlin 85 as an insurance against any failure of American supplies of Merlin 68s.

Whatever the risk of an insufficiency of two-stage engines it soon became clear that the immediate danger was of a shortage of the single-stage types. The two-stage Lancaster (or Lincoln) was a completely new aircraft and was soon well behind programme while additional single-stage Lancasters had to be built to bridge the gap. MAP begged for more Merlin 38s from Packard, which, as we have seen, were very readily supplied. But the shortage remained and in February 1944 there were 120 Spitfires in Air Storage Units without engines.

Consideration was naturally given to expansion of capacity in Britain. It was proposed to step up production at Ford from 700 to 1000 per month and to add to capacity at Glasgow.[8] We saw no great need for this since the shortage seemed likely to be over by the time the additional capacity was in production. But before negotiations could begin the Chief Executive gave the expansion his agreement. As in the case of Continental, Ford did not have long enough to bring the additional capacity into full use: their programme was cut in the autumn of 1944 before they had reached 1000 engines a month.

What disturbed us in DDG Stats P was to find the Chief Executive accepting the engine department's insistence that there would be a shortage of two-stage engines in 1945 without reference to us and basing his agreement to expansion on this presumed shortage. As events proved, there was no real danger of a shortage and the expansion programme set on foot in 1943 was quite unnecessary. Apart from anything else, it took no account of the Packard situation; any supposed shortage at the end of 1944 could easily have been met from newly created capacity in America. When Devons returned from the United States, where he had gone at the end of October, he told me that had he known while he was there that we meant to expand Ford output to 1000 a month and then let it fall in late 1945 to 700, and that Glasgow would be making some two-stage Merlins, he would never have countenanced letting Packard go completely over to two-stage engines.

Although other applications for the Packard engines were considered the Lancaster remained to the end the only British aircraft to which they were fitted. It may seem that to tie so large and expanding a requirement to a single source, not under our immediate control, was risky in the extreme; and the risks were particularly apparent when the installation of a two-stage engine in the Lancaster had to be aligned with the changeover from single-stage to two-stage engines in America. Once begun, the marriage of the Packard engine and the Lancaster could not easily be disturbed. The weight of inertia was strongly against any change in our planning of engines and accessories that would upset that relationship. As the two increased in bulk in proportion to the rest of the programme so room for manoeuvre with other types of aircraft and engine diminished. Fortunately things worked out well and we were able, to our great convenience, to let Packard's concentrate on the mass production of a single type of engine on our account and to confine its use to a single type of aircraft, and one that remained at UK bases. Had we fitted the engine to the Halifax and not the Lancaster we should have had a most unhappy time. But as Devons pointed out, we should then have acted differently. We knew that the Packard-Lancaster was a success and that in itself made the risks less grave than they may appear in retrospect.

While engining the heavy bombers and trying to coordinate American engine supplies with aircraft production requirements were our main problems, there was no lack of others. With Rolls Royce, as already explained,[9] there was something approaching a rival system of coordination since they were in close touch with all the aircraft firms, and with the squadrons as well, and had a profound distrust of MAP. It was necessary to demonstrate that we had information (e.g. on requirements) which they did not have, and that we would make good use of what they told us, before we could count on cooperation in programme-making.

Less than a year before we came to MAP, Rolls had submitted between 10 November 1940 and 20 February 1941 no less than four separate forecasts of Merlin deliveries in the first half of 1941. These had dwindled month by month from 7208 to 5406, causing one jaundiced MAP official to comment: 'this company's programme is a complete mess . . . the firm has shown the most lamentable lack of real planning ability and foresight'.[10] By comparison, the Glasgow factory had a much better record. But then Glasgow did not bear the burden of development as the parent factory at Derby did and was producing a single well-established mark of Merlin engine while Derby was busy developing a growing number of new marks of the Merlin and new types of engine like the Griffon.

After 1941 the Rolls programme became increasingly complicated, quite apart from Packard engines. It would have been very difficult to organise production of the long list of different types of Merlin without a programme of the kind we prepared.

BRISTOL ENGINES

Although Bristol had a much shorter list they too were badly in need of an official programme if only to sort out the distribution of work between their various factories. Bristol operated two shadow factories in the Midlands, managed by motor-car companies, a factory at Accrington in Lancashire and one underground at Corsham in Wiltshire, in addition to the parent factory at Bristol. They produced radial air-cooled engines used almost entirely in bombers and like Rolls Royce were steadily increasing the power of existing engines or about to introduce a new type with higher power. When we arrived in 1941 they were in production on the Pegasus, Mercury and Taurus, expanding production of the Hercules, and preparing to introduce the Centaurus. For most of the years 1942–45 the bulk of the output was of Hercules engines, starting with the mark XI, moving on to the VI, then the XV and finally the 100.

Bristol presented us with far fewer development problems than Rolls. The main problem was cooling, particularly with the Hercules 100 and the Centaurus,[11] but there were few conspicuous delays in the introduction of new marks of engine,[12] no multiplication of marks such as complicated the planning of Merlin engines, and no Bristol engines being manufactured in America.

Bristol did, however, suffer more than Rolls from manpower shortages since their factories were either in places like Coventry where war production was concentrated, or a rural area like Corsham where there was very little local labour to recruit. The Corsham factory, scheduled to produce 200 Centaurus engines a month by July 1944, had struggled up to 33 and this made it necessary to re-allocate capacity elsewhere as an insurance against continuing failure. On the other hand, the shadow factories could be relied on to meet their programme without fuss. Just as Bristol engines were less exciting in performance than Rolls's, so also there was less drama in the evolution of the Bristol engine programme.

This was due in part to the downward pressure on requirements. Of the heavy bombers that took Hercules engines, the Lancaster II was limited to 200, and the Stirling programme was for ever being cut to make way for Lancasters. Medium bombers, many of which were Hercules engined, were on a falling programme from the end of 1942; light bombers and fighters were nearly all fitted with Merlin engines. On the other hand, when the Halifax was switched from Merlin to Hercules engines in 1943 the pressure was, for the time being, very intense. There was also in 1943 great uncertainty about the future of the Sabre engine and a distinct possibility that all Tempest fighters would be switched to the Centaurus. Indeed, at that time, Centaurus requirements were well in excess of prospective supplies if new aircraft like the Brigand and Firebrand came into production as planned.

As it happened, the lateness of these aircraft and the fitment of Sabre engines to Hawker Tempests, dissolved the shortage. But, as with Rolls, 1943 was a year of alarm and planning for expansion that was very soon put into reverse. At the beginning of the year it looked as if lack of labour and tools would keep the shadow factories down to 1000 a month. By October, however, they had reached the level of 1350 a month that was originally planned. The shadow programme was increased to 1500, the Accrington plant was to be expanded from 400 a month to 425 and the parent factory was to continue at 120 a month, giving a total for Hercules production of 2045. Provision had to be made, however, for more Centaurus engines. Bristol, for some extraordinary reason, wanted to add to the Corsham programme by 100 a month beyond the planned output from the factory of 250–350 but were overruled by MAP, who insisted on turning over half Accrington's capacity to the Centaurus. The eventual balance in the programme was 1750 Hercules and 600 Centaurus.

The outcome was very different. Accrington never produced a single Centaurus and monthly output of the engine peaked at about 150. It may seem a rather inglorious record. But only a few years previously there were doubts whether it should go into production at all and it must be added that, apart from the Tempest, the aircraft to which it was fitted were not conspicuous successes.

The expansion planned in 1943 soon went into reverse. By April 1944, when the shortage of manpower made it necessary to cut the aircraft programme, the Bristol engine programme called for an output of 1360 engines in January 1945, not 2300. The proposed expansion to 1500 at the shadow factories was cancelled and so also was the smaller expansion at Accrington.

When the cuts were under discussion in February 1944 we found that the engine department was proposing to close either the underground factory at Corsham making Centaurus engines or the factory at Accrington which was due to turn over to the Centaurus late in 1945. We were told two stories about Accrington on successive days: first that it could come into production on the Centaurus in mid-1944 and then, more plausibly, that it could not come in until at least the summer of 1945. Our view about closures was that both factories should remain in production and Bristol's shadow factories should take the cut in requirements. To close Corsham would leave us short of Centaurus and to close Accrington denied us an opportunity of reducing labour requirements in an area of intense labour shortage.

There was a sequel to this when, just before Arnhem, we required Bristol's to arrange for the closure of the shadow plant and made a large cut in the contract for Hercules engines. Bristol protested, arguing that the engines were nearly complete, but were overruled. However, after Arnhem, Hercules engines from the glider tugs (Albemarles) began to flood in for repair and piled up in the maintenance units, far beyond the capacity to repair them. We had then to eat our words and let Bristol complete the engines at Shadow.

Some months later, at the end of March 1945, there was a dispute between us on the one side and Bristol and DGAP on the other. We had pressed for the Halifax transport to be fitted with Hercules XVI engines largely on supply grounds. When it was found that we had also a large surplus of Hercules 100 engines, Bristol and DGAP wanted to have the decision reversed. The Controller of Research and Development who was in the chair, had previously shown a preference for the XVI on the grounds: (a) that the ceiling was not important and up to 10000 ft the XVI was superior to the 100; (b) that the cooling of the Hercules 100 was chancy under tropical conditions. CRD was now inclined to back off and make the issue turn on supply considerations. When Brian Davidson (now with Bristol) asked what stock we had of the XVI and Devons said we had 7000 the Bristol party was visibly shaken. DGAP would have liked to continue the debate but Bristol, seeing that any advantage they secured would go only to Shadow, threw in their hand.

In these exchanges the Engine Production Department and DDG Stats P needed to keep each other informed, but this did not always occur. Arrangements were made to transfer a member of our staff, W. E. Bulley, who had worked on the engine programme, to the Engine Department to assist Brian Davidson and this proved helpful although it was not altogether successful. Bulley, with his knowledge of engine planning, was inclined at times to take on his own shoulders the job of coordination, in ignorance of highly relevant circumstances and without consulting us. Sometimes, too, senior officials discussed programme changes with him instead of approaching the planning department and we learned of the matter rather late in the day. But, on the whole, Air Commodore Banks and his staff were very understanding and helpful and actively encouraged direct exchanges with the engine firms on the engine programme.

NAPIER ENGINES

The Sabre engine was a constant headache. It had originally been 'regarded as the engine which would give the RAF qualitative superiority over the best that Germany could provide. But it was on balance a miserable failure'.[13] At one time it had been planned to manufacture it at No. 1 Shadow Group but the plan was dropped in December 1941 when it was clearly not ready for large-scale production. The design was too intricate and the sleeve valves caused endless difficulties until Banks took things in hand and forced Napier's to switch to sleeves designed by Bristol.[14] As Freeman told C-in-C Fighter Command in July 1943, 'the Sabre was designed without any idea of how it was going to be put together'. The truth was that the engine had been inadequately developed because the research and development staff was starved by an unadventurous management and numbered under 500 at the beginning of 1943 when Bristol had a development staff of about 1500 and Rolls Royce twice as many.[15] It cost five times as much to manufacture as the Merlin and two and a half times as much as the Hercules.

The Ministry was slow to take the measure of the problem. Many admired the engine and as late as January 1945 CRD was still lamenting that there were no new airframe applications for it. When fitted to the Typhoon and Tempest it gave us an effective tank-buster in the land battles after D-Day. But it proved as difficult to maintain as to manufacture, needing frequent replacement when in use operationally. The one man whose judgement of the Sabre's difficulties was uniformly reliable was Air Commodore Banks.[16]

Although Freeman, the Chief Executive, had no illusions about the Sabre he showed great solicitude for Napier. He persuaded English Electric to take them over and was determined to do what he could to keep them in production at their new Liverpool factory after the war. It was the turn of the RAF, he argued, to put up with any resulting difficulties for the sake of the aircraft industry. Freeman dwelt on the days in the 1920s when the name of Rolls Royce had been mud and they were on the point of going out of production altogether. He hoped that Napier might yet pull up in the same way as Rolls. So long as they stayed at Acton making a few engines with high overheads in a badly laid out factory, their costs would prohibit a wide sale and they would never establish themselves as a major firm. But once at Walton they might develop the Sabre to collar a much larger market than they could supply from Acton. He was thinking of a post-war output of about 40 Sabre engines a month. But of course neither he nor anyone else could guarantee an indefinite demand for Napier engines nor Napier's success in developing jet engines that were competitive with the post-war output of other manufacturers.

JET ENGINES

Although we were keenly interested in jet engines, we had little to do with them. An aircraft fitted with a jet engine had already flown before the war in Germany but although, thanks to Whittle, an early start had been made in Britain, development was slow and neglected by the leading aero-engine firms. Rolls Royce, as Hives once admitted, took far too long to be persuaded that jet engines would work and for a time development was left to the Rover Motor Company at Barnoldswick.

5 Propeller Planning[1]

When I took over responsibility for propeller planning I was in complete ignorance of the aircraft industry and its products. I was not even aware that an airscrew was a propeller under another name or that there were at least two kinds of propeller, some fixed pitch and some variable pitch, or that a change in the type of propeller in use was likely to require a simultaneous change of spinner and constant speed unit.[2] It took me some time to unravel these and other mysteries because, as was gradually borne in on me, some of the staff in the propeller production department were almost as much at sea in the technicalities as I was, while others had the greatest difficulty in communicating what they took for granted that everyone must already know.

SLOWNESS IN DEVELOPMENT

What I discovered, only after the war was long over, was how backward the Air Ministry had been in propeller development. To make the most effective use of engine power it was necessary to vary the pitch of the blades between take-off, level flight, climb and dive. For the biplanes in use in the 1920s the advantage might be minimal but with the faster monoplanes that succeeded them it could be crucial. Yet in 1938 Hurricane and Spitfire fighters were still fitted with fixed-pitch wooden propellers. Even at Dunkirk in 1940, when British fighters were fitted with two-position, variable pitch bracket propellers which allowed the pilot to vary the pitch manually between the pitch for take-off and for level flight over a range of 10° to 20°, German aircraft were superior in ceiling, rate of climb and diving.

The fitment of a constant speed unit (CSU) costing about £25 (which all German fighters had from the start) allowed the pitch to vary automatically, freed the pilot's hands for his guns, and improved the performance of the aircraft quite radically, increasing the rate of climb by a quarter and raising the ceiling by 6000 feet. But it was not until early June 1940 that de Havilland were able to start fitting CSUs retrospectively. Over the summer, before the beginning of the Battle of Britain, they converted 1050 planes in two months, helped by the recovery by a naval raiding party of packing cases containing CSUs

92

that had been left behind in German-occupied France. Not that the bracket propeller, complete with CSU, was the latest thing. In fact it was obsolete by the end of 1940 although production continued until the spring of 1944, by which time it was used almost exclusively on trainer aircraft.

The Air Ministry had been slow to recognise the importance of propeller design. A variable-pitch constant-speed propeller had been fitted in the United Kingdom as early as 1928, but to a slow biplane and with little improvement in rate of climb. Variable-pitch propellers were in general use in the United States by 1935 and by 1937 de Havilland were supplying the Japanese air force with variable-pitch propellers and had begun to manufacture CSUs. The official attitude can be judged from the fact that the staff of MAP dealing with propellers at the end of 1940 consisted of two men and a young girl.

THE PROPELLER PROGRAMME

When I came to the Ministry my first step was to obtain a clear picture of supplies and requirements. But it soon appeared that both presented difficulties. The only way of arriving at figures of output was to go through the weekly contract statements showing deliveries against each contract and add them up. Curiously enough, this had never been done. There was no run of figures showing total monthly production (however measured) from either of the two main firms or by individual plants. Yet without these figures there appeared to be no way in which the production department could judge whether production was rising or falling. As for requirements, it is not clear to me how these were communicated before our arrival in the absence of a credible aircraft programme. However it was done, more reliance appeared to be placed on 'chasers' who moved between the aircraft and the propeller firms applying pressure for immediate delivery of what they needed that month, without paying any attention to the shortages that might develop in the longer run.

There were two main firms, de Havilland and Rotol. The de Havilland parent factory at Stag Lane in Edgeware was supplemented by a large shadow factory at Lostock in Lancashire and by four smaller plants including one at Hebburn-on-Tyne, managed by Reyrolle and one at Mount Sorrel in Leicestershire managed by Alvis. The Rotol parent factory near Weybridge was supplemented by two large factories, one at Coventry managed by the Standard

Motor Company and designed to manufacture 1000 4-blade propellers per month and one at the Hoover factory in Tottenham.
There was also capacity elsewhere, making large numbers of fixed-
pitch and a few two-blade variable-pitch propellers.

The firms may have had their own production programmes but
until the arrival of DDG Stats P – indeed for many months thereafter
– there was no official production programme for propellers. There
was not even an unofficial production programme. The propeller
department spent many hours in translating the recently-issued
aircraft programme into propellers, adding conventional allowances
for spares and lead-time, and sending this to the propeller manufacturers as a statement of requirements. This was the procedure which
had presumably been used whenever aircraft programmes were
issued, and however unrealistic these programmes were, the statement of requirements sent to the firms was always based upon them.

This statement of requirements was not closely related to the
capacity of the propeller firms. The propeller department did not
have at its disposal carefully checked estimates of the capacity of the
firms, although it did have statements of peak capacity which were
used whenever a submission to the Supply Board for additional
capacity had to be made. No use was made in assessing capacity of
the records of actual production, which were supplied weekly but in a
form (deliveries against particular contracts) that made it almost
impossible to trace the week-to-week variations in output either in
any one type of propeller or of all taken together. The statement of
requirements assumed that one or other of the two main firms would
make the propeller required (if it was a variable-pitch type) and did
not attempt to match requirements over the ensuing months with the
capacity which was believed to exist. Instead, the production department simply accepted the specification laid down by the aircraft
manufacturer and approved by the research and development department, and assumed that if there was not sufficient capacity to cover
requirements arrived at in this way, the propeller manufacturer
himself would take the initiative and ask for additional capacity. It
was rare to consider bringing pressure on the aircraft manufacturer to
fit a propeller made by the other firm in order to relieve the strain on
production, since as a rule both firms tended to be fully loaded. New
capacity was being brought into existence almost continuously at
rates that could be adjusted to the preferences of the aircraft
manufacturers. There were however occasions when the supply

position was so tight, or the uncertainty as to future requirements so great, that the production department stepped in and, on supply grounds, fixed the type of propeller that a given aircraft would have to take.

The statement of requirements sent to the firms was unlikely to be in accord with the Air Ministry's views on requirements of spare propellers. Yet it was the Air Ministry, through the Director General of Equipment (DGE), that assessed requirements for the purposes of requisitioning. The contracts for propellers, with rare exceptions, were placed by MAP on an Air Ministry requisition, and these contracts could not be cancelled or modified without Air Ministry agreement. At the beginning of 1942 the contracts laid down rates of delivery which, if faithfully observed, amounted to a production programme; but they could not be faithfully observed because they added up to a total output vastly in excess of available capacity. This was not simply the outcome of shortage; it reflected the current practice of DGE in calling for delivery of spares at a high rate in the early months of the contract and leaving for later delivery embodiment requirements only. The sum total of DGE's delivery rates, therefore, was almost invariably a curve 'backed like a camel' with a pronounced peak in the middle. But the normal curve of output, and therefore of a good production programme, is shaped like a logistic curve of growth, flattening out at peak. Neither the production directorates nor the firms could take seriously delivery rates which, individually defensible, were collectively absurd. It was necessary for them to construct a bridge between their contracts and their capacity and no bridge could be built over the camel's back.

Instead, some working rule had to be devised that would allow them to translate future requirements for new aircraft into total requirements including spares. The rule inevitably took the form of a percentage addition, at first 10 per cent and later 20 per cent, for spare propellers. The rule was convenient since it made calculation easy and (apparently at least) definite; it was possible to compare available capacity and peak requirements immediately one knew which aircraft took this or that type of propeller and to what programme each aircraft was being built. The rule was, in addition, the basis upon which initial orders for propellers were placed, since the first Air Ministry requisition merely translated the first order for aircraft into propellers and added the standard percentage for spares.

The justification for the rule advanced by the Air Ministry – although I only once heard it in two and a half years' contact with DGE – was that it was necessary to hold a total reserve of 60 per cent spares behind aircraft strength and that normally aircraft strength was about one-third of cumulative deliveries of a given type of aircraft. Thus if deliveries of spare propellers came to one-third of 60 per cent, or 20 per cent, they would normally be adequate. If on review it proved that requirements were greater or less than 20 per cent, then the Air Ministry could raise a fresh requisition or cancel part of the initial requisition. Since the Air Ministry review took place at least six months after the propeller came into service, what generally happened was that the Air Ministry adjusted their *later* requisitions to cover additional orders by more or less than the standard 20 per cent.

Underlying this procedure was the assumption that the life of the propeller was roughly equal to that of the aircraft to which it was fitted. Experience showed that this was a fair assumption, although, of the two, the propeller had the longer life. Both aircraft and propellers were subject to frequent repair, however, and the assumption was possible only if both were repaired with equal care and speed.

But why was it necessary for the RAF to hold 60 per cent spares of a component that outlived its use? Why were any spare propellers needed at all? The answer was that a stock of propellers was required to cover delays and uncertainties; the delays that occurred between damage and repair because propellers took time in transit, or were immobilised on damaged aircraft, or not removed from the squadrons to the repair depots, or not immediately repaired when they reached the depots; the uncertainty that serviceable propellers might be mislaid during operations or in one of the maintenance units, and might not be immediately available when replacement was necessary.

Once it was recognised that the prime function of spares was to provide a float to cover delays and uncertainties, the idea of a fixed percentage for spare propellers lost much of its fascination. It was immediately apparent that the float was needed mainly in the early life of the aircraft, and would later be provided, largely or entirely, from propellers which had been recovered from crashed aircraft. The percentage, in other words, varied from well above 20 per cent to less than zero late in the life of the aircraft. The need for the float obviously diminished more rapidly the greater the longevity of the propeller in comparison with the aircraft. On heavy bomber types, for example, an overall percentage of 10 instead of 20 per cent came to be considered adequate because of the high rate of recoveries from crashed aircraft. On fighter and trainer types, and types in use overseas, however, the float requirement remained high and was assessed at 30 instead of 20 per cent.

The rigorous application of a 20 per cent rule, therefore, was liable to lead to error. But the error could generally be insured against by MAP if capacity was planned on a scale rather more generous than the rule suggested, and if deliveries were made at a higher rate on new types. The error could have been eliminated almost entirely by DGE if reviews had been conducted on a rational basis, for later orders would have compensated for the initial excess or deficiency, as indeed they were intended to.

Unfortunately DGE's reviews proceeded on a false assumption: the assumption that propellers were consumable items. The initial requisition assumed that propellers and aircraft had an equal life, subject to equal treatment in repair. Later requisitions assumed that propellers, like bolts and nuts, were issued for consumption as spares – although some might reappear later after repair. As a result, it constantly happened that large orders for spare propellers were placed when the aircraft to which they were fitted had long been out of production and the float requirement was consequently long past peak. The Air Ministry reviews habitually forecast a net consumption of spare propellers over the future although they demonstrated with equal regularity that more propellers had arisen for repair in the past than it had been necessary to reissue for maintenance and that net consumption had, therefore, been negative. Add to this, that the reviews were based upon statistics which were so freakish that they were repeatedly queried by the provisioning officers themselves, and were regarded with the utmost suspicion by anyone who was in a position to check them.

Yet throughout the war it was on these reviews that requisitions were raised and MAP was asked to plan. In contrast to aircraft and engines, the propeller programme was not the basis on which orders were placed. Since nothing could rid the reviews of their fundamental weakness – a morbid concentration on dying types of propeller – these types were almost invariably over-ordered. The propeller firms were thus invited to disregard the programme and allow their capacity to be clogged by the manufacture of junk. At the same time

orders for new types in the programme were frequently held up for
lack of orders because DGE did not know which type of propeller a
new aircraft would take or was not aware of an impending increase in
the programme for that aircraft. The tail wagged the dog; propellers
for new aircraft were requisitioned by an agency whose primary
function was to cater for spare propellers. The production department was invited, at times compelled, to plan spares first and think of
new aircraft requirements afterwards.

DESIGN CHANGES

In the course of the war, propellers underwent rapid development.
This at first took the form of a move to fully-feathering variable-pitch
propellers. Then came a multiplication of blades: 3-blade propellers
were superseded by 4-blade types, then by 5-blade types and
somewhere just ahead was the repeated promise of contra-rotating
propellers with three blades fitted to each half. The increase in blades
was most pronounced in fighter aircraft but there was constant talk of
fitting 4-blade propellers to Lancasters and Halifax bombers –
changes for which it was impossible to make full provision in advance
by setting aside the necessary capacity, so large were the requirements for those two aircraft.

A development that seemed promising in 1942 was a simpler and
cheaper design for a three-blade propeller using a rack and pinion
mechanism. This would also have constituted the front half of a
contra-rotating propeller and so was doubly attractive. But production was delayed and in the end it came to very little.

Further ahead lay the jet engine and, with the pure jet, the
disappearance of the propeller from the aircraft of the future. That
lay beyond our wartime horizon.

The differences in design between de Havilland and Rotol propellers were most obvious in the use of dural (aluminium alloy) blades
by the former and wooden blades made from Canadian birch by the
latter. The wooden blades were lighter than dural ones and could be
easily and quickly made in a variety of sizes. But they were not so
satisfactory in hot climates and less easy to repair (about 40–60 per
cent were repairable compared with 80 per cent for dural blades).

Most propellers worked on the hydraulic system but by 1941 Rotol
had also embarked on the production of electrically-powered propellers, for use mainly on the Wellington. Electric propellers were

used successfully on German aircraft (e.g. the Focke-Wolf 190) and ostensibly possessed many advantages (e.g. reversibility), but the pitch change was slow and there were constant design and manufacturing difficulties. In the middle of 1941 Rotol had not got beyond a dozen or so per month. By the beginning of 1943, output climbed to about 700 a month, but their previous history denied them fresh applications and they were phased out rapidly in the second half of 1944. Only a small number of Rotol propellers were produced in time for the Battle of Britain.[3]

By that time – indeed from the outbreak of war – de Havilland were turning out about 1000 bracket propellers a month. They had just begun production of the more modern fully-feathering 'hydromatic' propellers (made to an American design), which was similar in performance to a Rotol hydraulic propeller. It was not until 1942 that the supply of hydromatic propellers overtook that of the bracket type and after 1943 bracket propellers were rapidly phased out.

More than half the output of variable pitch propellers in wartime came from de Havilland. But in the later years of the war their share was reduced by two design difficulties. One related to 4-blade propellers. Although 4-blade propellers appeared in the de Havilland programme from March 1942 they had difficulty over constant speed units and production was delayed. Output rose only briefly above 100 a month, reaching over 300 in September 1944 and then fading out a few months later. Rotol on the other hand were predominantly on 4-blade types by 1944 and the main burden of meeting requirements for 4-blade propellers whether for fighters or for bombers rested on them.

A second difficulty with de Havilland propellers, especially in single-seater fighters, was that there was apt to be a leak of oil from the CSU onto the windscreen. Whatever the efforts made to correct this the trouble persisted, with the natural result that Rotol propellers tended to be specified for single-seater fighters. Since these were the aircraft most likely to take 4- and 5-blade propellers, both design difficulties combined to produce a trend towards the use of Rotol propellers on fighters.

There was a third factor unconnected with propeller design that pushed more of the load on to Rotol. Propellers are made in different engine shaft sizes and, as it happened, de Havilland output was heavily concentrated by 1943 on the large size suitable for use with the Hercules engine while Rotol were not in production on that size of hub except for electric propellers (and for these, new applications were banned). It was not easy, therefore, when the Halifax bomber was rejuvenated in 1943 by switching it from Merlin to Hercules engines, and the load on de Havilland increased sharply, to find ways of lightening it by calling in Rotol. Indeed, had any difficulty arisen over the de Havilland propeller there would have been no alternative available for fitment to the Hercules engine and the numerous aircraft employing it.

There were only two aircraft on which it was possible to switch from a de Havilland to a Rotol propeller and for one of those – the Welkin – it was decided to make no change. That left the Tempest and even there a switch was accepted with reluctance since it meant that Sabre-engined Tempests would be fitted with de Havilland propellers while Centaurus-engined Tempests would now take Rotol propellers. All the switches between propeller manufacturers were from de Havilland to Rotol and in the two principal cases where contracts had to be transferred Rotol were by no means keen to accept the additional load.

THE PROPELLER SHORTAGE

When the heavy bomber programme was under discussion in September 1941 a review was undertaken of prospective shortages in key components, including propellers.[4] The full calculation is not available and it is very doubtful whether it made any sense. For example, the only type of propeller that was expected to be in surplus in 1942 was the Rotol electric propeller – the shortage of which was so notorious three months later, with 300 Wellingtons accumulating propellerless on the beach at Blackpool. Rotol hydraulic propellers were expected to be in rough balance; and the big shortage, intensified by the enlarged bomber programme, looked like being in de Havilland hydromatic propellers. The mystery is how, without a production programme, any estimate was possible; but perhaps the two main firms were able to provide some indication of their likely total output for the year as a whole.

For 1943 the outlook on the programme as it stood before the drive to enlarge the heavy bomber programme, was one of surplus all round but on the enlarged programme, one of shortage all round (including Rotol electrics). No mention was made in the review of the large orders that had been placed in the United States under Beaverbrook to match the orders for Packard Merlin aero-engines.

The Ministry set about expanding capacity in a big way without any reliance on the supplies from America which began to trickle in early in 1942. It also proposed to go on fitting bracket type propellers to the Spitfire Vb and Vc in order to relieve the deficiency of hydromatic propellers.

When I joined the Ministry at the beginning of December 1941, the propeller shortage was real enough. It was not just the Wellingtons on Blackpool beach: the shortage extended right across the board. It covered Rotol hydraulic propellers for the Halifax and Whitley and de Havilland hydraulic propellers for the Stirling, Beaufighter, Typhoon and Albemarle. It had not reached the point, however, where large numbers of aircraft (other than the Wellington) were having to be delivered from the factories with 'slave' (i.e. temporary) propellers. The new capacity authorised would shortly begin production and the two main contractors were by no means at peak. Above all, American propellers were about to arrive in unexpected abundance.

The Rotol electric shortage eased fairly rapidly. Production rose from 19 in the second quarter of 1941 to 481 in the second quarter of 1942 and reached a peak of 800 a month by May 1943. Meanwhile the propeller was denied new applications (the pitch change was slow), the Hercules-engined Lancaster II, which was fitted with Rotol electric propellers, was limited to 300 aeroplanes, and almost the sole requirement was thus for the Wellington III.

The shortage of Rotol 3-blade hydraulic propellers was also soon overcome. In the course of 1942 output roughly doubled and continued to expand until the autumn of 1943 when it fluctuated around 1600 per month. Meanwhile two new factories were coming into production and with admirable foresight it had been agreed that they should produce only 4-blade propellers: the Standard motor-car factory in Coventry was to produce 1000 bomber-type propellers per month and the Hoover factory in Tottenham 500 fighter types. By the autumn of 1943 nearly 1000 4-blade propellers per month were being supplied and Rotol's production of 3-blade propellers could begin to ease off. By the end of the year it could be reduced sharply, ceasing in June 1944.

Rotol 4-blade propellers raised no major technical problems. In view of de Havilland's difficulties and the absence of any orders in America, this was fortunate. At the beginning of 1944, when Rotol's output of 4-blade propellers was roughly 1000 per month, no de Havilland 4-blade propellers could be fitted, although de Havilland had been in production for a year and were turning out 200 propellers a month. No constant speed unit had been cleared for operation with a de Havilland 4-blade propeller nor, for that matter, with a rack type or fully-feathering contra-rotating propeller. Rotol were also the only suppliers of 5-blade propellers, beginning in the autumn of 1943 and reaching an output of over 200 a month by the spring of 1944 – well ahead of requirements.

If there were few headaches over Rotol propellers once the initial difficulties with electric propellers had been overcome, there were plenty with de Havilland types. Here, too, the situation improved enormously in 1942. Three-blade propellers with a 5500 shaft size to fit Hercules and Centaurus applications increased rapidly from under 400 a month at the beginning of the year to over 1000 at the end of the year and reached a peak of over 1600 by the middle of 1944. Requirements, however, also expanded when it was decided to fit Hercules engines to the Halifax in place of Merlins, with a consequent switch from Rotol propellers, fitted to the Merlin, to the de Havilland propellers used with the Hercules. This was not a small change since there were five factories making Halifaxes but fortunately it did not affect propeller requirements until well into 1943 and by that time 5500 shaft size propellers were in fairly easy supply.

De Havilland's difficulties arose mainly over the heavy bombers. First of all the Stirling II, which was to have taken Wright Cyclone engines and American propellers, proved a flop and Hercules engines had to be fitted instead with de Havilland propellers. Then came the engine switch in the Halifax, an increased load on de Havilland, and pressure to have 4-blade propellers fitted – which de Havilland could not supply. More important than either of these was the problem of how to provide for the Lancaster. The early Lancaster Is took 4500 size de Havilland propellers and Merlin XX engines while the Hercules-engined Lancaster IIs took Rotol electric propellers. Only 300 Lancaster IIs were made. The large and continuing requirement was for the Lancaster III with Packard Merlin engines – at first single-stage 28s, 38s and 224s, but at some point in late 1944 or early 1945, due to change over to two-stage American engines.

At first we counted on using the rack-type propeller and planned for early production on a large scale. As explained below that came to nothing. Very soon it became clear that American propellers were arriving to match the Packard engines and with no other use than for the Lancaster and Mosquito. There were doubts, however, whether the propeller could be used in either application. It had paddle blades, very different from the blades in use in British propellers fitted to the Lancaster I and the Mosquito. There were also doubts whether there would be enough Packard Merlins for the whole of the Lancaster programme and for this and other reasons British propellers might be needed for some part of the programme. There was also a risk that at some point 4-blade propellers might be needed if there were a change of engine on the Lancaster, for example if two-stage Merlin engines replaced the single-stage engines first produced. But we obviously could not retain capacity for 2000 4-blade propellers a month against a contingency of this kind. We could and did keep Hoover in production, recognising that 500 propellers a month was only a limited insurance against so important a risk.

All these problems were compounded by the need to provide for Commonwealth production of Lancasters and Mosquitoes. Canada and Australia had their own requirements for Merlin engines and 3-blade propellers and these requirements were neither stable nor easily ascertained. We had to co-ordinate, on the basis of imperfect information, British, American and Commonwealth supplies of engines and propellers. There was no great difficulty over the propeller hubs which could be fitted to Packard Merlin-engined Lancasters and Mosquitoes with American splines. But the American 'paddle' blades were suited only to limited applications and raised problems over spinners and constant speed units. Fortunately there was ample blade capacity and by discarding the American blades it was possible in the end to fit a combination of American hubs and British blades that was entirely satisfactory and to find a suitable CSU (the AY 118). This was one case in which we, so to speak, invented a propeller, and it was by no means the only one.[5]

The Mosquito raised more complex issues. We had to fit different propellers to different marks of Mosquito with some taking British propellers and others American hubs with their blades removed and British blades substituted. We devised this solution ourselves and then got the research and development staff to approve it. At a great meeting of all concerned on 21 October 1942, it was agreed that the Mosquito F.II (after the first 250) and the B.IV (after the first 150) should be fitted with American hubs and British blades and CSUs. The FB.VI, however, would use both the American hub and American blades; and the T.III would make use of 400 propellers sent on from Canada.

THE RACK TYPE PROPELLER

The story of the rack-type propeller illustrates a number of our problems. It goes back to the propeller shortage in the autumn of 1941 when de Havilland's made arrangements to bring this new type of propeller into production at the Alvis and Reyrolle factories. Since the Ministry was committed to the expansion scheme it had to think of a use for the propellers which they planned to manufacture. Why the rack type was chosen before there was a known requirement is puzzling but not untypical of decision-making in MAP. Presumably what counted was that it was an easier and cheaper manufacturing job: it was reckoned that three rack-type propellers could be made for the cost of two hydraulic propellers.

In the spring of 1942 only one use suggested itself – the Lancaster (an earlier candidate, the Beaufort IV had been struck out of the programme). It looked as if the two factories, once in full production, could meet the peak requirements of the Lancaster and it was proposed, therefore, that when the opportunity arose the fitment of de Havilland hydromatic propellers should be discontinued and rack-type propellers fitted instead. What was not appreciated was that there was no constant-speed unit which could be employed with this propeller in a feathering application. This discovery was made only when efforts were made to fit rack-type propellers to the Sunderland after a disaster caused by inability to feather the propellers then in use. It was much later before a satisfactory constant-speed unit for use on the Sunderland was developed – indeed it was not cleared until March 1944. Had plans for fitment to the Lancaster gone forward not only would existing contracts for Lancaster propellers have been terminated but the RAF would have been left without any workable propellers at all for the Lancaster (much the most successful of the heavy bombers).

What is not clear to me now is whether it was realised in the spring of 1942 that propellers would shortly be arriving from America to meet the whole of the Lancaster requirements. Their arrival certainly came as a surprise to me and there had been no indication from the propeller production department that this was about to happen. Yet the additional propeller capacity on which we could draw in the United States from 1942 onwards revolutionised the situation and not only put an end to the propeller shortage but left us with surplus capacity.

By August 1942 (when American propellers were already arriving in quantity) the programme for the rack type had been boosted to 1260 a month at peak and it was hoped to use them in place of hydromatic propellers in all three-blade applications. This hope was entertained chiefly on grounds of cost but also because the pitch-change mechanism employed in the rack-type propeller was so much simpler that great economies in maintenance were expected and much less skill required operationally. Nevertheless if engine ratings had gone up, as was at one time expected, and made four-blade propellers essential, reliance on a 3-blade type of propeller which it was not proposed to develop for use in 4-blade applications might have led to a serious crisis.

It was partly this uncertainty that led to the decision not to proceed with the manufacture of rack-type propellers for use on engines with a larger (5500 size) shaft than the Merlin and to divert the capacity to 4-blade hydromatic types. The programme for the (4500 size) Lancaster propellers was pushed back but was not finally abandoned until the end of 1942. By that time it was abundantly clear that there was too much propeller capacity. There was also once again no use for the rack-type propeller apart from a relatively small Sunderland requirement.

There was, however, a further contingent requirement. One of the chief attractions of the rack-type propeller was that it formed the front half of a contra-rotating propeller and could pave the way for the introduction of such propellers at a later date. It was decided, therefore, to retain some of the rack propeller capacity and use it for purposes of development so as to enable newer types of propeller to be introduced more quickly. Not much came of this. Contra-rotating propellers were not cleared for fitment to aircraft until the war was over and in any event there was great difficulty in finding applications to match the programme. The York – a large transport aircraft – was proposed but it was decided not to proceed. The night fighter Mosquito became the only agreed application for rack-type propellers.

As so often happened, development took far longer than expected. Even so, the production of rack-type propellers was disappointingly late. Apart from a small batch in July 1943 it was October that year before production began. Output never exceeded 135 a month, or 700 propellers from start to finish, compared with the planned output of 1260 a month. Even the Sunderland requirement fell away when a different engine was fitted to newly produced aircraft, leaving 100 flying boats to be fitted retrospectively.

6 Conclusion

When I look back on those days in MAP what is it that stands out in my memory?

First and foremost the incessant uncertainty and confusion. Our world was in constant change, we knew very little of what was going on and what lay ahead was hard to foresee. No one could be sure how well an aircraft would perform until it had flown: even then, as with the Lancaster, its merits might not be fully recognised until later. No one could be sure what the enemy would put into the air: German jet-engined aircraft might have wrought havoc in 1944. We had to be ready for unexpected changes of mind in the Air Ministry: not just on aircraft like the Albemarle and the Merlin-engined Halifax, where the current quotation could fall abruptly or rocket upwards, but on matters such as armament, refuelling and tropicalisation – to say nothing of spares. There were equally unexpected changes in technical requirements: we might suddenly have to find 4-blade propellers for the Lancaster, the American propellers arriving in thousands might prove useless, de Havilland might be unable to stop their CSUs from oil-slinging and the whole propeller programme would be thrown into chaos.

But when I think of the confusion it is not these uncertainties that I have in mind: it is the difficulty of agreeing on a course of action that makes sense; the different levels of competence and knowledge in those who decide; the incalculability of the path towards a decision when it is almost a matter of chance who is consulted; the lack of continuity and the wide scope for rumour. At the time MAP seemed to me one gigantic muddle qualified by a little organisation. And yet, as I had subsequently to recognise, it was the way of the world. I little thought in wartime that the time would come when MAP would be represented to an admiring British public as a model of careful planning: still less that I myself should look back on MAP – as I did in Berlin in the winter of 1945–6 – as an example to be drawn upon.

Nobody who served in it would pretend that MAP was a particularly efficient body. The speed of change, the scale and variety of MAP's activities, the low calibre of much of the staff, all told against a really high level of performance. Of course it would have been possible to do better. But if it had been less frustrating it would probably also have been less fun.

A second reflection is how much alike communist and wartime planning are. Both rely on controls and suppress the price-mechanism. Both replace monetary by physical indicators of action. Both profess a single objective to which all else can be subordinated. Even the disorders of the one have much in common with the disorders of the other. A good example is what the Russians call 'storming': trying to push through everything at the end of the month so as to meet the target. Or the difficulty of devising an appropriate target for an assortment of items (for example, spares) some of which are easy to produce but not much needed, while others get in the way of new production and are badly needed. The parallel was one that struck me forcibly in Moscow in 1952, when I was able to distinguish those who did from those who did not understand planning by the importance they attached to stocks (which of course play the role of prices in a competitive system).

This leads on to another reflection. War is a great centraliser since it is fought by governments which, in conducting the war, are not slow to use their powers of control. But centralisation implies a multiplication of interrelated decisions and requires far more decision-takers: decision-takers, not as consumers or producers on their own account but as officials acting as part of the government. The decision-takers or officials who are washed into government from civilian life are likely to be a mixed bag, and those who enter late (as with MAP) will not be the ablest, nor will they be accustomed to the kind of decision-taking that government normally requires. MAP was a process of acculturation to which some took and some did not.

Another lesson I learned was the supreme importance of technical change. It dominated my life for four years and largely determined the balance of air power. It was impossible not to take away a sense of its equal importance in economic development. I could never believe after watching the struggle between rival designers of aircraft that capital investment, management, or any other factor ranked equally with technical change in its influence on competitive success on the one hand and the standard of living on the other.

At the same time it was impossible not to become aware of the many snags in giving effect to new techniques and introducing new designs. Again and again firms proved to be too optimistic over the time it would take to gain technical clearance or to introduce a new model. Similarly they nearly always underestimated the loss in production in a changeover from one model to another. It was a simple corollary that in the absence of technical change productivity would be much higher – but only by forswearing all the advantages of change.

It is common among scientists to read into wartime achievements (and later events like putting a man on the moon) the lesson that men have only to put their minds to a problem for the thing to be done. This is not the conclusion that an economist would draw. It is easier in wartime to know what the problem is and find a market for the solution. There is a narrowing of the range of problems, a concentration of talent on them without regard to cost, and above all a known requirement in almost every case. This is not true of economic problems in peacetime where consumers' wants are far wider and new wants frequently emerge only after new products are put on the market. Cost plays a much larger part in controlling development to meet a specific civilian want than in development of weapons indispensable to the larger aim of victory. This is not to decry the great importance of research and development. But its role in improving the standard of living is very different from that in improving munitions of war – as is indeed only too obvious when one looks at what has happened in the transition from the atomic bomb to atomic energy.

My immediate impressions were more of what went to planning: the narrow margin between shortage and surplus; the importance of the trend in stocks as an indicator of how the margin was changing – an indicator rarely understood by those with no experience of planning; the tendency to overreact so that, as we were constantly reminded, 'there's nothing like a shortage for creating a surplus or a surplus for creating a shortage'.

We were, of course, engaged only in *production* planning, like any very large firm, and that is a more limited form of planning than trying to plan the whole wartime economy. That the planning we did helped to raise the level of production of aircraft I have no doubt. The big question, in the light of foreign experience, is not whether we should have done less planning but whether we should have done more: whether, without damaging loss in aircraft performance, we (or some other group with more knowledge of engineering problems) could have taken firmer control over modifications in design and reaped the impressive advantages of standardisation that Speer achieved in Germany. Personally, I attached more importance to expanding the output of proven aircraft and cutting out what I thought of as junk. Above all, I think that there was not the close collaboration that was needed between the staffs engaged in development and the staffs dealing with planning and production.

I could see the need for more planning within the firms with which I dealt. But central planning of the entire economy such as we engaged in during the war seemed to me not at all adapted to a free civilian economy. It was obviously reasonable to carry over some wartime controls for a time while various shortages persisted and the government ran down its demands on manpower and other resources. There might, too, be a continuing enlargement in the role of government compared with pre-war years and a sustained effort to maintain 'full' employment through budgetary or other means. Economic policy directed towards the coordination of economic activity necessarily incorporated a form of economic planning. But that it should supplement, not supersede, the planning engaged in by business enterprise in response to market pressures and price signals seemed to me almost beyond question.

Planning in Wartime

TABLE 6.1   *UK output of aircraft, 1938–45*

	Heavy bombers	Fighters	Other types (excluding trainers)	Total combat aircraft	Trainers, etc.
1938	–	371	1 022	1 393	1 434
1939	–	1 324	2 407	3 731	4 209
1940	41	4 283	4 310	8 634	6 415
1941	498	7 064	5 598	13 160	6 934
1942	1 976	9 849	5 905	17 730	5 942
1943	4 615	10 727	6 096	21 438	4 825
1944	5 507	(10 730)[a]	(7 347)[b]	23 584	2 877
1945[c]	1 669	(4 156)[a]	(2 952)[b]	8 807	549
Peak rate per month (March 1944)	520	1 098	?	2 324	(669)[d]

[a] Including (a negligible number of) light bombers.   [c] Six months only.
[b] Excluding light bombers.   [d] July 1940.
SOURCE: M. M. Postan, *British War Production* pp. 484–5.

TABLE 6.2   *UK aircraft programmes, 1938–44*

Programme of	Planned output in	Heavy bombers		Fighters		Total combat aircraft	
		Plan	Actual	Plan	Actual	Plan	Actual
July 1938	March 1941	–	–	–	–	1738	1140
Jan 1940	Oct 1941	211	57	540	676	1389	1213
Oct 1940	Dec 1941	205	55	1150	644	2143	1104
July 1941	Dec 1942	418	233	770	823	1608	1576
Dec 1941	Dec 1942	418	233	898	823	1865	1576
July 1942	Dec 1943	612	420	1119	848	2484	1753
Jan 1943	June 1944	566	487	966	(970)	2263	2143
Sept 1943	Sept 1944	618	486	1169	(864)	2498	1985
Aug 1944	June 1945	549		1025		2058	

SOURCE: Based on M. M. Postan, *British War Production*, pp. 472–83.

TABLE 6.3   *Employment on munitions for MAP and structure weight of aircraft delivered, 1939–45*

	Employment for MAP[a] (000s)	Structure weight of aircraft delivered (in million lb)
1939 Q1	265	–
Q2	300	–
Q3	355	7.50
Q4	492	8.31
1940 Q1	628	8.86
Q2	757	15.67
Q3	866	18.23
Q4	964	16.07
1941 Q1	1073	18.70
Q2	1168	20.90
Q3	1238	23.57
Q4	1319	24.14
1942 Q1	1405	27.51
Q2	1490	32.41
Q3	1562	35.46
Q4	1630	38.00
1943 Q1	1654	42.64
Q2	1680	46.61
Q3	1736	46.11
Q4	1812	49.89
1944 Q1	1792	56.46
Q2	1746	55.28
Q3	1700	50.41
Q4	1581	46.32
1945 Q1	1447	42.87
Q2	1263	31.95
Q3	993	–

[a] At end of second month of the quarter; part-time workers counted as half.
SOURCE: MAP Statistical Review, 1939–45, PRO AVIA 10/311.

TABLE 6.4   *UK output of aircraft, engines and propellers, 1939–45*

	Aircraft	Engines	Monthly average Propellers[a]	Heavy bombers
1939 Q3	681	1026	1051	–
Q4	714	1168	1165	–
1940 Q1	794	1313	1214	–
Q2	1417	2215	1600	1
Q3	1536	2387	1845	3
Q4	1370	2109	1741	10
1941 Q1	1503	2424	1807	25
Q2	1621	2814	1762	35
Q3	1792	3201	1838	49
Q4	1746	3745	2275	57
1942 Q1	1880	3985	2641	59
Q2	1982	4439	2992	144
Q3	1980	4552	3529	192
Q4	2049	4996	3908	224
1943 Q1	2136	4821	4112	328
Q2	2201	4651	4386	399
Q3	2172	4593	4603	383
Q4	2246	5266	4755	427
1944 Q1	2473	5490	4282	482
Q2	2396	5070	3998	481
Q3	2038	4507	3562	461
Q4	1893	3943	2944	412
1945 Q1	1755	3397	2134	358
Q2	1331	2824	1461	199

[a] Excluding fixed pitch.
SOURCE: 'MAP Statistical Review, 1939–45', PRO AVIA 10/311.

TABLE 6.5   *Output in structure weight of USA, UK, Germany and Japan (million lb)*

	USA	UK	Germany	Japan
1939		29		
1940	14	59		
1941	90	87	88	21.2
1942	315	134	114	36.5
1943	759	185	163	65.5
1944	1101	208	199	111
1945	580	95		70

SOURCES: USA: Craven and Cate, *op. cit.*, p. 353.
    UK: 'MAP Statistical Review, 1939–45', PRO AVIA 10/311.
    Germany and Japan: Overy, op. cit., p. 150.

Part II

Germany

7 Planning Aircraft Production in Germany

BACKGROUND

There are plenty of studies of Germany's part in the air war from 1939 to 1945. Some of them deal in general terms with the production of aircraft, and a few touch on the problems of planning, usually from the high ground of strategy. It is obviously much more important to establish whether the right decisions were made as to the scale of aircraft production, the type of aircraft to be built and the balance between different types than to pursue the question how these decisions were translated into production programmes or how the activities of all the firms involved were coordinated. How planning in this sense proceeded is also much more difficult to establish because it requires an intimate knowledge of what went on within the Air Ministry and within the firms over the six years of war and much of what one needs to know is not recorded. When one does come across a book that throws light on the subject it is apt, like Homze's *Arming the Luftwaffe*,[1] to deal exclusively with pre-war arrangements or, like Overy's PhD thesis on German aircraft production,[2] stops, nominally at least, half-way through the war.

Both of these studies provide a very thorough account of developments over their respective periods and Overy in particular throws a flood of light on the performance of the German aircraft industry in wartime. But neither is much concerned with the problem of coordination which dominated life in MAP. Although there are occasional references to engine shortages, their key role in production planning is not pursued. I had expected to find circumstantial accounts of frequent shortages of components and the difficulties of adjusting the supply of each of them to sudden changes in requirements. What I read provided surprisingly little evidence of such shortages until I came on a passage half-way through Overy's thesis in which he refers to:

> continual difficulties over components' supply which the central firms blamed on the suppliers. This kind of complaint was heard from every firm and at all times from 1939 onwards. . . . Aircraft

would be left with parts missing for weeks before delivery . . . and
larger sub-contractors . . . would find themselves forced to delay
their own deliveries because of hold-ups in small parts. At the end
of the war components' supply was singled out by those researching
the aircraft industry as one of the most important general limitations on increasing war production in the early years of the war.[3]

But the point is not elaborated or illustrated (apart from a reference
to engine crankshafts) and very few references are given. There is no
explanation why the *early* years of the war should be singled out nor
whether there are grounds for supposing that shortages of components were markedly less frequent in the *later* years of the war –
which would seem highly unlikely. Overy appears to regard the
shortages as the outcome of the system of sub-contracting to small
and dispersed firms in use in Germany, but although this may have
aggravated the problem of coordination it was certainly not the
source of it. Without more material, however, it is impossible to
embark on an examination of German planning in terms of the kind
of shortages familiar in British experience in those years. I return to
the subject below (see page 146–8), but it is on other aspects of
planning that I have been obliged to concentrate – aspects affording
fewer parallels with the normal run of problems in the British
Ministry of Aircraft Production.

   Apart from the work of Homze and Overy I have read very little of
the literature on the German aircraft industry. All that I can bring to
an account of German planning methods is what I learned from
engaging in British planning, from visits to a number of German
factories as a member of the Farren Mission in July 1945,[4] from
interrogation by the Mission of the staffs of three aircraft manufacturers (Blohm and Voss, Messerschmitt and Heinkel) and from earlier
interrogations by Ely Devons of Speer, Heinkel and Frydag. This is
obviously far from enough for a full and systematic account; but it
does make possible a broad picture of German planning and provides
some parallels and contrasts with British experience.

   One of the difficulties in describing German planning is that the
arrangements in force changed radically from one period to another.
Just as what went on in Britain before Beaverbrook, under Beaverbrook and after Beaverbrook represented three very different regim-
es, so in Germany the system was transformed at various stages with
changes in the higher direction of armaments production. At the
beginning in 1933, Göring was very much in control and Milch did a

very effective job of planning for expansion. By the autumn of 1944, as Speer told his interrogators in June 1945, transport disorganisation and other effects of heavy bombing had made the planning of aircraft production completely impossible and from that time on, aircraft planning was done on a hand-to-mouth basis with instructions to the firms only two or three months ahead. In between, there was a phase from 1937–41 when Udet took precedence over Milch in the Air Ministry and planning was neither effective nor efficient; and then came a galvanic spurt in production from 1942 to 1944 when Milch was given charge again, Göring took a back seat, and Speer, in combination with Milch, imposed fundamental changes on the industry. It is round the contrast between these two periods that Overy shapes his thesis; in seeking to explain the contrast he provides a vivid picture of the weaknesses of planning under the Nazis in the critical years up to 1941 and at the same time demonstrates the potentialities of planning when well directed. We shall come to the spurt in production later (see pp. 125 *et seq.*). But first we must sketch the pre-war development of the Luftwaffe and the organisation of aircraft planning.[5]

PLANNING ARRANGEMENTS

Before Hitler's rise to power in 1933 the production of aircraft in Germany was very small and confined to civil types. The framework for rapid expansion, however, had been established under the Weimar republic and 'the secret rearmers of those years' became in the 1930s 'the builders of the Luftwaffe'.[6] The output of combat aircraft was already 70 per month by 1934 and rose to 400 per month by 1939, when the corresponding figure for the United Kingdom was a little over 300. Expansion in Germany was given the highest priority by Hitler from the start in the allocation of materials and money, without much regard initially to the capabilities of the aircraft under construction. Even with obsolete planes, the Luftwaffe posed a threat indispensable as a shield to rearmament in the mid-thirties and to Hitler's diplomacy in the years immediately before the war. By 1936–37 the industry was changing over to new models of aeroplane and aero-engine while additional capacity was coming into production. Expansion was unchecked except in 1937–38 when the strains on the budget and the balance of payments created raw material and financial difficulties reflected in 'a series of convulsive jolts' in the aircraft programme.[7] But the Luftwaffe's plans did not envisage war before 1942 and the rate of expansion after 1936 was remarkably slow: so much so that British production had overtaken Germany's by the outbreak of war.

From 1933 onwards responsibility for aircraft production rested with the Air Ministry (the RLM) under Göring. In the light of what they understood to be the general strategy they had to draw up 'general staff requirements' indicating the proposed size and composition of the Air Force at some future date, the number of squadrons to be equipped, and the number and models of aircraft that the squadrons would require, both in operational units and in reserves. The Air Ministry would also lay down the performance characteristics of particular aircraft and items of equipment. The stock of aircraft at the date specified had then to be translated into an inflow from production at a rate that bore some relation to production possibilities. This was the procurement programme which showed how much of each type of equipment was to be produced by a given date, which factories were to produce it and the official designation of the various aircraft and pieces of equipment. The procurement programme did not require consultation with the firms but the production programme based upon it did. It also made allowance for delays in development and loss of output in the changeover as new types were phased into production. As in Britain the production programme was the basis for placing contracts, planning capacity, allocating materials, hiring labour, ordering contractors' parts and obtaining items on embodiment loan (engines, propellers, guns, turrets and other armament, radio equipment and the automatic pilot).

The procurement programme was drawn up within the Ministry by the Technisches Amt which was a very different body from DDG Stats P since far more of the production planning in Germany was left to the aircraft firms. From first to last no less than 42 procurement programmes were prepared (excluding variants), six of them in the twelve months before the outbreak of war. Of this total, 36 were finally issued to the firms in the form of industrial production plans.[8]

The aircraft programme thus reflected a mixture of influences. On the one hand, it gave expression to military plans and strategy. At the same time it had also to express economic realities in schedules of what it was reckoned industry could produce and the government could finance. The reckoning might be done by the aircraft industry or by the Air Ministry but whoever did it needed a special expertise which was rarely possessed by military leaders.

An example of the interaction between military and production planning was Hitler's directive in 1938 shortly after Munich, that the Luftwaffe should be 'immediately enlarged fivefold' and given top priority. The Air Ministry came to the conclusion that such a programme might be possible in theory, in the absence of difficulties and delays in developing key aircraft, but that it was not possible in practice. They prepared a more realistic interim programme, calling for about one-third of the production asked for by Hitler. This received almost universal agreement at a full conference of the RLM and the Luftwaffe but was rejected by Göring who insisted that the Führer's programme must be carried out in full.[9] Nevertheless Germany's output of combat aircraft in, say, 1941 was less than two and a half times output in 1938 while Britain's had increased nearly tenfold and was more than half as large again as Germany's (see Table 7.1).

TABLE 7.1   *Output of German aircraft 1939–45*

Year	Fighters	Bombers	Transports	Trainers	Others (incl. gliders)	Total
1939	1856	2877	1037	1112	1413	8295
1940	3106	3997	763	1328	1632	10826
1941	3732	4350	969	889	1836	11776
1942	5213	6539	1265	1170	1369	15556
1943	11738	8589	2033	2076	1091	25527
1944	28926	6468	1002	3063	348	39807

SOURCE: USSBS

Efficient planning required not only competence in the planners, whether politicians, military leaders or administrators, it also required close cooperation between the different parties involved: Hitler and Göring, the Luftwaffe, the Air Ministry and the different elements within it, and the aircraft firms. In Germany the links between them, as we shall see, were totally inadequate. For example, Hitler never revealed to the staff of the Air Ministry his full intentions, so in making their plans they had to guess whether there would be war and if so, when it would occur, how long it might last and what sort of war it would be.

The plans authorized by Göring in 1938 visualised an Air Force that would be capable by 1942/3 of undertaking long-range bombing, would include a much enlarged number of medium bombers and would add a whole generation of new or modified fighter aircraft. Instead, when war broke out in September 1939, the Luftwaffe had neither completed their economic mobilisation plans nor taken delivery of all the new equipment planned to be in readiness for 1942/43.

Hitler himself rarely took much interest in aircraft planning – at any rate not until 1941 when things were clearly going wrong. But he would intervene from time to time with a demand such as that in the middle of 1940 for a 75 per cent increase in fighter production or in 1941 for a quadrupling of aircraft production. He was content, as a rule, to leave matters to Göring and it is to his decision to do so that Overy traces the failure of the Luftwaffe.[10]

The Air Ministry under Göring was from an early stage almost a fief of the Nazis, organised on the *Führerprinzip*. All major decisions of policy involving one or more major departments had to be taken at the top by the single individual in command. There was no encouragement of the solution of problems by cooperation at a lower level. On the contrary, Göring split the military and technical branches of the Air Force. From February 1939 the air staff was made fully responsible to Göring for the conduct of the air war and the formulation of aircraft requirements. The technical and engineering staff were made separately responsible for producing and developing the aircraft and they too reported directly to Göring without discussing requirements with the air staff. The military were thus kept in ignorance of what industry might produce if asked and the engineers in ignorance of what direction air strategy might take.[11]

Göring was sensitive to any threat to his own authority and in appointing subordinates preferred to appoint officers or party comrades whom he could successfully dominate rather than choose men of distinction who would expose his own shortcomings. Though he himself had no lack of energy and drive, his responsibility for aircraft production was only one of a long list of offices, including that of Commander-in-Chief of the Luftwaffe. 'Discounting his many minor offices', he was responsible 'for Prussia, for the Four Year Plan (and most economic policy after 1938), for rearmament, and for certain areas of justice. In addition there were many party offices and an informal role in Hitler's own field of national policy'.[12] As Overy points out, no one, not even Churchill, could have run all these activities simultaneously without some form of Cabinet structure such as Göring made no attempt to create.

Göring's interest was primarily in the strategic development of the Luftwaffe, leaving 'the routine work of technical procurement and organization to the military experts'.[13] The practical work of organization was undertaken by his Deputy and Secretary of State, Milch, a keen Nazi and former Managing Director of Lufthansa.

> A bull of a man, with a tremendous vitality and appetite for work, Milch had impressive industry and ability. His mastery of aviation technology, his gifted sense of administration and his keen nose for scenting the prevailing political winds . . . offset his personal liabilities of outspokeness, arrogance and unusual personal sensitivity. He became the perfect complement to his boss, Göring, who . . . was incapable of long and methodical labour.[14]

Milch surrounded himself with able civilian advisers while the Reichswehr, anxious to counterbalance the influence of the Nazi party and Milch's advisers, released about 200 officers to serve in the Ministry.

The chief of the Air Staff at the outbreak of war was a young officer of 39, Jeschonnek, who had been head of the planning staff throughout the previous year and had risen from the rank of major in 1935. He was no friend of Milch, who had had occasion to reprimand and threaten to court-martial him, but he was 'unshakably loyal to Hitler'. It was he who had been alone in 1938 in supporting Hitler's directive for a fivefold expansion of aircraft production. He was aggressive, ambitious, hard-working and something of a loner. Unlike nearly all his senior colleagues in the Air Ministry he had not served in the Luftwaffe in the First World War.

The head of the Technical Office from 1936 until 1941 and in charge of procurement from 1939 was Udet. A daring pilot ranking second in his war record only to von Richthofen, the 'Red Baron', Udet was a man of great charm and many gifts but no administrator. Heinkel described him as 'a bohemian, an artistic, light-hearted, frivolous man'. 'I don't understand anything about production', he confessed when he took office. 'I understand even less about big aeroplanes'.[15] It was typical of his lack of technical background that when shown the Messerschmitt 109 he should say: 'that would never make a fighter'.[16] Yet for two critical years at the beginning of the war he was Göring's No. 2.

Under Udet the strict control that Milch had exercised over the aircraft programme up to 1936 disappeared. Göring, Milch, the Technical Office under Udet, the general staff under Jeschonnek, and the various producer-designers in the aircraft industry vied with one another for control. 'Instead of a uniform, consistent policy towards the aircraft industry, there was confusion and chaos. Each firm tried to build everything from single-engined trainers to multi-engined bombers, and every effort of the ministry to squeeze them into specialization was successfully countered.' [17]

The key men at the head of the Ministry were all in their way remarkable figures but they did not combine to give effective direction to the aircraft industry. Göring was too confident of the invincibility of the Luftwaffe, had little grasp of production problems and never took the trouble to scrutinise production policy in a regular and systematic way. In 1936 when he made the Luftwaffe general staff responsible to himself, he undercut the position of Milch, who was the one really capable administrator in the group, and with the appointment of Udet a week later, added to Milch's difficulties. Although Milch remained Göring's deputy, he was effectively down-graded and in eclipse until the autumn of 1941 in a period when the full exercise of his talents would have been of particular value. Even Milch, however, had his limitations and was not only at loggerheads with Jeschonnek but on bad terms with Udet. There was little cooperation at the top of the Ministry and little respect for the Ministry in the aircraft industry.

THE AIRCRAFT INDUSTRY

When the Nazis came to power the aircraft industry consisted of eight firms struggling to keep alive. Some of these were rescued by government loans, most were directly subsidised and all were assisted by government orders. The three largest – Junkers, Heinkel and Dornier in that order of size – each employed between 7000 and 10 000 workers by July 1935. A year before the war each employed more than twice as many and in wartime far more (Messerschmitt in 1944 employed 120 000 workers). Of the other five Arado, BFW (later Messerschmitt) and Focke-Wulf were the biggest, Fieseler a good deal smaller and Klemm no longer of much consequence. No other manufacturer except Blohm and Voss was classed as a main developmental firm but there were two other large entrants, Henschel and Weser (a subsidiary of Krupps), who were allowed to do some development and there were half-a-dozen or so smaller firms able to undertake manufacture.

Junkers, the largest and most efficient firm, continued to have an outstanding record after nationalisation and met its programme regularly. Heinkel and Messerschmitt were great rivals and full of new ideas. Heinkel was brilliant and versatile as a designer and a highly successful business man but a difficult person to work with. The chairman of the main commission for airframes, Frydag, was also Managing Director of Heinkel's and the firm was clearly on good terms with the RLM. Messerschmitt was another brilliant designer, a friend of Göring and with access to Hitler but at odds with Milch since 1929 – a circumstance with which the Messerschmitt company had to contend repeatedly. Messerschmitt himself was not particularly interested in details – a failing of other successful designers – but liked to come in as soon as a new design had become a production possibility. The company had narrowly avoided bankruptcy in 1933 but had repaid all its debts to the government by 1940 and claimed to be the only aircraft firm thereafter that remained 100 per cent private. This did not prevent the government from putting in their own controller, Degenkolb, in February 1945 with SS officers in all the works, although the production manager, Linder, was left undisturbed in charge of production. Of the other designers, the most prominent were Dornier, who had started with the Zeppelin Company and designed cars and flying boats, and Kurt Tank, the chief designer with Focke-Wulf.

The designer-owners who ran most of the industry in the thirties 'were primarily inventors and only secondarily entrepreneurs'.[18] As a group, according to Homze, they were 'vain, ambitious, intensely jealous of each other, suspicious, and extremely gifted'.[19] Later, a number of other manufacturers, some of them large firms with interests in other industries like Henschel and Blohm and Voss, entered the industry. There were large profits to be made, grants of funds and guaranteed bank credits were on offer, and the government showed no inclination to embark on wholesale nationalisation. An important exception was Junkers which was nationalised in April 1935 after Junkers personally had shown opposition to rearmament and distrust of the Nazis.

The policy of the Air Ministry in the early days was governed by the need to encourage rapid expansion. The Ministry pushed for standardisation of procedures and parts, uniform methods of financing and accounting, pooling of patents, and the institution of scientific management, treating the industry as an integrated unit. Competition was eliminated, cooperation stressed, and firms assigned a specific role within the industry. Development work was concentrated on the older firms; newcomers and smaller firms were treated primarily as producers with only limited development work; other newcomers were regarded as shadow plants attached to companies with strong design teams. Companies were given considerable latitude in designing, scheduling, pricing and testing new equipment so long as there was still slack in the economy. But as the slack in labour, materials and capital markets disappeared, the Ministry assumed far more extensive control over the activities of the companies.

The aircraft firms organised themselves in the early stages so as to make the maximum use of sub-contractors, usually located in the same neighbourhood, but long before bombing began the Air Ministry insisted on dispersal to sites at a safe distance, preferably in rural areas well away from possible targets. Shadow factories of the English type were not constructed but each of the main airframe and engine firms had at least one back-up plant that could produce the same equipment. There was ample spare capacity and single shift working so as to permit of a rapid expansion in output on mobilization.

Following the example of Junkers, groups of firms ('complexes') were organised around the leading firms engaged in design and development so as to make the maximum use of sub-contracting. The parent firm 'controlled the manufacturing methods, operations sequences, and machining methods employed by sub-contractors and licensees'.[20] It provided the basic tools and jigs, maintained rigid control over engineering design, made sure of proper quality control, administered inspection and took care of materials and facilities requirements. To ensure full interchangeability of parts through the use of elaborate assembly jigs, Junkers devised a basic type of jig which became the standard for the Manufacturers' Association although Dornier used a different system.[21]

An example of the division of work within the group is provided by the Ju 88 before the institution of main commissions in 1943. Of five plants contributing, three made fuselages and two made wings but only Junkers themselves made both. This allowed comparison of the cost at each producer and enabled the main commission when appointed to drive down the price for Junkers' output to that for the other firms. A complete report was made every week to a central station at Junkers on the state of production at each of the various factories. Details were received of the number of components in the jigs, out of the jigs, in pre-assembly and out of pre-assembly, so that it was possible to see that all factories were working in line. This system had been forced by the Air Ministry on a reluctant industry but it was later agreed that such specialisation had tremendous advantages, the main disadvantage being the difficulty of adjusting to a cut in the programme when it might be necessary to run several factories well below capacity instead of closing one down completely.

Relations between the firms and the interchange of information until late in the war were far from satisfactory. Dornier, Junkers and Heinkel, for example, were not prepared to build a Messerschmitt machine however overloaded they might be. Equally, relations between the firms and the Air Ministry left something to be desired. The judgement of the top direction in the Ministry earned little respect; the firms were full of stories of misjudgements that had proved fatal in one way or another. The most obvious example was the insistence that an otherwise satisfactory heavy bomber, the He 177, should be redesigned as a dive bomber.

For the industry as a whole, one of the biggest drags on efficiency and progress was the multiplication of types. No less than 53 types of aircraft were in production at the same time. Heinkels had only one really successful model, the He 111 medium bomber; but it was producing ten other models in prototype or in small series. When an aircraft was successful, moreover, there were endless modifications that absorbed development time but might yield no corresponding improvement in performance. There were 250 000 modifications to the Ju 88 and the improvements to the He 111 from start to finish took four million hours of designing time.[22] Frequent efforts were made to reduce the number of types but never with sufficient resolution, presumably because the changeover to favoured types would have lost output. When BMW sought to limit the number of engine types undergoing development by stopping work on an 18-cylinder engine, the Air Ministry expressed disapproval, not relief.

In every country one of the biggest problems in expanding aircraft production lay in the difficulty of reconciling quantity and quality: the obstacle posed by frequent modifications in design to production in quantity and at low cost. In peacetime, when orders came in penny numbers, batch production by skilled craftsmen was the only possibility. There could be no fitting together of interchangeable parts made to exact specifications because of the limited demand and the high overhead cost of the necessary fixtures. To keep pace with design, fitment by hand, with no assurance of interchangeability, provided the necessary flexibility. But in wartime, with volume production, it was natural to aspire to the mass production methods of the car industry in the way Ford attempted at Willow Run.

In Germany, however, the pressure to adopt such measures was checked by two important factors. One was the very limited role played by the automobile industry in the manufacture of aircraft. The other was the greater insistence by the Luftwaffe on the introduction of modifications in design. German weapons took a lot of development and they were very expensive. This was because the officers selecting and developing weapons who were highly educated and critical were also extremely demanding. 'They insisted that the weapons should be constantly changed and modified to keep abreast of current research and the demands of the front-line soldiers. . . . Even at the end of the war the actual cost of British weapons per year did not reach two-thirds of the amount spent in Germany in 1940.'[23] As we shall see later, when the spate of modifications was halted, the effect on output levels was dramatic.

THE PATTERN OF PRODUCTION

The pattern of production during the war was largely set in pre-war years. Given the length of time required to develop a new aircraft, it was not easy to move from an Air Ministry specification through all the stages of development and get into full-scale production within the six years of war; and if it seemed likely that the war would soon be over, as it did in 1940–41, it must have seemed hardly worth while to try. It is true that the Heinkel 162 was in production in well under a year from the time when a specification was agreed. The Messerschmitt 262 was completely redesigned in 1942 and was in production two years later. But most aircraft, if they are to be thoroughly tested and developed, need twice that time. Similarly with a completely new engine, development usually takes several years, and where a new principle is involved, like the substitution of jet for piston engines, it takes correspondingly longer.

It is a different story where the change is from one mark to another within an existing design. The result may be a dramatic difference in performance, as when the thrust of a jet engine is doubled, but the time required may be quite moderate. BMW claimed to be able to scale up a jet engine, if no new features were introduced and priority were given, within eighteen months. One difficulty is to be sure that the aircraft or engine will be given clearance within some specified time so that the inevitable loss of production in changing over is limited. But it is far from true, as some writers imply, that even a complete change in design is impossible within the limits of a five- or six-year war. There is certainly no difficulty, within a much shorter period, in bringing into production new types of aircraft and engine already under development or in introducing new marks that improve aircraft speed, engine thrust and other performance indicators.

In Germany virtually no new design of aircraft, whether from pre-war years or later, was successfully introduced until the Me 262 in 1944. As Telford Taylor points out, 'Me 109 and 110's, Dornier 17's, He 111's, Ju 87 Stukas and Ju 88's were all on hand before the war began. With the sole exception of the FW 190 . . . not a single new major aircraft type was added to the Luftwaffe until the last year of the war. . . . The Luftwaffe reached its peak of effectiveness before the war had even begun.'[24]

The planning in which the Air Ministry engaged envisaged a short war in which aircraft were used in a tactical role in support of army operations. The only four-engined bomber still on the drawing board in 1939, the He 177, was still under development to turn it into a dive bomber and was produced only in very small numbers until 1942. No preparations had been made for long range bombing of British ports and shipping and there had been no development of night fighters. To quote Telford Taylor again, Jeschonnek 'took no interest in training, neglected air transport, opposed the development of a long range bomber, and focused all his considerable ability on army support, and especially on the dive bomber.'[25] In the case of air transport, the Ju 52 had been in service to bring Franco from North Africa to Spain in 1936 and it was still in use in 1945 as the standard transport aeroplane. The absence of new types did not mean that there had been no effort to bring new types into production; on the contrary, there had been a tremendous effort. But it had all gone on aeroplanes like the Me 210 fighter, of which only 352 were ever made, and the He 177 four-engined bomber of which less than 100 were made in 1940–41 and 1260 (i.e. an average of 35 per month) in the next three years before it was scrapped. Yet these were two out of the four aeroplanes to which Göring wanted to give top priority in his 'concentration programme' of August 1939.[26]

In pre-war years when it was important to intimidate other countries by a rapid build-up in Germany's bomber strength, the aircraft programme was heavily weighted in favour of bombers. It was a bias that remained well into the war: not until 1943 did the number of fighters produced exceed the number of bombers. The bias persisted even in the closing stages. Hitler delayed the delivery of Me 262 fighters by insisting that they must be used as fighter-bombers. As late as January 1945, when the Americans were already at Würzburg, Messerschmitt, Junker and Dornier were asked to submit designs for a four-engined bomber to be used in bombing the United States in 1946. Practically all the larger firms had a heavy bomber on the drawing board right into 1944 although few heavy bombers were made and no new types of bomber, heavy or medium, ever came into large scale production. The amount of preparatory and development work done on bombers was nonetheless enormous. Messerschmitt were still proceeding with development of the Me 264 bomber in 1944. At Heinkel the He 177, the only heavy bomber in production, was not cut out until the summer of 1944. The Arado 234C, a four-engine ground-attack bomber, was abandoned about the same time, and the use of the BMW jet engines originally assigned to it on the He 162 fighter was very much an afterthought.

The same conclusion emerges from the figures of employment. More than half the workers making airframes in October 1938 were employed on the programme for the Ju 88 bomber alone. If we look at things the other way round, the output of fighters in June 1938 was 112 out of a total aircraft production of 498. The average monthly output of fighters in 1941 was just over 300 against a peak in September 1944, when a great effort had been made to redress the imbalance, of 3129: ten times as many (see Table 7.1). From the middle of 1942 the programme was repeatedly increased until in 1943 Milch announced a target of 4000 fighters, but all this was too late in the day.

The preoccupation of the Air Ministry was not just with bombers but with a limited range of them. They concentrated on two-engined tactical support types of aircraft; these were not only indispensable early in the war but continued to be needed in large numbers from 1942 onwards on the eastern front and in the Mediterranean area. On top of all they were already doing, the Air Ministry found it impossible to build up, in addition, a strategic air force of heavy bombers. One may doubt how much effect this would have had, given the experience of Allied bombing of Germany. But Britain was far more vulnerable to attacks on ports, shipping and the coastal approaches, and the Russian transport and power systems were also highly vulnerable. As Overy points out, no special-purpose aircraft had been fitted with torpedoes by September 1939.[27] Co-operation between the air force and the navy was poor and Göring refused to give priority or train crews for the specialised work of attacking shipping and ports.

THE ACCELERATION IN PRODUCTION

One of the remarkable features of German aircraft production in wartime was the contrast between the slow growth in output in the early years, when the territory under German control was expanding and the bombing of Germany had hardly begun, and the marked acceleration after 1942 in less favourable circumstances when the tide of war turned against Germany and the weight of bombs dropped on Europe rose well above a million tons a year.[28] Much of Overy's study of German aircraft production deals with the reasons for the initial slow growth and the subsequent acceleration. What follows reproduces parts of his argument which he develops in great detail.

There is no doubt that the aircraft industry at the outbreak of war was well below the level that full mobilisation called for. Production in the whole of 1939 was little greater than a rapidly disintegrating Germany produced in the first four months of 1945. Even after war broke out, the mobilisation plans for each factory were not brought into operation; many factories continued single-shift working instead of working a second shift as planned. In 1940, with victory in the west and the Luftwaffe confident that it could destroy the Russian air force, the Luftwaffe was no longer assured of top priority and sank to No. 5.[29] The production of aircraft in 1941 was little higher than in 1940 and between April and November 1941 fighter output dropped by 50 per cent. It was only in 1942, when America had entered the war and Russia had unexpectedly begun to hit back instead of being overwhelmed, that a fresh effort was made to expand production. Output climbed by 32 per cent in 1942 and climbed even faster in 1943 when aircraft production was more than double by numbers, and nearly double by structure weight, the level in 1941.

The reasons for the poor performance of 1939–40 are summarized by Overy as: 'poor planning, lack of strategic direction from the inept Göring, competing areas of jurisdiction and poor co-ordination between administrative sectors'.

He also emphasises the weaknesses of the industry: the conservatism of the management and work force, dependence on supplier firms that used outdated methods of production, and political difficulties due to the clash between state and private economic interests.

The fundamental weaknesses were organisational. There was no real direction from above, friction at all levels and, as Milch noted in his diary, 'virtually useless people acting as administrators'. There were conflicts within the Ministry, conflicts with the Luftwaffe, and conflicts with industry.

One such conflict, even before the war, was between what the Luftwaffe wanted and what the Technical Office planned to give them. The General Staff of the Luftwaffe had been planning for mobilisation since 1936 and envisaged requirements when it happened of 1753 aircraft per month, both in a study undertaken in 1936 and in a plan of 1 April 1938. But the Technical Office continued to produce plans right up to the war that stuck to an average monthly output of 1000–1100 aircraft over the period to March 1942 and output in that period at no time reached even that level. Similarly, the General Staff wanted 12 000 bombers by 1942 and 45 700 aircraft in all and were promised only 7700 bombers and a total of 31 300 aircraft.

The mushrooming of the Luftwaffe created other problems. Within the Ministry, men of little experience were given high office. There was no staff tradition or *esprit de corps*. Power was sought for its own sake and corruption and intrigue were rife. There was also a division into two social groups working side by side in the Ministry under men whose qualifications were absurdly inadequate. Engineers were treated as an inferior caste by the army officers, who resented the rise of newcomers like Milch and never got used to their presence in top positions without having followed the career of a regular officer. There was no adequate development of a workable collaboration between the military planners and the technical staff and relations between the Ministry and the aircraft industry were also poor.[30]

One of the greatest weaknesses of early wartime organisation was the handling of development. As war approached Germany had enjoyed technical superiority in the air but lost it within a short time. This was partly because of defective arrangements in the choice of models, partly failure to decide sufficiently far in advance what was wanted, and partly from a lack of understanding how innovation really worked. Tank, the Focke-Wulf technical director, pointed out that at least three and a half to four years were needed from first thinking of a new type of aircraft to bringing the finished model into production. But Udet insisted on limiting the time to three years by cutting the time allowance for adapting the design to series production. New development contracts were then given too quickly, causing firms to split their resources and fail to meet the targets set.[31] In 1940 he imposed a halt on all development work that could not be completed during the year. This shortening of the time horizon for development led to too many projects being under development and too few in readiness for full production. Faults in design that should have been eliminated earlier were discovered only when production had already begun and had to be corrected at heavy cost in output sacrificed when the rhythm of production was interrupted by modifications.

Other difficulties arose over the determination of the larger design firms to multiply designs so as to keep a place in each market. When development contracts were placed, no choice between models was made until the prototypes had flown. At that stage the unsuccessful models were supposed to be dropped. But again and again this did not happen. Heinkel continued to develop the Heinkel 280 without Ministry approval. Of 17–18 types on which they worked, only a third saw serial production on any scale. Heinkel, Junkers, Arado and Messerschmitt all worked on jet aircraft independently, delaying any exchange of information, in the hope of being first. The wishes of the Air Ministry were thus without effect. Heinkel were supposed to concentrate on bombers and Messerschmitt on fighters but both firms covered each type of aeroplane. No authority controlled aircraft development effectively and the result was large-scale waste of highly-skilled labour and dissipation of the lead that Germany had earlier enjoyed.

All this began to change in August 1941 when Milch took over from Udet (who shortly afterwards committed suicide) as Chief of Luftwaffe Procurement and Supply and resumed the position of authority he had earlier exercised. His first act was to establish definite production goals and aim at a substantial increased in output. In a year and a half the outlook was transformed. Clear decisions were now taken without reference to Göring, changes were made in the staff, an advisory council of industrialists was appointed, and a new system of industrial organisation was introduced. Milch instituted industrial rings on the model of the system devised by Todt for tank production. The rings, which were similar in form to the 'complexes' described above on p. 124, were later rechristened 'special commissions' and given wide powers by Speer. The scheme was launched in August 1941 and grouped 5600 firms into 92 production rings with responsibility placed on a central manufacturer of which there were twelve among the aircraft firms. The move brought industry into the planning process in a way impossible before. By the middle of 1942 aircraft production was tied up inextricably with the armaments sector and control over it was exercised jointly by Milch and Speer.[32]

In his explanation of the improvement in production after 1941 Overy points to these changes as removing many of the weaknesses of organisation already discussed. The changes were accompanied by positive steps to use the resources of the aircraft industry more effectively. The action taken can be summarised as rationalisation. This had been a slogan from an early stage in the expansion of the industry but in practice the prescription was not followed. The industry was far too conservative in its methods, relying heavily on manual skill, sub-contracting to small firms unfamiliar with modern methods, failing to reap the benefits of specialisation and exchange of information and unable to take advantage of flow production free from constant interruption and stoppages. Other measures concentrated effort on increased volume, if necessary at the expense of quality, by means of simplification of design, suspension of modifications, and elimination of inferior types of aircraft. The less efficient small firms were eliminated, the more efficient expanded and an intensive educational campaign was set on foot to familiarise industry – and the smaller firms particularly – with modern methods of production. The results were striking. The output per man in terms of structure weight rose from 1 lb in 1941 to 1.5 lb in 1943. The shortages of materials and labour that were alleged to set limits to production were largely overcome. Unskilled labour, suitably equipped, proved capable of sustaining a higher level of production; and with materials like aluminium it was soon evident that there were large hidden stocks, wide possibilities of substitution by other materials, and a supplementary flow of secondary metal which could be recovered from crashed aeroplanes.

Overy's account is full and convincing but he seems to me to exaggerate a little. Some at least of the weaknesses of earlier years persisted to the end. The manpower at the disposal of the industry had outstripped the growth in output between 1940 and 1942 and some of the expansion in output in 1942–43 may have been catching up with the earlier input of labour even if there was a dilution of skill and greater dependence on foreign workers.[33] Finally we know very little about component shortages as a constraint in 1939–42 except that BMW met only 44 per cent of their programme in 1940 and that aircraft remained consistently below programme until 1942 when the programme was finally exceeded.[34] Some of the limitations on output may have taken the form of component shortages that were only gradually overcome. In that case the rise in 1943 would in part reflect a faster rate of expansion in the supply of components.

If the expansion in output mainly corresponded to the suspension on the drag in productivity exerted by frequent changes in design then it would not be surprising if engine production, for example, expanded simultaneously with aircraft. All we know is that, of the large aero-engine plants for which Göring called early in 1938 not one was built and operational by the end of the war. One only – at Wiener Neustadt – was completed but was put out of action within a week by accurate bombing so that the machinery had to be dispersed. But it seems plausible that there was a general improvement in productivity across the board. Whatever the explanation the remarkable fact remains that, with little or no expansion in the resource base of the industry, the output of aircraft was almost four times as great in 1944 as in 1941.

Most of the credit for the improvement in 1942–43 must go to Milch. But from 1942 onwards Speer played an increasingly important part. He had been brought in to head the Ministry of Weapons and Ammunition on the death of Todt in February 1942. A year later, he was put in charge of a powerful new Ministry of Armament and War Production with coordinating functions but no control over aircraft production: that remained with the RLM. Göring had no wish to surrender his authority to Speer but by this time Göring had been pushed more and more into the background and effective control rested with Milch who, according to Overy, collaborated closely with Speer. As part of his Ministry, Speer set up a Planning Office under Saur and this set about planning the war economy on a thorough and systematic basis.

Speer was a convinced believer in decentralisation. He devolved responsibility on the firms and left them to coordinate their efforts without constant intervention from headquarters. At the same time, a special drive was made after Stalingrad to expand output, and armaments production grew by 56 per cent in 1943. Credit for this expansion was given to Speer. He had, however, had no direct part in the big increase in aircraft production in 1943 and it was even alleged by the head of the Araments Supply Office in his Ministry of

Armament that there was an unofficial policy within it 'to short-ration aircraft materials'. It was also alleged that the Ministry was opposed to the big increase that occurred in aircraft production, in spite of pretences to the contrary.[35] Speer's Ministry was by this time an increasingly powerful rival to the Air Ministry.

In the spring of 1944, after heavy bombing of German fighter plants, Speer was invited by Milch to take a hand in organising the production of fighter aircraft. On 1 March 1944 the Jägerstab (Fighter Staff) was set up to control all fighter output under the direction of Saur, the head of Speer's Ministry. This included representatives of the RLM, several industrialists and a staff of technical experts. Fighters were given top priority. A month later Hitler changed his mind and ordered an increase in bomber production but changed back again in July when he agreed to this being drastically reduced. Meanwhile, in spite of bombing, dispersal, and interruptions to transport and communications, aircraft production had increased by over 50 per cent in the year to July 1944.[36]

It was at this point that Speer's remit was extended to the entire aircraft industry. The system he favoured was one of delegation to the industry to the utmost extent. Three commissions had already been brought into existence staffed by men drawn from the industry who worked full-time for the commissions but were not government officials. One of these, under Frydag, covered airframes, one was for engines and engine accessories and one for aircraft equipment. Under each of these main commissions (*Hauptausschusse*) were a number of sub-commissions (*Sonderausschusse*) made up of representatives of the firms. For example, under the airframe commission there were sub-commissions for Junkers aircraft, Messerschmitt aircraft, Heinkel aircraft, and so on. The representatives from the industry worked part-time on these sub-commissions and part-time in their own firms. They might also be required by the head of the main commission to work for it full time for a short period if he thought this necessary; or he might instruct them to work full time for a period in any aircraft firm that was in difficulties. The head of the Junkers sub-commission, for example, was once sent to work for eight weeks in the Messerschmitt factory to help them resolve a difficulty.

The system of commissions was not fully developed in the aircraft industry when Speer came on the scene. Until then they had been responsible to the Air Ministry. Now they were allowed to settle their own programmes. Speer's opposition to Service control was based on the inefficiency which resulted from their constant changes of view about what they wanted from the industry. He put the loss of output resulting from the frequent changes in models and the excessive number of types and models in production at 20 per cent. Self-government would not only reduce the variability and variety of output but would also effect economies in administrative manpower. The main commission for airframes, for example, comprised about 120 officials compared with about ten times that number who had previously served the same purpose in the Air Ministry. Naturally the policy was highly popular with the manufacturers who, it was claimed, worked together in harmony.

In parallel with each of the main commissions there was a permanent official called the *Beauftragter* who was attached to Speer's Ministry (and presumably before that to the Air Ministry). With a small staff he acted as a kind of liaison between the main commission and other government departments, dealing on behalf of the commission with problems of transport, call-up, etc., and offering general criticism and advice on the programmes it prepared. The *Beauftragter* held a meeting in Berlin every morning of representatives of the aircraft companies who reported on the state of production. He also took part in the morning meetings under Saur, known ironically as '*Standenkonvent*', which were intended to last only a few minutes and allow heads of departments to inform one another of their latest problems but came to last for two to three hours with up to forty officials present. These were meetings in which the discussion turned mainly on shortages, especially those due to bombing, not on changes in the aircraft programme, although the meeting could record its view that a change in programme was necessary.

Delegation of control on the development side to the Armaments Ministry and to the aircraft industry was more gradual and delayed. It was not until late in 1944 that a Development Commission for aircraft (*Entwicklungskommission*) was set up. This was composed of representatives of the industry, the main commissions, the Luftwaffe, long-period research and the Beauftragter, with an industry representative in the chair. It main job was to examine design changes proposed by the Air Ministry and designs for new types at the very earliest stage so as to get the views of production before decisions were taken. Speer felt strongly that production management should be brought in at the design stage so as to avoid decisions that made manufacture unnecessarily difficult and he had already promoted similar arrangements in other branches of armaments production.

Until previous arrangements, any firm proposing a new aircraft design went straight to the Air Ministry.

Speer complained bitterly of the constant changes of mind on the part of the Air Ministry. There had been a committee of the general staff which was supposed to restrict modifications of design but which, according to Speer, never let a weekly meeting go by without recommending two or three new changes. The aircraft firms, although they complained loudly about these modifications, were just as bad. Dornier complained about the changes in type they had to make (they never made more than 70 aircraft of one mark) but when their complaint was investigated most of the changes were found to have originated with Dornier themselves.

It was another complaint of Speer's that the Luftwaffe kept asking for the immediate cessation of production of unwanted types of aircraft without appreciating that they might get no other aircraft in place of them. The demand showed no understanding of production problems but it was not one that could be challenged. All that could be done was to transfer workers to other factories until another type of aircraft was ready to go into production in place of the one discontinued. In June 1944, for example, a sudden decision was made to cease production of the He 177 long-range bomber. It was intended to change over to the Dornier 335 but tooling for this aeroplane at the daughter firms was not nearly complete. Many of the workers in factories making the He 177 were transferred to Dornier to help in making Dornier 335 jigs for the daughter firms. At the same time, workers were moved from Dornier to Heinkel with jigs for the Do 335 so as to allow a start to be made again at the Heinkel factory.

A similar situation arose over the Me 210. There were design difficulties which Messerschmitt kept promising would soon be overcome. Eventually the Luftwaffe lost confidence that things would ever be put right, just when Messerschmitt claimed that this had at last been done. The Luftwaffe ordered the project to be scrapped and a switch to the Me 410 to be made although there was no tooling available. In those circumstances all that Messerschmitt could do was to boost the production of their standby aircraft, the Me 109, and allow a large volume of labour to be transferred to other factories.

Many other illustrations could be given of hesitations and delays. Göring had promised the construction of factories to make 1000 engines per month and in 1940 Junkers were asked to undertake the construction of one urgently at Wiener-Neustadt for the manufacture of Jumo 222 engines. In 1941, when construction had not yet begun, the Air Ministry handed over responsibility to Daimler Benz but no progress had been made by the end of the year and yet another firm – BMW – was brought in. By this time much of the machinery had been transferred in error to Italy. In 1943 the building was at last completed and only 150 engines had been produced when the factory was bombed and its contents dispersed.

Junkers were said to have delivered no aircraft for a year. Another example is the programme for BMW 801 engines (from all sources) which was changed nine times in 1944, not always in the same direction, between a maximum of 3000 and a minimum of 500 per month. I can remember nothing of that kind in MAP.

A particularly good example of the changes of mind of which Speer complained is the Ju 188. Henschel's had been turning out Ju 88s for some years when they were asked in 1943 to develop the Ju 188. Just when they were ready to go into large-scale production, the Air Ministry cancelled the order and directed the firm to concentrate on Me 410s. Again preparations were made, over eight months, to tool up for production and just as everything was ready, the entire programme was scrapped. Next, Henschel were asked to produce the Ju 388 and had procured 50–60 per cent of the tools when the plan was abandoned. The end result was an output of Ju 88s with the wing of a Ju 188.[37]

THE FARREN MISSION

When the Farren Mission examined German research and develop-ment methods in 1945 they found no great difference from British arrangements except in three rather important respects. One was the large number of prototypes which it was customary to make. It was usual to order 10 prototypes of single-engined machines and up to 20 of twin-engine machines and larger types. For the Dornier 335, for example, 15 prototypes were made. These aircraft were usually produced in rapid succession so as to allow tests to proceed at short intervals for stability, engines, and armaments, as well as ordinary navigational tests. The drawings were checked on the penultimate prototype, and series production commenced immediately afterwards from the same drawings. According to the Germans the making of so many prototypes cut the time necessary for testing and allowed production to start earlier. For the Me 262, which may have been exceptional, the interval between the first prototype of the revised version in 1943 and series production was a little under one year. At each firm, before production began, the drawings were vetted by production specialists and had to be certified free from production difficulties.

For most aircraft there was also a zero or pre-production series which might be as large as 100. Zero aircraft were made in the production shops, with the exception of Junkers who made them in their development shop, and for some of the parts it was quite frequent for no use to be made of jigs. It was always understood that while an aircraft was still in zero production the Air Ministry was free to ask for what might be substantial modifications in design or, as Frydag put it, they had more time to change their minds before series production started. Small wonder that, even before Speer took over, there was a tendency to drop the zero series altogether and rely entirely on prototypes as happened with the Dornier 335.

A second difference was the higher calibre of the staff and the greater abundance of skill available to the technical director. Messerschmitt, for example, had a staff of 800 and 1000 other workers engaged solely on the development of new projects. On the other hand, scientific knowledge was not so well mobilised for the purpose of assisting the industry. There was no operational analysis. One result was that the high speed of the Me 163 was wasted in futile attempts to protect oil installations rather than make interceptions at the frontier because the Air Ministry had not done the necessary calculations. The scientists were also less well placed to familiarise themselves with current operational problems and so were more likely to follow false trails of argument.

A third difference was the government-provided development facilities that the German firms enjoyed. These were often much more lavish than in Britain for the whole of the armaments industry. Within the aircraft industry, one could point to the test plant for high altitude BMW engines at Munich, costing £½ million and without equal at any engine factory in Britain. On the fringe of the industry was the even more striking example of the Waltherwerke at Plon, east of Kiel. This was founded in 1935 by Walther, a chemical engineer, in order to exploit the potentialities of hydrogen peroxide as a provider of concentrated energy, primarily for high-speed underwater propulsion of submarines. The activities of the firm had spread and during the war had included designing the catapult for launching the V1 (the 'buzz bomb'), the rocket drive for the

Messerschmitt 163 and for the glider bomb HS 293, and the motive power for the fuel pumps on the V2. The government not only met most of the firm's capital expenditure but paid all its running costs (about £1½m. per annum at current prices – perhaps £20m. at 1990 prices) regardless of the success or otherwise of any of the work undertaken. Nevertheless it gave Walther a free hand, leaving the technical direction entirely to him, with no government appointee on his staff or resident government representative. He confined his activities to research and development, never carrying manufacture beyond a 'pre-production' scale. No firm remotely like Walther's existed in Britain; and no firm in Britain had explored the kind of developments on which it was engaged.

The Farren Mission was greatly impressed by the lavish scale on which the German government had supported research and development by a private firm, employing in 1945 5000 workers in five separate establishments, and stressed the contrast with what it regarded as the parsimony of the British government in financing research and development in aviation. On the other hand it suggested that the absence of any link with a large manufacturing company might explain the relatively limited use made of Walther's products in the war and felt that his efforts had been spread over too wide a field.

There was one other important difference between British and German arrangements that affected development. There were strict regulations in Germany against visits by officers of the Luftwaffe, except of the highest rank, to any of the aircraft factories, although in fact such visits did take place. No representatives of the Luftwaffe were attached to the airframe manufacturers except for purposes of acceptance and testing. There were no resident representatives such as the RTOs and RPOs in Britain. Even more important, the firms had no staff with the squadrons, such as Rolls Royce maintained, to draw attention to the lessons of operational experience for future manufacture and design. All suggestions had to go from the operating theatre to the top of the Air Staff, from there to the Ministry of Armaments, and then down again to the firms. The firms might find ways of getting round the regulations but they limited contact and the flow of information.

While Speer agreed that there was not enough contact at the working level between firms and the Services he was determined not to do anything that might offer the Air Ministry further opportunities of dithering or changing its mind and opposed direct contact of any sort between the two. In his view these hesitations and changes were a principal source of confusion and inefficiency and were paid for in a heavy loss of production. Heinkel, on the other hand, wanted the maximum contact between manufacturers and those who piloted their aircraft.

There were few cases, perhaps only one, in which a high air force officer had actually gone behind the back of the Air Staff and fixed up production arrangements. Heinkel quoted the Heinkel 219 as such a case, and he was by no means alone in thinking it the best night fighter that Germany had ever made. But when he went into production after encouragement by the officer he was never given more than a very small order and was convinced that this was the Air Ministry's revenge.

JET AIRCRAFT

A disastrous error was the failure to speed up development of jet-engined fighters as Speer tried to do with the He 162. A mock-up of the Me 262, a twin-engined jet fighter, was on display in July 1939, but did not come into production until April 1944. Even this was ahead of any jet-engined Allied fighter and production had reached 300 a month before the end of the war. It was alleged by Messerschmitt that the aircraft could have come into production a year earlier with proper backing from the government. It was also alleged that General Milch told Heinkel in the spring of 1942, after Udet had flown successfully another twin-engined jet very similar to the Me 262 – the Heinkel 280 – that there would soon be no Russian air force to shoot down and that, while he looked forward to the production of jet-engined types once the war was over, he had no immediate use for them. There were stories of similar remarks by Göring: the war, he is said to have maintained in 1941, would be won with piston engines and there was no immediate need to develop jet engines.

It is certainly true that there was a very long interval between the time when the first German jet-engined aeroplane – the Heinkel 178 – flew in 1939 and the production of the first Me 262 in 1944. The Heinkel 280, which was first flown in the summer of 1941, never entered into production. In view of the obvious threat of a major bombing offensive against Germany after 1941, there was every reason to press on with the development of jet-propelled fighters. Why then the delay? While part of the explanation may lie in the lack of government pressure, there were other causes of delay. One was the absence of an adequate engine.[38] The first satisfactory power plant did not become available until the middle of 1942 when the Me 262 first flew with jet engines. It was at this point that Professor Messerschmitt became fully alive to its possibilities. A second obstacle was the need to retrain pilots because of the complexities of the aircraft: it was this that led to its rejection in 1941. In addition, Messerschmitt themselves had not been prepared to plump unreservedly for the Me 262 and stop work on to Me 209 (a record-breaking successor to the Me 109 which was originally due to come into serial production in May 1940 and was then delayed from one year to another).

These factors were all of importance. The evidence suggests, however, that the government was also to blame. In 1941 Milch refused to order a speeding-up in development work or make capacity available (which did not, however, prevent Messerschmitt from carrying on with experimentation and arranging that Junkers and BMW should continue the development of jet engines). In 1942 the government persisted in showing little enthusiasm for jet fighters when they could have given the industry a lead. For example, they did not accord priority to the Me 262 over the development of the Me 209 or 309 and this alone involved a delay of several months. Even in the last year of the war Messerschmitt, always overloaded and rarely able to meet their programme, were still struggling to produce three different aircraft: the Me 109 fighter, the Me 262 and the Me 264, a four-engined bomber which flew in prototype in 1944 and absorbed a high proportion of the skilled manpower making prototypes.

At Heinkel the story was the same. The firm were told in 1941 to regard the He 280 as a post-war project and it was not until three years later, in 1944, that they were suddenly invited to submit designs for a new jet fighter – an invitation that finally led to the construction of the He 162 as described below.

Perhaps the most important handicap suffered by the Me 262 was Hitler's intervention. He was an early enthusiast, sending a telegram in December 1943 to say that 'delay in the jet engine programme would be tantamount to irresponsible negligence'.[39] But when he sent Göring to make enquiries it was to convey, in November 1943, the Führer's wish for bombs to be fitted. The following April, he was enraged to discover that the aircraft, which was just coming into production, was not equipped to carry bombs and gave orders that they must all be converted to fighter-bombers. Repeated efforts to get him to change his mind had little effect and it was not until November that he agreed to series production of the Me 262 as a fighter, always provided it was able to carry a 550 lb bomb. As a result, a great many of the aircraft had to be sent to modification centres and relatively few were able to engage in combat before the end of the year.[40]

The Me 262 is also an example of vacillations in policy of which other examples will be given later. Not only did the planned peak rate of production jump about from 800 to 1000, then to 550, and back again to 1000, but the later programmes show that typical bending upwards of the production curve of which Speer complained but in which his staff continued to indulge (see Table 7.2). The aircraft was clearly some months later than planned but the June 1943 programme was probably not unrealistic, to judge from the eventual rise in output. On the other hand, the programmes prepared after production were already becoming progressively more unrealistic in May and June 1944, and still more so in December, when the evidence available was only too conclusive. This happens to be the only detailed series of programmes to which I have access and its chief characteristic would appear to be wishful thinking. If the later programmes were drawn up by the Messerschmitt special committee one can only suppose that the factories concerned paid not the slightest attention to them and that they were intended for consumption elsewhere. The interesting question is what the engine makers did about them but presumably they had their own difficulties in meeting an equally unrealistic programme.

The star example of rapid development under Speer's new system, and his favourite evidence of what could have been done on new types had he been in charge earlier, was the Heinkel 162, a single-engine jet fighter of which about 100 were built before the war ended. When the project was approved by the Development Commission on 10 September 1944 it had been worked out only in general terms without drawings or any production preparations. Yet the first aircraft flew on 5 December and a production programme rising to 400 a month by April was prepared which Speer, Heinkel and Frydag all maintained would have been achieved had the first machine not crashed on its second flight. The first drawings were issued to the shops on 30 September and series production started five weeks before the first flight. Indeed, Heinkel could claim to have started work before receiving an order; to have been delivering jigs before the drawings were complete; to have begun manufacturing of the first, experimental aircraft before the jigs were available; and to have embarked on series production before the first aircraft had flown.

TABLE 7.2 *Planned and actual output of the Me 262*

	Programme Number[b]						Actual[c]
	223B 15 June 1943	223C and 224 30 Aug 1943 and 1 Oct 1943	226 15 May 1944	Saur 22 June 1944	227 15 Dec 1944	Emergency Programme 21 Feb 1945	
1944 Jan	1	1					—
Feb	8	8					—
March	21	21	15				1
April	40	40	22				15
May	60	60	40				7
June	60	60	60	24			28
July	60	60	60	60			58
Aug	60	60	80	100			15
Sept	60	60	100	150			94
Oct	60	60	120	225			118
Nov	70	70	160	325			101
Dec	125	125	210	500	200		131
1945 Jan	180	210	260	500	350		228
Feb	280	280	350	500	550		296
March	360	360	450	500	750	450	240
April	440	440	500	700	800	600	101
May	500	520	550	900	900	750	—
June	580	600	550	1000	1000	900	—
July	670	700[a]	550	1000	1000	1000	—
Aug	770	840[a]	550	1000	1000	1000	—
Sept	800	1000[a]	550	1000	1000	800	—

NOTES

a Programme 225 of 1 Dec 1943 reduced the peak to 660 in these three months, falling to 550 in 1946.

b In addition to the seven programmes shown (and Programme 225) there were also programmes for 15 July and 30 September 1944 for which details are given only for Augsburg (with a peak of 500), and no mention is made of Regensburg.

c The first 50 of these were pre-production models. It was originally intended to make 575 pre-production machines at a rate of 60 per month (as shown in the 1943 plans).

   The speed with which the He 162 was developed and produced was remarkable. It was made possible only through the elimination of all Air Ministry technical and other controls and by flooding the job with the maximum practicable number of men working the maximum number of hours.[41] Work on other aircraft was abandoned and parts from them diverted to the Heinkel 162. The undercarriage was taken complete from the Me 109, the engines from the Arado 234c. The wings were sub-contracted and made of wood in order to eliminate elaborate jigging. Fuel tanks were dispensed with and the wings themselves used as fuel tanks. In the fuselage, welded construction was used in preference to castings and no new forgings were employed.

   At the same time it was a high risk strategy. Heinkel's chief test pilot was killed when the aircraft made its second test flight on 6 December 1944 and the technical weaknesses of the design persisted long afterwards. In 1950, for example, *Le Figaro* carried reports from a returned prisoner of war of a succession of pilots killed in Russia flying He 162s there. Messerschmitt maintained that they could have made more effective use of the resources employed in making more Me 262s during the winter months and that they would have been more likely to meet their promises.

   It is always possible to short-circuit the development process by limiting the tests to which the original design is submitted; and it may be wise, when designs become so quickly obsolete, to put ample manpower behind a chosen design, make several prototypes simultaneously, and speed up development as much as possible. But there is always the risk that speed may be at the expense of safety and that failure to make thorough tests may lead only to unnecessary loss of life and waste of effort.[42]

SPARES AND SPARE PARTS

The aircraft programme prepared by Frydag and issued in agreement with the Air Ministry was the basis of the planning of components by the other two main commissions. The programme was translated into requirements for each of the more important items of equipment on Hollerith calculating machines and a percentage added to cover spares that was appropriate to the item. The list of items was a long one even if it was by no means complete. In the case of aircraft equipment it was divided into three parts: instruments, electrical equipment and hydraulic equipment. As an indication of the detail involved, the instrument list for the Junkers 88 included 500 items. It took over a month to complete the translation for any one aircraft programme – a delay that could not be regarded as satisfactory. In exceptional cases, therefore, steps were taken by the main commission concerned to warn large manufacturers of an important item of equipment of an impending change in requirements. A firm like Siemens would be sent a copy of the new aircraft programme immediately and left to adjust its planning of items of which it was the sole producer without waiting for official notification of the change in requirements.

An important difficulty was that many aircraft instruments were also used in other kinds of armament. The total load on the manufacturer of some item might therefore escalate suddenly for reasons unconnected with the aircraft programme and endanger the supply to the aircraft industry. This had occurred over instruments needed for the V2. Since this had been a closely guarded secret, the industry had no means of anticipating the heavy load placed on them and was unable to prevent substantial interference with the supply of instruments for aircraft.

There were bound to be other difficulties of the kind experienced in Britain. Some evidence of these difficulties was given by Frydag. It appears, for example, that there was a major row in 1942 between the German Air Ministry and the *Industrierat* (a body representative of German industry). At that time the Air Ministry fixed the margin over installation in new aircraft that was to be provided as spares and also stated the requirements for spare bits and pieces. The *Industrierat* complained that the basis for ordering spares had been bungled and took their complaint to the highest level where a decision was given in their favour. From then on responsibility for spares passed to the sub-commissions.

The sub-commissions had power to allocate orders for spares between the firms and even to exempt a firm, if they thought fit, from producing spares. It was the sub-commissions that determined the percentage to be added for spares for new types of aircraft, engine or other equipment. They presumably also established the production programmes to which the different members worked.

Spares were sent from the manufacturers to military stocks, from which the squadrons drew when necessary. Issues from the military stores were carefully tabulated every month on Hollerith machines and the tabulations sent to the sub-commission. This allowed the sub-commission to compare issues to the squadrons month by month with the production programme and make any necessary adjustments. However, as was only too apparent in Britain, figures of issues can be highly unreliable for a number of reasons, one of which is that the squadrons might draw from military stocks not for immediate use but to build up stocks of their own. The sub-commissions, therefore, were given powers to go to squadrons and inspect stocks held there. These powers, according to Frydag, were frequently used and provided a useful check on the figures of issues.

Much the same arrangements operated for spares going to repair factories. Issues from a government-controlled stock were tabulated and a list sent monthly to the sub-commission concerned.

If no spares were available in stock to meet an urgent requirement the squadrons could issue an order to the manufacturers concerned and the item could be taken from current output. There was always difficulty in persuading firms to produce spare parts at the expense of new production but Frydag was in a position to threaten serious offenders that he would withhold payment for completed aircraft. This was a threat that he never had to put into effect.

COORDINATION OF PROGRAMMES

In the later years of the war – and perhaps earlier as well – there was no central staff such as existed in the Ministry of Aircraft Production to scrutinise the aircraft programme and coordinate the supply of components. This was left to the officials on the main and sub-commissions who were largely drawn from the industry. It is not altogether clear how the firms manufacturing components were enabled to draw up production programmes nor how the supply position in components impinged on the aircraft programme itself.

So far as the second of these points is concerned, I have found little evidence of a hold-up of aircraft production through lack of major components such as engines or propellers or of the ferrying of aircraft with 'slave' components. There were those who claimed that up to the middle of 1943 aircraft programmes were, broadly speaking, met. On the other hand, Speer claimed that the programmes were usually extrapolations of recent trends in output over the next few months, followed by upward curves that seemed about to bend back on themselves because of the pushing into later months of what failed to be produced earlier. Frydag in 1945 insisted, in contradiction to Speer, that the programmes he drew up were in fact realistic estimates of what would have been achieved had the Air Ministry not kept changing its mind. But no one dwelt on the difficulty of reconciling the aircraft programme with that for engines and other components.

Frydag seemed more concerned to make accurate estimates of manufacturing capacity and for that purpose collected data on man-hours, on floor space and on machine-tools, much like the Technical Costs experts in MAP. The man-hour data were carefully analysed and comparisons by company for the various processes involved in the manufacture of a given type of aircraft were circulated freely and openly throughout the industry. This might help to improve efficiency but had little bearing on production programmes.

There were, however, occasional references in Frydag's evidence to engine shortages. In describing the production position on the He 162 at the end of March 1945 he referred to 30–40 airframes at Vienna and 60–80 at Rostock awaiting engines. In fact only about 70 aircraft were engined compared with 160–200 awaiting engines. It is not unlikely that it was precisely because they foresaw delays in the production of jet engines that the RLM changed the specification in July 1944 for the aircraft from a twin-engined to a single-engined fighter. Frydag also said that when a manufacturer wanted a higher programme he usually gave way even if engines were not likely to be available to meet it. In short, the position was probably akin to that under Beaverbrook when the engine manufacturers were left to make their own arrangements with the airframe manufacturers and account was taken of the current supply position in specifying the engine to be installed in new types of aircraft.

One can find other episodic references to engine shortages. For example, in the early summer of 1939 the Technical Office reported that engines and auxiliary equipment (unspecified) were falling from 3 to 37 behind while airframes were more or less on target.[43] There was also the case of the Ju 88 which usually kept close to programme but was in danger of being held up over a change in the engine. When the mark 211D failed to come forward in time for the changeover from the mark 211C it was necessary to change back the airframe line to use the old mark of engine. But this is more a case of unexpected delay in development than of outright shortage.

This was perhaps the major difficulty in the coordination of components in Germany. The Germans felt at a disadvantage in engine development compared with Britain and were constantly struggling to improve the quality of their engines. Thus the form that shortage took was likely to be a delay in supply resulting from an effort to make use of a higher-powered engine before it was really ready.

Engines were certainly never in excess supply. The Germans like the British, aimed to supply 20 per cent spare engines behind those installed in aircraft, with a lead of one month for engines and two months for power plants. They tried to raise this, when it proved not quite adequate, to 30 per cent but were never in a position to do so. The margin they could produce was too small for their full requirements.

It is, however, significant that when shortages are mentioned they almost invariably turn out to be of metals of one kind or another, not engines and engine accessories. Even the Me 262 was held up for lack of sheet metal. Thus the problem of coordination would seem in the German case to have been mainly one of priority in the allocation of materials – a problem that rarely troubled DDG Stats P.

In the end, however, the biggest shortage after bombing of the hydrogenation plants was in aircraft fuel. There was not even enough in the spring of 1945 to make it worth while to produce more aircraft.

CONCLUSION

From the planning point of view, there is one striking similarity and one striking contrast between British and German experience. The similarity lies in the eventual detachment of aircraft planning from the Air Ministry and its assignment to civilian direction under Speer. The Germans did not, like the British, create a separate Ministry of Aircraft Production. But they did, late in the day, let the Ministry of Munitions take charge and reorganise the planning arrangements with remarkable success. In that respect the similarity ends: for although there was also a spurt in production under Beaverbrook it was a spurt leading to disorganisation of the industry immediately afterwards, not one reflecting a continuing improvement in organisation.

The most striking difference is that whereas German planning seems to have revolved round the supply of materials, British planning – after 1941 at least – revolved round engine supply and development. It was the allocation of materials that gave the German planners some purchase on the aircraft manufacturers: once the manufacturers had the necessary materials they were apparently able to look after all the other components, even when they were on embodiment loan and supplied on government account. It would be astonishing, however, if different manufacturers, using the same engine from the same supplier, never found themselves in competition for an inadequate supply. When the big spurt in production occurred in 1943–44, there could hardly fail to be divergences between the rates of expansion in airframes and engines: not just in total but in each type of airframe compared with the engine fitted to it.

In British planning, these divergences were treated as inevitable while raw material shortages were rarely the source of a hold-up in production. But the deeper problem was not in juggling with an inadequate supply of engines – although there was plenty of that – but coping with engine development and its consequences. The German air force may have been conscious of a more rapid advance in engine power in British fighters – first and foremost in Merlin engines – but they are unlikely to have been aware of the problems that this posed for the planning of all that went with the Merlin: the constant effort to redesign and manufacture the engine accessories necessary to take advantage of the additional engine power; the frequent change of engine, not just by mark but by type in order to get an improved combination of engine and airframe.

The Germans had their development problems but they are not easily traced in the surviving papers. There were a whole series of delays in clearing engines for use by the time they were needed but these seem to have been handled rather mechanically by prolonging the life of older marks (which still creates the obvious headache of finding more of the older mark of engine at short notice). Until the arrival of the jet engine there was nothing in German aircraft planning to compare with the wholesale re-engining of the Halifax with Hercules engines or the upsets caused by the move to two-stage Merlins or the problems associated with tropicalised power plants.

APPENDIX: THE HEINKEL 162[44]

As the Germans appeared to regard the design and manufacture of the Heinkel 162 as one of their most outstanding achievements, we made a special point of collecting evidence on the history of this aircraft.

Heinkel had had experience with jet-engined aircraft for many years before they started to design the 162. Their first machine – the

Heinkel 178 – was flown at Rostock in 1938 with an 001 unit designed by von Ohain.[45] This aircraft was used mainly as a flying test-bed for jet engines. Next came the Heinkel 280, a twin-engined type very similar in appearance to the Me 262. This was flown in July or August 1941 but never went into production. The attitude of the RLM seems to have been that jet-propelled aircraft would not be needed or would not be ready during the war and that they should be treated as post-war types. General Milch is said to have told Heinkel in the spring of 1942, after Udet had flown an He 280 successfully, that there would soon be no Russian Air Force to shoot down and that while he looked forward to the production of jet-engined types once the war was over, he had no immediate use for them.

Partly because of this attitude and partly for lack of suitable power units there was something of a lull for the next three years. Heinkel kept working on projects for new jet types and got as far as a mock-up for a four-engined aircraft (presumably a bomber), but no prototypes were made, and so far as we could gather, no specifications for a jet-propelled machine were put forward by the RLM to Heinkel until the beginning of June 1944. Heinkel were then asked to tender for a two-engined fighter. Their proposals, when put forward about four weeks later, were for an aircraft with one engine above and one below the fuselage and involved rough calculations of the aerodynamic characteristics rather than a complete design. It was their intention to conduct a full aerodynamic investigation in parallel with the actual design and drawing-office work.

This original project, submitted to Göring on 12 July 1944, was accepted. The RLM subsequently changed the specification to call for one engine instead of two, and asked for simplifications in the design so as to allow the aircraft to go into mass production rapidly and at low cost. Heinkel hastily modified their design, but in view of the reduction in power, insisted on a reduction in size, armament, wireless equipment, etc. The RLM agreed to the new specification in August, and an order to produce was finally received on September 10th.[46]

In the meantime, Heinkel were getting on with the job. They were able to alter fairly quickly many of the detailed drawings for the two-engined aircraft on which they had started in July. In the drawing office, the stressman worked alongside the draughtsmen and jig and tool drawings for the experimental aircraft were made simultaneously with the drawings for the aircraft itself. The designers of the jigs worked closely with the aircraft designers and were able to arrange for alterations to the aircraft parts so as to simplify the jigs. In all, about 1000 drawings were prepared. The first drawings were issued to the shops on 30 September and by that date 80 per cent of the small jigs had been completed. The fuselage jigs took somewhat longer and the first wings were made with a minimum of jigging, using wooden set-ups.

On 5 December, 1944 the first aircraft made a successful flight. Series production had started five weeks earlier. Thus Heinkel started work before receiving an order, started to deliver jigs before the drawings were complete, started manufacture of the experimental aircraft before the jigs were available and went into series production before the first aircraft had flown.

The speed with which the He 162 was developed was partly due to the willingness of the Government to leave the work in the hands of the firm and to accept whatever design modifications the firm considered necessary in order to accelerate production. The mock-up was approved after production had already been decided upon and only a week or two before actual manufacture commenced. There was no flight trial in the ordinary sense. On the second flight of the prototype the aircraft crashed and the chief technical designer, Herr Franke, insisted on making the next flight himself after various modifications had been introduced. A Rechtlin pilot then flew the aircraft and expressed satisfaction with the machine but this was largely a formality since Franke's flight had already established that there was no question of further major changes in the design.

Apart from the willingness of the Government and of the firm to accept big risks in what was essentially a gamble the major reason for the rapid development of the aircraft was that it was possible to avoid the use of new parts to an extraordinary degree. No parts used in previous jet-engined experimental machines were incorporated but extensive use was made of parts used in the He 177 and 219. Those were standard parts either in stock or half-finished and the resort to those standard parts did not appreciably increase the all-up weight of the aircraft (the estimate given to us of the increase was 4 kg). Not a single new forging was required and because of the welded construction there were practically no castings. The fact that the wings were designed in wood was also of assistance.

In order to assist the firm in bringing the He 162 into production the Government allowed them to drop work on the He 219. Use was also made of the dispersal plant near Rostock which at that time was making wings for the Me 109. No additional draughtsmen were required.

The major limits to large-scale production, apart from those associated with the modifications introduced after the trial flights, were in the supply of engines, wings and wooden parts. The engine was the BMW 003 unit which was not considered very satisfactory and was to have been replaced by the He 011, with higher power, in the summer of 1945. The BMW 003 had originally been intended for use on the Arado 234C, a four-engined bomber which was not proceeded with. Some minor modifications to the engine were necessary as a result of this change but there was no difficulty over the installation and no hold-up in the supply of engines for the proto-types. Later, however, the supply of engines failed to keep pace with the production of airframes although these fell far short of program-me. The engine, moreover, over-heated when used at full throttle and it was necessary to impose limitations which reduced the speed by 50 km per hour below the estimated maximum. The top speed reached with the higher engine rate was 910 km per hour at 6000 metres.

Although the use of the Junkers 004 unit was not considered in the early stages it had apparently been proposed later that the Ju 004 should be introduced if the difficulties over the production of the BMW 003 continued. The two types of unit were not interchangeable at the mounting points but a special mounting platform could have been introduced to enable the Ju 004 to be fitted.

The supply of wooden wings was also inadequate. This may have been associated with the decision to draw supplies from a group of sub-contractors. There was no single works large enough or experi-enced enough in work of this kind to cope with the production of wings and in the end a number of small firms were formed into a group to take on the job. They were supplied with drawings from Heinkel's drawing office and liaison engineers were sent to live at the sub-contractors' works with full powers to deal with any design difficulties. The wooden wings were used as fuel tanks since it was essential to increase the fuel load as much as possible and there were no suitable drop tanks. The alternative of using metal wings was considered on grounds both of weight and of possible fuel leaks but was rejected.

We were given no illustrations of the wooden parts (other than for the wing) that were in short supply. Apparently there was some difficulty in finding a suitable glue, but the glue itself did not seem to present any difficulty once decided upon.

Heinkel's estimated that once they were in full scale production the man-hours required for the aircraft including wings and excluding undercarriage would fall from about 10 000 to about 2500. Thus, the machine would have been a very cheap one to produce as well as one which could be made quickly in large numbers. The original programme called for 1000 aircraft per month by May 1945 but by the time the war was over only about 80 to 100 aircraft had been completed. It would seem from this that the criticisms made by Professor Messerschmitt in the autumn of 1944 (see ADI(J) report No: 340) had some justification and that Heinkel's promises were probably about six months too optimistic. Allowance should however be made for the confusion and dislocation resulting from allied bombing and the advance of the allied armies in the early months of 1945. It is impossible to predict what the actual production would have been if the conditions prevailing in the autumn of 1944 had continued. Obviously however, it would have been much easier to have put additional pressure on Me 262 production from the autumn of 1944 onwards than to have built up production of a new type in conditions that were bound to deteriorate.

Effect was given to one of the major criticisms passed by Messerschmitt. The petrol load was doubled and in the final model was sufficient to provide for 40 minutes flying at an all-up weight including fuel and war load of 2600 kgs. Curiously enough nothing had been done to develop a suitable drop tank.

Heinkel themselves seemed prepared to admit that they had been fortunate in the modifications that were found to be necessary to the original design. For example, although on their other machines, particularly on the He 219, they ran into trouble on ailerons, the He 162 was free from those difficulties. The other modifications – to the tail unit, wings, etc. – were considerable but insufficient to prevent production from continuing without a prolonged hold-up.

Heinkel also expressed the view that their methods in developing the He 162 by an all-out effort designed to get production started quickly were preferable to the normal machinery of prolonged testing before allowing production to begin. It is doubtful, however, whether the firm which designed the He 177 would have been prepared to express the same confidence over the development of a four-engined machine.

13.8.45   *A. K. Cairncross*

PART III

The United States

PART III

The United States

8 Planning Aircraft Production in the United States

EXPANDING PRODUCTION

When war broke out in Europe in September 1939 the American aircraft industry was a tiny one employing about 80 000 workers and ranking fortieth in size among the industries of the country.[1] Within four years it had risen to the top with an employment of 2.1 million by the end of 1943. The story of aircraft planning is therefore mainly one of mobilisation for expansion rather than of coordination at or near full-capacity operation.

In the 1930s most of the aeroplanes produced were civil types costing a few thousand dollars each. The output of military aircraft did not exceed 2000 a year until 1939, by which time the output of civil aircraft, including a small number of transport planes costing on the average about $60 000, had crept up to over 3000. By value, however, more than half the output throughout the 1930s was of military aircraft with an average cost of about $40 000.

American rearmament had hardly begun in 1939: expenditure in that year on military aircraft was no more than $68 million. In the fiscal year July 1939–July 1940 the Air Corps ordered only 435 aeroplanes. As late as April 1940 Congress was considering a cut of 9.5 per cent in the War Department's request for 1940–41.[2] Even at the time of Pearl Harbor in December 1941 the number of transport aircraft on the strength, including 8 Boeing 'Clippers' and 11 converted B-24s, was 27.

Not that the aircraft industry lacked for orders. French and British missions had visited the United States in 1938 and 1939 with the procurement of military aircraft and aero-engines as their main objective. The industry accumulated a backlog of $680 million in orders in those two years, including $400 million in orders from abroad.[3] By the end of 1940 American aircraft companies had spent $83 million of their own money on new plant and equipment in addition to $74 million provided by the United Kingdom.[4] The British also persuaded Lockheed, then the largest of the American

157

firms but with no previous experience of military aircraft, to take on military orders. The net effect of these foreign orders, and of the financial assistance provided for expansion when the industry's own financial resources were severely limited, was to advance aircraft production in the United States by a full year through plant expansion and tooling.[5]

Meanwhile production lagged badly. Against European orders totalling over 10000 aircraft in July 1940, deliveries at the beginning of 1941 were only 250 per month.[6] The collapse of France in May/ June 1940, however, injected a new urgency into American policy and on 16 May 1940 Roosevelt called for the production of 50000 aeroplanes a year, raising this in January 1942 to 60000 in that year and 125000 in 1943. These figures were so far above current levels and expectations that there was a tendency to deride them as completely unrealistic. But they did set a target that accurately reflected the scale of effort required. Military planners insisted on taking the President's statement as an order and production schedules were prepared accordingly.[7]

From 1940 onwards the United States expanded the production of aircraft on a scale and at a rate that astonished the world. From the beginning of 1940 to the end of the war with Japan on 14 August 1945 over 300000 military aircraft were produced – 90 per cent of them after Pearl Harbor – and production built up from 200 to 300 a month to a peak of over 9000 in March 1944. By that time the United States was producing more aeroplanes by number, and far more by structure weight of airframes, than Germany, Japan and the United Kingdom combined. The swiftness of the expansion was as impressive as its scale. Output in December 1943, two years after Pearl Harbor, was already close to its peak although it was not until America entered the war that an all-out effort of expansion had begun.

With such a record it might seem that that effort was faultless and beyond criticism. This was not so. There were the usual battles between different agencies, the usual shortages and muddles. These will be touched on presently. But first what were the planning arrangements behind the expansion of the industry? How were the various plans coordinated?

PLANNING ARRANGEMENTS

The need for coordination became more pressing in the spring of

1940 when the war in Europe was going badly for the Allies. The United States felt compelled to look to its own defence and take more active steps to re-arm. Up to this point the military had not obtained priority for their requirements and had had to give way to the more urgent needs of France and Britain. Now it was necessary to do more to coordinate the various demands falling on American industry. An Office of Emergency Action was created on 25 May 1940, closely followed by a National Defence Advisory Committee. This had no executive authority to plan munitions production and had to rely on persuasion but did its best to secure a measure of coordination, especially in aircraft production.[8] Its aircraft section included a number of well-known engineers, such as Ted Wright; and from an early stage it had the services of Stacy May who remained in charge of what became the War Production Board's Bureau of Research and Statistics until September 1944.

After the formation of the NDAC a meeting was called in July 1940 of representatives of the Army, Navy and British Supply Council which reach agreement that there should be a single committee – the ANB Purchasing Commission – to make binding decisions on the apportionment of productive facilities, the flow of materials, and so on. This had two outstanding advantages.

First, it made it possible to move on from placing orders to drawing up production programmes that were in conformity with the agreement in July on the division of output. These programmes, as in Britain, were indispensable in judging what expansion in productive capacity was needed and in planning the production of materials and components.

Second, it made for greater standardisation of design with the attendant advantages of single assembly lines, longer production runs and lower unit costs. The need for greater standardisation of design could be illustrated from the example of the Douglas Aircraft Company which was manufacturing seven models of the same aircraft with only minor variations to satisfy different customers.[9]

Since programmes and designs were constantly changing, there had to be some agency charged with responsibility for revising programmes and approving changes in the design of items of equipment. It was increasingly recognised that the coordination and control of production called for 'centralized, high level, decision-making bodies.' Once the presidential election was out of the way, the President set up in January 1941 a new body, the Office of Production Management, to replace the ineffective NDAC in coordinating mobilisation and to pay particular regard to the aircraft programme. The OPM, replaced a year later by the War Production Board (WPB), took over most of the functions of the NDAC as well as its aircraft division while the group preparing the aircraft programme was formally constituted in April 1941 as the Joint Aircraft Commission.[10] From then until the end of the war, it was the JAC that prepared and revised the American aircraft programme.

The JAC had two high-level representatives each from the Army, Navy, Office of Production Management and British Supply Council. Its job was to 'consider and decide matters pertaining to aircraft standardization and aircraft delivery schedules.' It had power to allocate capacity for aircraft and aircraft components and to prepare delivery schedules on the model of NDAC programmes.

It would not have been possible, however, for such a group, located in Washington, to keep track of all information from the aircraft industry and the directive establishing the JAC provided for a working echelon, the Aircraft Scheduling Unit, to act as a central clearing house for the exchange of information between the industry and the JAC. The ASU, indeed, already existed in another form. Officials of the OPM charged with the coordination of aircraft production had realised when it took over from the NDAC in January that there was a trained staff of the Air Corps already doing the detailed job at Wright Field, Ohio, and that it would be futile to recruit a second staff for the purpose. They were required in February to make use of the Production Engineering Section of the Air Corps Matériel Division at Wright Field, as a working staff. When it became clear that this did not make for impartiality between different interests, the Unit was modified by the addition of representatives from the other services so that it represented Army, Navy, British Supply Council and OPM. By 1942 it had a staff of over 3000 dealing with over 6000 different types of end-item involving over 9000 different bills of materials, any one of which might relate to up to 100 types of component and raw material.[11]

The ASU's job was fundamentally to deal with 'critical shortages' of raw materials, components and equipment, such as machine tools, and it did this either by issuing directives or preparing preference lists. While the JAC prepared the engine and aircraft programmes, the programmes for other aircraft components, including propellers, were left to the ASU.

The procedure in the case of the engine programme consisted at first of the submission of requirements to the JAC from all the various users of aero-engines (Air Force, Navy, British, etc.) and the preparation of production programmes by the JAC based on the capacity of the aero-engine factories to produce the required units. This procedure took too long and the programmes when finally issued were apt to conflict with the engine producers' contracts. A new procedure was therefore introduced leaving it to the Air Force to make direct contact with contractors 'under Army cognizance' and decide on their ability to meet programmes based on Air Force requirements before submitting the programmes to the JAC for approval. This was judged to be a preferable arrangement because the Air Force could establish programmes satisfactory to themselves and designed to make the best use of existing facilities. Where contractors could not match requirements for new aircraft the aircraft programme could be modified accordingly so as to avoid serious shortages or excessive stocks. Other services followed a similar procedure, each submitting requirements and programmes to the JAC sub-committee on engines which then combined the programmes and issued them as the official JAC Engine Programme. Much the same procedure was followed for propellers except that representatives of the Services went to Wright Field where the whole of the propeller programme was combined into a 'Black Book' and approved by the ASU.[12]

EARLY PROGRAMMES

The first aircraft programme was issued in August 1940 by the NDAC, following informal discussions between the various purchasers of aircraft including the United Kingdom. Programmes for engines followed in September, and for propellers in November. These showed production by type, model and manufacturer over a period of 15–30 months and were comprehensively revised every few months and amended at more frequent intervals, much as in the United Kingdom. Between the autumn of 1940 and March 1943 there were twelve revisions of the original programmes. For the first two years these were guides to the expansion of capacity required rather than firm indications of prospective deliveries. They were pitched from the beginning at a level in excess of what manufacturers thought they could do and more in keeping with Presidential bids.

At the beginning of 1942, after the President's call for 60 000 aeroplanes in that year, an attempt was made to reconcile totals that tallied with the presidential statement and totals in keeping with what manufacturers judged that they could deliver. One set of figures showed 'the initial objective' and was intended as a realistic working schedule consistent with contracts placed and providing a basis for the allocation of equipment and materials and the planning of additional capacity. The other set of figures, 'the ultimate objective', showed what was required to meet the President's target. What use there could be for the second programme is hard to see except as a reminder of shortfall and a guide to eventual capacity requirements. It was discontinued in November 1942, when a single working schedule (Programme 8L) was issued. In March 1943 this was revised downwards in order to bring it into line with actual production trends and from then onwards the programmes were generally based on manufacturers' estimates of their probable output in the period covered.

A picture of the situation in December 1942, just after the issue of Programme 8L, is given in a report by Professor Jewkes who was then on a visit to the United States as a member of the Lyttelton Mission (Lyttelton being the British Minister of Production).[13] Programme 8L planned for a peak rate of production by the end of 1943 of 11 000 aircraft per month, although Ted Wright, a key figure in the War Production Board, doubted (rightly as it turned out) whether production would ever exceed 9000 per month[14] and output in the autumn months of 1942 had been consistently about 4000 only per month (which was, however, roughly twice the rate of production in the United Kingdom). The planned total for 1943 was 109 000, of which 62 000 were combat aircraft. This fell short of the President's target of 125 000 but it was clear that the programme was designed to get as close as possible to the President's objective and paid only limited regard to manufacturing prospects.

In comparison with the previous programme (8K) a cut had been made in the first three months of 1943 and the amount cut had then been added back, in order to maintain the total for the year, to the last three months of 1943 by raising the end-year peak from 10 000 to 11 000 a month. For combat aircraft alone this meant a climb from 2700 in the autumn of 1942 to 10 000 at the end of 1943. Within this total, the output of heavy bombers was scheduled to rise from 290 in October 1942 to 1326 in October 1943, having been only 42 in October 1941.[15]

At this stage American programmes were clearly of the Beaverbrook vintage: the planners were deliberately over-ambitious. Yet when one looks at the actual record of production it must be admitted that it came within reach of what seemed impossible totals, especially as the numbers greatly understate the expansion in *volume* of production because of the move to heavier and more complex aircraft. The 48 000 aircraft produced in 1942 certainly matched the original call from the President for 50 000 aircraft in that year and the 86 000 aircraft produced in 1943 was at least a creditable approach to the formidable Presidential target of 125 000 and enough to raise American output above that of Britain, Germany and the Soviet Union combined. Indeed, to say this is to do less than justice to the spectacular increase in production in 1943 from 5000 aircraft in January to nearly 8800 in December and the still larger increase in structure weight of aircraft over the same period from 31.9 million lb to 74.7 million lb (i.e. by 134 per cent in less than a year).

TABLE 8.1   *Production of military aircraft, 1939–45*

	USA	UK	Germany	USSR	Japan
1939	2 141	7 940	8 295	10 382	4 467
1940	6 086	15 049	10 826	10 565	4 768
1941	19 433	20 094	11 776	15 735	5 088
1942	47 836	23 672	15 556	25 436	8 861
1943	85 898	26 263	25 527	34 900	16 693
1944	96 318	26 461	39 807	40 300	28 180
1945	46 001[a]	12 070[b]	7 540[c]	20 900[a]	8 263[b]

[a] Jan–June   [b] Jan–August   [c] Jan–April

Source: For United States, Germany and Japan, Craven and Cate, *The Army Airforce in World War II*, p. 350; for USSR, R. J. Overy, *The Air War*, p. 150; for UK, *Statistical Digest of the War*.

Over-ambitious programmes, however, have their drawbacks. One is that they create phantom shortages in components and materials. If the programmes for these match an unrealistic aircraft programme they may not only lead to the creation of excess capacity but multiply shortages that are in fact imaginary since the take-up into complete aircraft remains well below what the programme shows. Unfortunately it is not easy, without elaborate research, to document the waste and muddles that must have resulted. We know only of shortages in relation to requirements, not the proportion of those requirements that were bogus. For engines and propellers there were programmes, but how closely these were geared to the aircraft programme we cannot tell. What we do know is that aero-engines, propellers, and engine accessories were lagging behind and constituted a bottleneck in the early years and that it required a great effort to bring capacity into line with aircraft requrements.[16] There the shortage was real enough, though probably exaggerated in relation to actual as opposed to programmed requirements.

A View of the Position in 1942

In 1942, however, things were the other way round. To quote Jewkes:

> In Great Britain we produce 20 per cent spare engines and find it sufficient. The Americans plan to produce about 50 per cent spare engines. But in the past eight months [i.e . since March], because the engine programme has been achieved and the aircraft programme has not, about 90 per cent spare engines have in fact been produced. . . . We have, therefore, the paradoxical situation that aircraft are not being produced because too many engines are being produced.[17]

Jewkes made some further comments on the situation at the end of 1942. The Americans, he said, were aggravating chronic raw material shortages 'by adopting a system of distribution which is wholly irrational in principle'. The fundamental difficulty was reliance 'upon a system of *priority* as opposed to our own system of *allocation*'. A priority system involved three insoluble logical difficulties (which he elaborated) and was bound to break down as priorities multiplied.[18] No doubt he had in mind Beaverbrook's attempt in May 1940 to give first priority to fighters alone, followed by an extension within a week to all combat aircraft and within a month to trainers as well. The introduction of the Controlled Materials Plan in 1943 met Jewkes's criticism and did indeed improve the distribution of materials.

A second comment was on the allocation of manpower. There was nothing in the United States corresponding to the British Schedule of Reserved Occupations. Enlistment to the Services was unrestricted and large numbers of workers were leaving the aircraft industry either to join up or in pursuit of higher wages elsewhere. The Douglas Aircraft Company had lost nearly 7000 workers in the month of September alone and labour turnover appeared to be on the increase. The proportion of female workers in the industry was still only half that of 30 per cent reached in Britain. Finally, too many workers were earning too much in luxury trades because of the failure to restrict civilian consumption. Retail sales were increasing and profits were high in the production of luxury articles.

A third comment related to sub-contracting. There was no organisation in the United States for controlling and disposing of sub-contractors' capacity. Some were flooded with orders while others stood idle. This was more serious than it would be in Britain because of the vast distances over which materials and components moved from one process to the next. The result was the absorption into wide and numerous pipelines of large quantities of scarce materials, a strain on transport, delays and disturbance to the smooth flow of components to the point of final assembly. In Jewkes's view these conditions called for regional organisations that could disperse the burden on sub-contractors.

These comments have to be seen in the context of the hectic pace of expansion in 1942. They were intended, not as a reflection on industry's response, which was clearly remarkable, but on the inadequacy of the higher direction by the Services and the WPB. This was just about to change at the time of Jewkes's visit. A prolonged debate had been in progress all through 1942 between the War Department and the WPB over planning arrangements.

THE WPB AND THE MILITARY

As one writer sums up, 'Washington . . . never resolved the incredible administrative clash between a War Production Board responsible for total production and an armed forces "establishment endowed with, and acutely jealous of, its authoritiy over military procurement"'.[19]

The armed forces were happy to leave to the WPB under Donald Nelson the allocation of materials between the major agencies through the Controlled Materials Allocation (CMA) scheme introduced in May 1943. But they insisted that the WPB should confine itself to materials and not seek to control the scheduling of war production. The matter came to a head after Charles Wilson of General Motors was brought in as Vice Chairman of the WPB in September 1942. He set about preparing an orderly scheduling programme and reducing the excessive stocks of materials and components in short supply that were hoarded by manufacturers. The

Navy and the Maritime Commission agreed to Wilson's proposals but the Army did not.

'The crux of the matter', Donald Nelson wrote later, 'was whether we would have centralized control over an operation which involved all war agencies, or whether it was going to be every man for himself, with scheduling handled by those who were interested only in their own particular programme'.[20] Centralised control he never achieved.

A quite different interpretation is that Nelson aimed to build up a staff in Washington to act as a Ministry of Supply and replace the staff at Wright Field. As General Arnold, Commander of the Air Force pointed out, the War Production Board could neither speak authoritatively for the Armed Services as the JAC could, nor did it possess a detailed knowledge of the situation in the aircraft industry like the ASU. Although an Aircraft Production Board was created in January 1943 under Wilson's chairmanship as the top decision-making body for air matériel within the WPB, its membership was similar to that of the JAC, including representatives of Army, Navy and Air Force as well as Ted Wright from the WPB. It was soon located in the Pentagon and the JAC and ASU carried on as before.[21] Wilson's functions were extended to give him 'general supervision of the scheduling of the programmes between the various services to see that they do not conflict'. But the programmes had also to accord with the views of the Chiefs of Staff and had to carry their approval.

The Aircraft Production Board (APB) was made responsible for 'the scheduling of the aircraft production programme or any part thereof' but as already explained the JAC retained a firm grip on the aircraft and engine programmes leaving other components on embodiment loan to the ASU. In March 1943 the Aircraft Resources Control Office (ARCO) was created as the executive agency of the Aircraft Production Board and the Aircraft Production Division of the WPB was abolished. The ASU was now attached to ARCO 'to work out in detail most of the assigned functions of ARCO, APB and JAC'.[22]

ARCO was specifically required to:

> co-ordinate and publish the joint schedules for the production of airframes, aircraft engines and aircraft propellers, which, after co-ordination with the JAC and approval by the APB, shall become directives to the established production agencies' carrying out the programmes.[23]

Although this seems clear enough, the rivalry between the WPB and the JAC continued. When ARCO was established, the Secretary for War reissued the directive establishing the JAC giving it power to prepare delivery schedules. It was now asked to act 'with the concurrence of the Aircraft Production Board' and to prepare programmes on the model of Programme 8L which were to be approved by the Board before issue as a directive.[24] The two bodies were left, as so often under Roosevelt, with overlapping powers.

The ASU was now to act through ARCO with the authority and approval of the APB, and acquired from ARCO by delegation all the WPB's powers with regard to the aircraft industry instead of by direct delegation. It remained primarily concerned with critical shortages and preference lists, approved the propeller programme, and was 'utilized [by the Services] for production and control of GFE [embodiment loan] items other than engines and contractor furnished equipment (CFE)'.[25]

The British member of the ASU (Britain was represented throughout both on the JAC and the Aircraft Scheduling Unit) described its role as follows:[26]

> to reduce the conflict in industry as much as possible; to foresee requirements and provide for the whole industry before the specific problems struck the individual manufacturer; to break the bottlenecks in material supply; and to aid the production of one manufacturer in preference to another so that the industries' combined output best suited the war effort.[27]

SHORTAGES

In its battle with critical shortages the ASU never lacked for work; but the more work it had the more doubt was thrown on the efficiency of the machinery for preparing programmes. Some shortages were inescapable: for example, the acute shortage of machine tools in the early years of the war. Even an output of 300 000 machine tools a year was insufficient to keep pace with the headlong expansion of 1940–42. In those years 'almost every other aircraft manufacturer, and more particularly the producers of aero-engines, ascribed their production problems chiefly to machine tool shortages'.[28] Shortages of raw materials were the next to develop. Aluminium requirements had been underestimated and there was no proper system of allocation until 1943. In March 1942 Ford claimed that if they had the necessary aluminium they could double the output of aero-engines. The War Production Board blamed the manufacturers for hoarding, late ordering and lack of inventory control while the Air Force disagreed sharply and took the side of the manufacturers. The main shortages disappeared from the middle of 1943 thanks to technical advances in fabrication and by the end of the year it was possible to cancel the construction of three new extrusion plants.[29]

There were shortages also of steel and steel products and of magnesium. At the end of 1942 Jewkes referred to shortages of forgings and castings. Other shortages in 1942 included carburettors, spark plugs, electric motor controls, jewelled bearings, valves, crankshafts, heat exchangers, fans and blowers.[30] In September 1944 a list issued by ARCO of 31 items 'under guidance' as critically scarce includes turrets, carburettors, wheels and brakes, also struts, aircraft pumps and steel forgings.[31]

Critical shortages arose at the rate of over 1000 a month and in the years 1942–45 when the ASU was in operation the total reached 47 000. On a sample taken in 1943, more than half were in materials, with steel and aluminium each accounting for over 20 per cent, non-ferrous metals for nine per cent and non-metallic items for four per cent. Of components the most common shortages were in bearings, pumps, valves, fittings, etc. (23 per cent); electrical equipment (13 per cent); landing gear (five per cent); engine accessories (two per cent) and radio and instruments (three per cent).[32] But none of this tells us how balance between airframes, engines and propellers was preserved.

The ASU in 1944 blamed late ordering, engineering changes and frequent changes in programme for most of the shortages. Late ordering, they said in their annual report for 1944, had been a problem for over a year and increasingly serious in the second half of 1944, no doubt because of efforts to cut down inventories as the war neared an end. As for programme changes, 'each time one airframe schedule is revised, hundreds of component schedules must be immediately revised. Component schedules . . . must be . . . scheduled far in advance of completed aircraft. . . . When schedule revisions are made to take effect too soon to allow for this, and which is usually the case, critical shortages of both materials and components naturally increase', operations at all levels are kept 'in a constant state of flux and revision'.[33]

This glimpse of the familiar problem of coordination between the programmes for components and aircraft seems to imply a failure of the co-ordinating process. Programme changes should take full account of the supply position over time in major components. The quotation suggests less than adequate regard to supply problems such as might result from surrendering control over the aircraft programme to the military and leaving it to civilian agencies to cope with shortages in materials and components. With America's vast resources and greater flexibility it is likely also that the planners felt it more important to maintain the momentum of expansion than to check at prospective shortages which they could not investigate in detail.

The flexibility, however, was not unlimited. The ASU Report says nothing about the length of time it took to re-schedule components and on this Jewkes's comments in the summer of 1943 are of some interest. To get agreement that Packard should introduce 1500 extra single stage Merlin engines into their programme in place of two-stage engines, he commented, would never take less than six to eight weeks and would have to go through twelve different stages before it received the approval of the JAC.[34] Packard had taken sixty days to make the comparatively simple change from Merlin 32s for the Mosquito to Merlin 38s for the Lancaster. From this he drew the conclusion that if the United Kingdom wanted to draw more heavily on American resources – as in his view it should – more thought would have to be given to what could be contracted for well in advance, with no scope for a change of mind. But as he complained, in too many instances, which he went on to exemplify, attempts to obtain supplies from America were nullified by just such changes of mind. The United States was too often treated as 'a shop to be entered at any time' instead of 'as a farm to be harvested'.[35]

Apart from Jewkes's comment on the Packard programme (which is in keeping with his views on the American propeller programme) nothing survives, in the literature I have been able to track down, on changes in programme and how they were made, the balancing of risks and provision for uncertainties that lie at the heart of programme-making. Nor has it been possible to find anything from the American point of view on the problems of coordination with British production planning. Even those on the inside, like Colonel Lowe, are more concerned with the formal structure, procedure and relationships than with what it was like to handle the planning of 9000 aircraft a month and what problems it presented.

The Engine Programme

In the vast literature on American aircraft production in the last World War there is hardly a mention of the engine programme, the cornerstone of aircraft planning in Britain. Similarly there is no discussion of Embodiment Loan and how government purchase and planning of major components fits in with the production intentions of aircraft manufacturers. Coordination, although a favourite word, is used almost exclusively in relation to aircraft and aircraft requirements, hardly ever to aircraft components. There is plenty of talk of 'critical shortages' but these represent a *failure* of planning if allowed to occur and the efforts to cope with shortages have more in common with the efforts of 'chasers' in British aircraft factories than with the efforts to amend programmes so as to avoid shortages.

It is only when we study *British* sources for changes in the Packard Merlin programme, or the changeover from the Allison to the Packard Merlin engine that transformed the performance of the Mustang that we are alerted to the abiding problem of coordinating the component parts of the aeroplane. But I have looked in vain for other examples or for some account in the literature of the difficulties posed by competing claims for an engine undergoing rapid development or a changeover from one type of engine to another in a front-line aircraft.

One way of getting a general impression of major shortages is to look at a rather crude measure of coordination: the divergences in rates of growth between aircraft, engines and propellers. One would expect, for example, that engines and propellers would be produced in roughly the same quantity since there were no jet-propelled aircraft in production. Some divergence might result from foreign orders for engines unaccompanied by orders for propellers. But in practice orders for Packard engines and Nash propellers went together. The final column in Table 8.2 shows that over the whole period engines exceeded propellers by 15 per cent and that the excess fell steadily until 1945. This picture is consistent with an acute shortage of propellers in 1940–42 and with a tendency to more ample provisioning of spare engines than spare propellers. The decline in the ratio of engines to aircraft is more puzzling in view of the expansion in the programme for four-engine heavy bombers. It is consistent with Jewkes's comments on the high proportion of spare engines in 1942 but only if there was an equally high proportion in 1941 and an even higher one in 1940. Allowance must, however, be

TABLE 8.2   *US output of aircraft, engines and propellers, 1940–45*

	Aircraft	Engines	Propellers	Engines per aircraft	Engines per propeller
1940	6086	22667	14290	3.72	1.59
1941	19433	58181	39123	2.99	1.49
1942	47836	138089	106136	2.89	1.30
1943	85898	227116	213937	2.64	1.06
1944	96318	256911	243741	2.67	1.05
1945	46001	109651	96690	2.38	1.13
Total 1940–45	301572	822615	713717	2.73	1.15

SOURCE: Craven and Cate, op. cit., p. 350.

made for the need to produce engines some months in advance of aircraft. Engine requirements will therefore be moderated once aircraft production starts to flatten out as in 1944 and will be relatively high when aircraft output is accelerating.

THE PROCESS OF EXPANSION

In mobilising resources to meet Presidential targets, America had the great advantage of ample capacity not fully employed. In 1940 GNP was still only 9 per cent higher than in 1929 and unemployment was a little under 15 per cent. Once at war, it was possible for the United States, as it was for no other belligerent to expand military and civil production simultaneously.

Even so, the aircraft industry's base was a narrow one. In 1940 there were 41 recognised aeroplane, aero-engine and propeller plants with less than 14 million square feet of space. Only 10 per cent of the work done was sub-contracted. By the end of 1944, floor space had increased to nearly 170 million square feet, 35 per cent of the work was sub-contracted, and the output of military aircraft, under 200 a month in 1939, had grown to over 9000 a month. Between 1940 and 1944 engine production grew twelvefold and propeller production seventeenfold. Since output had almost reached peak in 1943, nearly all the expansion was accomplished in three years.

The process of expansion had begun in 1940–41. After June 1940 new plants were authorised and new production goals were agreed which largely anticipated the targets set by the President at the beginning of 1942. By that time the government had already become committed to new construction projects totalling $1 billion. In May 1942 the President accepted a programme for 500 four-engine bombers per month and before Pearl Harbor the programme had been doubled. Only a fraction of the capacity of the automobile industry was then in use, partly because of resistance by the aircraft manufacturers to proposals to bring them in and partly because of the reluctance of automobile firms to convert their plants. But they had already enlarged their facilities for aero-engine manufacture and were undertaking to manage new plants in course of construction.

The expansion programme was eventually to involve the government in an outlay on new aircraft plants of 89 per cent of their total cost of $3.84 billion. Only a fifth of this related to plants authorised after 1942.[36] By the end of that year it was clear that there would be sufficient capacity to meet the production programme and indeed in 1943 few companies made full use of the capacity available. Improvements in production technique reduced the need for the floor space and equipment originally planned.

There was also a considerable interval before the new capacity came into production. 'Not one of the new plants authorized after June 1940 and designed to build combat aircraft had yet produced a single plane and none of them was destined to get into full production before 1943.'[37] An airframe plant on a greenfield site took an average of 24 months for fighters and 40 months for B-29 bombers to get into full production, and even additions to existing factories took 21 months.[38]

The process of expansion was at its most hectic in 1942. In the first six months following Pearl Harbor, when contracts amounting to $20 billion were already outstanding, contracts were placed to the value of over $100 billion, which was more than the United States had managed to produce in the best pre-war year.[39] It was clear that something had to be done to spread the load and that sufficient labour was not available in the vicinity of the existing plants. There were no new entrants into the industry, the latest arrivals, Northrop and McDonnell, having started in 1939. Three different avenues of expansion were followed: plant extensions, sub-contracting and licensing. Of the total airframe weight produced during the war it has been estimated that 10 per cent was licensed, 35 per cent sub-contracted and the remaining 55 per cent produced by prime contractors in existing, extended or newly constructed plants.[40]

The concentration of orders on a small number of companies was a source of concern throughout. There were complaints in February 1942 that, out of the hundreds of thousands of plants in America (there were a quarter of a million *companies*), 56 manufacturing establishments had been awarded three-quarters of all Army and Navy contracts. Between June 1940 and September 1944 over one-third of the prime contracts, totalling $175 billion, went to the top 33 corporations. Moreover when the large corporations placed sub-contracts, most of them went to other large corporations employing over 500 workers. When a group of 250 of the largest contractors sub-contracted about one-third of the value of their prime war contracts, three-quarters of the sub-contracts were with other large concerns. [41]

There were two reasons for the complaints levelled against this concentration of orders. One was that it denied small companies a chance to contribute to the war effort. The second was that it made for a less competitive structure of industry and a greater danger of dominance by giant corporations. Firms with over 10 000 employees accounted for over 13 per cent of all manufacturing workers in December 1939 and 30 per cent in December 1944 by which time manufacturing output had doubled. [42] Congress responded to the complaints by establishing a Smaller War Plants Corporation responsible to the War Production Board and great efforts were made to make fuller use of small manufacturers. Not surprisingly, however, these efforts had limited results. Out of contracts placed in 1943 only 3.5 per cent by value went to firms with under 100 workers and a further 9 per cent to manufacturers employing between 100 and 500 workers.

Given the need for rapid expansion and the complexity of aircraft manufacture, it was only to be expected that the US government should place its orders with the larger corporations and leave them to sub-contract as far as possible. The managerial load on the aircraft companies was extremely heavy and imposed limits on the number of suppliers with whom they could deal. The smaller companies had skilled labour that it was important to bring into play but the productive facilities at their disposal were not well adapted to most aircraft work and could be used only for the smaller items and simpler operations. This was particularly true when aircraft were still made by hand and the changeover to line production was still in progress. What offered a more likely prospect to small firms was work for the larger sub-contractors. It is not clear from the figures how much of the sub-contracting was passed to sub-sub and sub-sub-sub contractors, as happened in Britain. But that would have been the natural way to devolve work on the smaller firms.

Three other points are relevant. First of all, so far as government orders changed the structure of industry in favour of large concerns, the cessation of these orders when the war was over would go far to restore the pre-war structure. A prominent position in the aircraft industry in wartime could not be assumed to be a major competitve advantage in peacetime. Secondly, the rapid expansion of the industry was heavily dependent on the provision of government finance for the new facilities required. Without that finance the bulk of the new capacity would not have been created or not created in time. But since most of the finance inevitably went into large new plants such as the big aircraft assembly factories, they had to be managed by corporations that were *ipso facto* large. It was much easier and (what really mattered) quicker for the government to make a limited number of large-scale additions to capacity than to finance the expansion of a mass of small companies. Thirdly, so far as the government could use resources outside the aircraft industry it was to the automobile industry that it inevitably turned first, precisely because they were large corporations with ample premises and equipment, an enormous reservoir of skilled labour and management familiar with mass production techniques and the assembly of a multiplicity of component parts.[43]

The Contribution of the Automobile Industry

The contribution of the American automobile industry was very important and is in striking contrast to German experience. In Germany the motor industry never produced complete aircraft, major firms like Volkswagen and Opel were greatly under-utilised and the industry as a whole brought to the aircraft industry only a fraction of its potential usefulness.[44] In the United Kingdom by contrast, contractors outside the aircraft industry and mainly in the automobile industry, produced 45 per cent of the heavy bombers, two-thirds of the light bombers and 22 per cent of total wartime production of airframes. In the United States these proportions were even larger.[45] Ford alone, in its Willow Run plant, produced at peak the equivalent in structure weight of half German aircraft production, also at peak.[46] The industry also produced about half the total output of aero-engines, mainly from new facilities, and a substantial propor-tion – over a quarter – of the propellers. It formed the largest single group of suppliers to the aircraft industry and also provided, by conversion, an enormous number of machine tools (66 per cent of its stock) for aircraft and engine manufacture.

Not that aircraft production was as easy as the automobile manufacturers supposed. There was too ready an assumption in 1940 that the production techniques of the industry would be readily adaptable to aircraft manufacture.[47] Walther Reuther, the Union leader, had a plan to make 500 fighters a day and Henry Ford showed equal confidence that he could undertake large-scale manufacture without more ado.

But what had first to be adapted was not the technique of the automobile industry but the technique of the aircraft industry.[48] The processes it was accustomed to using were those that went with small-scale production: handmade production in lots or batches, using parts that were, in consequence, not interchangeable and requiring special fitting during assembly. Since there were no adequate jigs and fixtures it was necessary to rely on a high degree of skill on the part of the fitters. With small volume and frequency of design-changes the key characteristics in fabrication and assembly of sheet metal parts were simplicity, inexpensiveness and flexibility. For volume production by the automobile industry it was necessary to move to line production – a technique unknown in the aircraft industry in 1940 – with a controlled flow of production through work areas in which balanced operations are laid out in a progressive sequence.[49]

Moving to line production in aircraft assembly not only made special demands on factory space and heavy investment in tooling but required production studies, extensive redrawing and some redesign of aircraft parts. The first aircraft firm to adopt line production was Consolidated, combining it with labour training and the contracting out of sub-assemblies. Line production was also used in the four large new assembly plants at Fort Worth, Kansas, Omaha and Tucson which the government built in 1941 for operation by the airframe companies with parts and sub-assemblies supplied by automobile firms. At the Convair factory at Fort Worth, for example, 40 per cent of the fabrication on bombers and transports was prepared by subcontractors while feeder shops produced bulkheads, electrical harnesses, sheet metal sub-assemblies and most of the upholstery for B-24s.[50] Of the total man-hours in the construction of aircraft at the four factories only 22 per cent went on final assembly.[51]

The most celebrated new airframe factory was the Ford plant at Willow Run (operated in conjunction with Douglas and Consolidated) which took so long to come into production that it came to be called 'Will It Run?'. There were indeed problems in moving from hand production to line production but Ford hoped to expand the rate of production within a year from zero to 490 per month, i.e. to more than the contemporary rate of production of heavy bombers in Britain, reached after many years. Ford did in the end produce 1315 B-24s in 1943 and 5476 more in 1944–45 – a volume that would have been impossible with job shop production methods.[52]

The automobile industry played an equally important role in aero-engine production. Here there was not the same conflict in approach and the adjustment to aero-engine production was easier. There was, however, little or no saving in time in converting existing floor space as compared with putting up a new factory since the time taken up by tooling was longer still. There were, moreover, considerations of labour supply, housing and transport that might be of even more importance. Manufacturers might prefer to concentrate within easy reach of the parent factory but the government had to think of dispersal to underemployed areas for the sake of maximum production. As will be seen from Table 8.3, floor space for engine manufac-

TABLE 8.3   *Growth of floor space in US aircraft industry, 1939–44*
(million square feet)

	Airframes	Engines	Propellers	Total
1 Jan 1939	7.5	1.7	0.25	9.5
1 Jan 1940	9.6	3.0	0.49	13.1
1 Jan 1941	17.9	6.5	1.05	25.5
June 1943	77.5	31.8	5.24	114.6
Dec 1943	110.4	54.2	6.84	171.4
Dec 1944	103.0	54.9	7.89	165.7

SOURCE: Craven and Cate, op. cit., p. 318.

ture grew far more than for aircraft assembly: from less than a quarter of that area in 1939 engine floor space had grown to half by the end of 1943. The largest plant in the aircraft industry in terms of floor space was not Willow Run but the Dodge engine factory in Chicago costing $175 million and covering nearly 6.5 million square feet – as much as the entire area occupied by aero-engine manufacture at the beginning of 1941.

Development

As in other countries wartime production was of aeroplanes designed before the war.[54] Many, including the B-24, B-29, P-47 and P-51 were designed as late as 1938–40 and in that respect the United States had an advantage over other countries. The prototype of the P-51 (the Mustang) was turned out in 117 working days. From design to the 500th aircraft took only two to two and a half years for the P-47 and P-51 (fighters) and about four years for the B-24 and B-29 (bombers). This was fast going by the standards of other countries and distinctly faster than with aircraft designed before 1938. It reflected the importance US manufacturers attached to development. A single large firm like Consolidated employed a design staff almost as large as that employed by the entire British aircraft industry.[55]

While large design staffs made it easier to introduce modifications, line production made them far more costly. The Americans were very much alive to the penalty in lost production that modifications involved. As Sorensen of Ford commented: 'the most annoying feature of our bomber operation was change in design during production. We would agree on freezing a design, then be ready to go ahead. Back from the fighting fronts would come complaints or suggestions regarding certain features; and the plane designers came through with alterations in design with no consideration for the production programme'.[56]

The government was at first hesitant, ordering deferment of research and development that might interfere with the production of existing types. Opinion swung the other way in 1941 and then swung back again after Pearl Harbor. A way out was found in the use of modification centres using at first the maintenance shops of civil air lines and adding to them new factories adjacent to assembly plants. The system was said to have originated from the example of British efforts to adapt American aircraft to use British equipment. It was costly in its use of skilled manpower and reversion to handicraft methods but was judged to be successful in the lift it gave to new production.

Productivity

American aircraft production provided a striking example of the economies of large-scale production combined with 'learning by doing'. Although 'every model became larger and more complex as more armour, armament, communications equipment and fuel tanks were installed', the average unit cost fell progressively. The man-hours on a B-17 bomber, for example, fell from 54 800 in 1942 to 18 600 in 1944; and between the 400th and 1000th aircraft the construction time on B-29 bombers was halved.[57] It has also been claimed that, in spite of a 50 per cent increase in earnings between the early months of 1941 and the summer of 1944, labour costs had fallen by two-thirds.[58] The figures on which this is based are, however, suspect and in conflict with other more plausible estimates showing on the average a doubling of output per man-day between 1941 and 1944.[59] Such an increase is well above the improvement in productivity recorded in any other country. Germany's best performance was in 1943 when output per man-day was not much more than half America's best and 30 per cent higher than in 1941. Japan's labour productivity was about half Germany's.

Spare parts

Like other countries the United States found difficulty in maintaining an adequate supply of spare parts. The pre-war practice was to place orders concurrently with orders for new planes up to 25 per cent by value of the latter. In 1939, however, General Arnold took a chance on getting funds for additional spares promptly and pressed for concentration in the meantime on complete new aircraft. Unfortunately the necessary funds were not available when needed and a spares shortage developed in 1941 with 30 per cent of planes in a typical unit out of commission for lack of spares. First claim on spares at that time went to the RAF for American aircraft used in combat and American squadrons had to cannibalise new deliveries for the spares they needed.[60]

Although General Arnold now sought to insist on concurrent delivery of spares, manufacturers still gave priority to new production and continued to do so after Pearl Harbor. An alarming number of planes were grounded and in 1942 engines had to be removed from aircraft for shipment to overseas bases. The Air Force expressed willingness to delay delivery of finished aircraft if this would add to the supply of spares and by the middle of the year were pleading for spares whatever the effect on new production. Early in 1943 however the JAC was urging strong measures to cut down the supply of spares, especially large extrusions for airframes. Yet in August 1943 the manufacturers of B-29s were asked to cut their programme by up to 200 planes in order to improve the flow of spares to aircraft in active service.

Shortages (and surpluses) continued for the rest of the war in spite of all efforts to improve the procedure. The Air Force was never able to devise an effective system for calculating requirements and planning production in time to prevent the critical shortages that occupied the Aircraft Scheduling Unit.

CONCLUSION

The most impressive aspects of American experience are the boldness of the planning and the speed of execution. The government, once decided on rearmament, was whole-hearted in the goals it set and in the scale on which it financed the necessary facilities. American industry, for its part, was swift and resourceful in making full use of those facilities, demonstrating the flexibility and managerial skills that are bred in a competitive economy.

It was also, in wartime at least, a cooperative economy. There was cooperation between government and industry. Within the aircraft industry there was cooperation between manufacturers normally pursuing their own private interest and intent on guarding from their rivals the secrets of their success. First on the West Coast and then on the East, War Production Councils were formed by the large aircraft companies to exchange experience and help to overcome each other's difficulties. Every major firm ended up making someone else's planes in addition to its own.

It is true that the United States enjoyed many advantages: remoteness from the battlefront and the absence of bombing and other disturbances to well-planned production that this implied; ample space for large and efficient units without need to seek safety in dispersal; under-employed manpower and capacity on the grand scale; a vast engineering industry, including much the largest automobile industry in the world, with unique experience of mass production. This may help to explain but does not belittle the American achievement.

It is true also that there were some limitations to American success. Where America excelled was in the production of large planes – heavy bombers and transports – and the thrust of the aircraft programme was towards such planes. This went happily with a strategy that hoped to bring the enemy to submit by bombing alone, without invasion of the European continent. But it went less happily with a comparative neglect of fighters, especially long range and night fighters.

Planning, too, was less successful in detail than it was in terms of broad strategy. As we have seen, it suffered from the usual imperfections of coordination, with shortages and surpluses, conflicts of authority, delays, muddle and waste. But there is no reason to suppose that it suffered more than other countries from these imperfections.

Notes

INTRODUCTION: PLANNING AIRCRAFT PRODUCTION

1. There are some files which I preserved and deposited in the 1980s. These are in PRO AVIA 10. A sackful of papers which I handed over in 1949 after receiving suitable assurances appears to have been lost.
2. M. M. Postan, *British War Production*, HMSO and Longmans Green, 1952; J. D. Scott and R. Hughes, *The Administration of War Production*, HMSO and Longmans Green, 1955; M. M. Postan, D. Hay and J. D. Scott, *The Design and Development of Weapons* HMSO and Longmans Green, 1964.
3. E. Devons, *Planning in Practice*, Cambridge University Press, 1950.

CHAPTER 1: PLANNING AND COORDINATION

1. Devons, *Planning in Practice*, pp. 14–15.

CHAPTER 2: PLANNING IN MAP

1. An aircraft programme *was* issued under Beaverbrook in October 1940 (the Hennessy programme) but it bore little relation to actual performance. For example, it called for an output of 2143 combat aircraft in December 1941, while the actual output in that month was only 1104 combat aircraft. For heavy bombers the corresponding figures were 205 and 55.
2. These were: Jewkes himself, David Champernowne, Ely Devons, Walter Hagenbuch, Frank Paish, Brian Tew and myself. In all, the staff totalled a little under thirty.
3. As Ely Devons pointed out in his review of Postan (reprinted in *Planning and Economic Management*, p. 60): 'Early in 1942 was the crucial period. It was then not too late to change production plans. . . . But heavy bombing was the sacred cow of British strategy, and the programme went on virtually without question'. A switch to Mosquitoes was suggested in the middle of 1943 but by then it was too late.
4. Devons, *Planning in Practice*, p. 133.
5. The last three paragraphs are from a note I prepared in April 1944.
6. Nevertheless not a single copy of any issue seems to have survived.
7. Devons, *op. cit.*, pp. 161–2.
8. Devons, *op. cit.*, p. 178; see also his discussion of 'the limits of co-ordination' in 'The problem of co-ordination in aircraft production', first published in *Lessons of the British War Economy* (ed. D. N. Chester) and reprinted in his posthumous *Planning and Economic Management* (ed. A. Cairncross).

9.   For the sources of confusion see Chapter 5, 'Propeller planning'.
      Apart from the conflict between contracts and programmes, there was
      confusion among the suppliers as to what was meant by a programme.
      When I visited Rotol's – one of the two main propeller manufacturers
      – in 1942 and asked to see their production programme, they produced
      what I identified as the statement of requirements sent to them by MAP.
      This was a translation of the current aircraft programme into propeller
      requirements, set back two months and with a 20 per cent allowance
      for spares added all the way along. It bore no relation to the current
      level of production but it was no doubt used in procuring materials.

10.   J. D. Scott and R. Hughes, *The Administration of War Production*,
      p. 396. Even the 'heavy bomber' programme, according to Sir Wilfrid
      Freeman, was decided 'by asking firms what they could produce and
      then adding a percentage' (Freeman to Cripps, 3 November 1942, in
      PRO AVIA 9/9).

11.   Sinclair to Llewellyn, 9 October 1942, in PRO AVIA 9/9. The July 1942
      programme had shown 950 heavy bombers in those three months; actual
      production was 684. Llewellyn ceased to be Minister a few weeks later.

12.   Devons, *op. cit.*, ch. VI, especially pp. 118–24. Only eight per cent of
      the labour employed on work for MAP worked for main aircraft
      contractors.

13.   The argument is more fully developed by Devons in 'The problem of
      coordination in aircraft production' (*Papers on Planning and Econo-
      mic Management*, pp. 37–44).

14.   The point is developed in Devons, 'The problem of coordination in
      aircraft production' (*Planning and Economic Management*, pp. 52–4).

15.   Jewkes, 'Changes in the Production Programme', 12 April 1942, in
      PRO AVIA 10/381.

16.   'Shortages of Aluminium and Light Alloys', EGS(40)1 in PRO CAB
      72/24, 7 June 1940. This was based on the report of a sub-committee
      (on Air Services) of the Select Committee on National Expenditure.

17.   'The Future of Aircraft Production', memorandum by the Minister of
      Aircraft Production, PR(43)98, 10 November 1943, in PRO CAB 87/13.

18.   Only 57 Warwick bombers were ever made and about the same
      number of Buckinghams. The interested reader will find a record of
      the cumulative production of each and every type of aircraft from 1939
      to 1945 in PRO AVIA 10/311. No less than 27 marks of Spitfire and 18
      marks of Mosquito were manufactured and 42 marks of British-made
      Merlin engines.

19.   For the growth of the MAP labour force see Table 6.3, p. 111, and
      Figure 2.1, p. 9.

20.   Meeting of War Cabinet on 14 August 1944.

21.   I may be mistaken in saying that the programme assumed an end to the
      war with Germany by 30 June. Cripps told the Cabinet in October that
      it was based on the indefinite continuation of the war. My recollection
      is that we allowed a further eighteen months for continuing hostilities
      against Japan.

22.   'The Aircraft Programme', Memorandum by the Minister of Aircraft
      Production, WP(44)572, 14 October 1944 in PRO CAB 66/54.

CHAPTER 3: ORGANISATION

1. Bridges to Rowlands, 1 September 1941, in PRO AVIA 15/3677. Before the war, Jewkes had been Professor of Economics at the University of Manchester and some years after the war became Professor of Economics at the University of Oxford.
2. At one point he told the Permanent Secretary that unless the Minister (at that time, Llewellyn) would protect him from foolish enquiries from outside and relieve him of the need to draft letters which were subsequently spoiled in the rewriting, he would be obliged to move to another job.
3. See below, p. 90.
4. For a fuller discussion of the organisation of the Ministry see Scott and Hughes, op. cit., ch. XIV and Appendix 3, and Devons, op. cit., p. 13.
5. PRO AVIA 15/3677.
6. PRO AVIA 10/379.
7. For the similar case of Merlin crankshafts where a new factory would have been needed to meet an unreal shortage, see Air Commodore Banks, *I Kept No Diary*, (Airlife Publications, 1978) p. 147.
8. These and other details will be found in PRO AVIA 10/398.
9. The problem is reviewed in D. A. Parry, 'The Spares Problem' in PRO CAB 102/52. Indications of the supply of spare parts from leading aircraft firms as a percentage of total output are given for the years 1942–45 in Table VII, 'Statistical Review 1939–45' (PRO AVIA 10/311).
10. Rolls not only maintained close contact with the aircraft firms which they supplied. They also had representatives with the squadrons who reported back to them on experience in combat operations, so allowing Rolls to make prompt use of the latest information in their engine development plans. In this respect Rolls were at an advantage over German aero-engine firms whose information had to be routed through the Air Ministry.
11. In October 1943 Cripps told the Prime Minister that 280 modifications had been made to the Lancaster since April 1941 at a cost of 2000 man-hours per aircraft, and 140 modifications to the Spitfire IX in a little over a year at a cost of 1000 man-hours per aircraft. Modifications to Catalinas, which the Americans flew without modifications, cost 3000 man-hours. In all, 6.3 million man-hours had gone on modifications to these three types of aircraft since they came into service.
12. Not that we were unaware of the Lancaster's virtues. I noted in March 1942 that so far not a single Lancaster had been lost over Germany. What interested us as laymen was that the Lancaster was such a success when no one had been able to predict it. It emerged from the two-engined Manchester and its over-stressed wings might have been expected to tell against its success.
13. Overy (in *The Air Way*, p. 123) points out that the bombing of Germany did limit their aircraft production through damage and dispersal, large numbers of finished aircraft were destroyed on the ground, plans to produce 80 000 aircraft a year in vast new factories in 1945 had to be abandoned, and the supply of aviation fuel was fatally

reduced. It is true, as he contends, that bombing destroyed Germany's freedom to plan war production without interruption and achieve a smooth flow of war supplies. But only a limited proportion of the damage to production was brought about by the *area* bombing on which most of the night bombers were employed.

14. In October 1942 Jewkes told me that when 100 Flying Fortresses (B-17s), escorted by 500 fighters, bombed Germany, the B-17s shot down 50 German aircraft and the fighters only 5. The Flying Fortresses, armed with 13 half-inch guns, could each pump out 600 bullets a minute (or over half-a-million from the 100 Fortresses in the raid) and could outrange the FW190 fighter.

15. Its rated performance with a Merlin 61 was over 430 mph – some claimed 500 mph – at 35 000 ft and Packard expected to be in production with their version of Merlin 61 by January 1943. The two German aircraft had a top speed of about 400 mph at 20 000 ft.

16. In a two-stage engine, air was pumped into the cylinders by two centrifugal blowers, and was thus compressed twice, which gave a much improved performance in the rarified atmosphere of high altitudes. In between the two blowers the air passed through a radiator, the 'intercooler'. The two-stage engine was inappropriate for low-level operations, e.g. torpedo dropping.

17. For a full account of the dilemma in engine programming see Devons, *Planning in Practice*, pp. 193–8, 204–6.

18. Beaverbrook, like Hitler, had an exceptionally good memory for figures. He kept asking for all kinds of statistics as sticks with which to beat us. Some of his requests were distinctly odd. He once asked us for an estimate of the change in the speed of aeroplanes *per man-hour*.

19. Llewellyn to Sinclair, 1 October 1942, in PRO AVIA 9/9.

20. Freeman to Cripps, 3 November 1942 in PRO AVIA 9/9. Cripps wanted no blanket priority but specific requests confined to specific factories.

21. There was also an unintentional cut, since labour allocations were made before the end of the year on the basis of an assumed figure for employment at 31 December. In 1943 this was some 40 000 above the total actually reached.

CHAPTER 4: THE ENGINE PROGRAMME

1. Merlin production in the United Kingdom remained flat at a little under 2400 per month between the last quarter of 1943 and the second quarter of 1944. In November 1943 we were still planning an output of over 2100 for the first quarter of 1945 by which time Packard Merlins were arriving in quantity.

2. There is a full account, on which I have drawn heavily, covering the period up to early 1944 in PRO AVIA 10/376. This was drafted by Ely Devons.

3. His report on the mission is in PRO AVIA 9/40.

4. Australia, however, still pressed for 100 sets of Mustang parts.

5. The early arrivals had faulty connecting rods and had to be sent to Rolls Royce's Glasgow factory for rectification. The Merlin 28 resembled the Merlin 22 rather than the Merlin XX in that they had a two-piece cylinder block which enabled a higher boost to be used. This increased power at take-off and the weight of bombs that could be carried. (D. A. Parry, 'Reciprocating aero-engines and engine accessories', PRO CAB 102/51).
6. Ibid.
7. For example, the Chief Executive feared early in 1943 that the Sabre would be a failure, adding to the burden on Rolls when they were also working on the development of jet engines at Derby. (Parry, op. cit., para. 199).
8. The construction of yet another aero-engine factory had been considered and rejected. There was a managerial limit to the number of units that Rolls could supervise and a problem of assembling the necessary skilled labour.
9. Above, p. 66.
10. Parry, 'Reciprocating Aero-Engines and Engine Accessories: Production and Programmes, 1939–45'. CAB 102/51. The official, according to Air Commodore Banks, was 'a most obstructive individual' and was soon removed.
11. The Centaurus was intended originally as a bomber engine but at bomber speeds its cooling was quite inadequate. Banks complained that no work had been done on designing the complicated ducts needed to convey an air flow round the cylinders. At Typhoon speeds, however, cooling was adequate and when the Typhoon was redesigned as the Tempest to take the Centaurus, the result was a very satisfactory fighter aircraft.
12. There was, I think, a delay in the introduction of the Hercules VI early in 1942 when we had to agree to the manufacture of an extra 800 Hercules XIs.
13. D. A. Parry, *op. cit.*
14. Banks's part in overcoming the development difficulties of the Sabre is described in his *I Kept No Diary*, pp. 134–9.
15. D. A. Parry, *loc. cit.*
16. In Banks's view it was not possible to run a Sabre long on a test bed since it soon broke down when on a firm foundation. Flying it in an aircraft gave you a rather longer run.

CHAPTER 5: PROPELLER PLANNING

1. In this section I have drawn on an admirable war history by D. McKenna in PRO AVIA 46/211. A long account which I prepared in April 1944 from which she quotes has disappeared except for fragments in PRO AVIA 10/390 and a section which I still retain.
2. A spinner is the metal fairing that streamlines the nose of an aircraft engine. It is attached to, and revolves with, the propeller boss. A constant-speed unit is a small hydraulic pump fed by oil from the engine that regulates the pitch of the propeller blades.

3.   D. McKenna, 'Development and Production of Propellers', CAB 102/
      47.
4.   PRO AVIA 10/377.
5.   For some of the problems involved in the use of American propellers
      see Devons, *op. cit.*, pp. 218 *et seq.* The story of Mosquito propellers,
      hardly touched on by Devons, is highly complicated and that of the
      Lancaster only a little less so.

CHAPTER 7: PLANNING AIRCRAFT PRODUCTION IN GERMANY

1.   E. L. Homze, *Arming the Luftwaffe*, University of Nebraska Press,
      1976.
2.   R. J. Overy, 'German Aircraft Production 1939–42', PhD thesis,
      University of Cambridge, 1978.
3.   R. J. Overy, *The Air War*, p. 186. Although I have not found in Overy
      the material I most wanted, it will be evident to the reader how much
      indebted I am to him in what follows for his analysis of German
      experience.
4.   There is a copy of the Report of the Farren Mission in PRO AVIA 10/
      411.
5.   For the early build-up of the Luftwaffe, see Homze, op. cit., and
      Professor W. Deist, *The Wehrmacht and German Rearmament* (Mac-
      millan for St Antony's College, Oxford, 1981).
6.   Homze, op. cit. p. 42.
7.   Ibid., p. 149.
8.   Homze, op. cit., pp.79–81 and 230.
9.   Homze, pp. 223–4.
10.   R. J. Overy, *Goering*, p. 165.
11.   Ibid., p. 169.
12.   Overy, ibid., pp. 153–4.
13.   Ibid. p. 152.
14.   Homze, op. cit., p. 58.
15.   R. J. Overy, op. cit., p. 99.
16.   Ibid., p. 107.
17.   Homze, op. cit., p. 262. This may exaggerate since however much
      overlapping there was in R and D, production of bombers was
      concentrated on Junkers and Heinkel and fighters on Focke-Wulf and
      Messerschmitt.
18.   Homze, op. cit., p. 63.
19.   Ibid.
20.   USSBS, *Aircraft Division Industry Report*, pp. 15–17.
21.   Homze, op. cit., p. 78.
22.   Homze, op. cit., p. 213.
23.   R. J. Overy, *Goering*, p. 159.
24.   Telford Taylor, Preface to Richard Suchenwirth, *Historical Turning
      Points in the German Air Force Effort*, USAF Historical Division, Air
      University, 1959.

25. Ibid.
26. Homze, op. cit., p. 229.
27. R. J. Overy. *The Air War 1939–45*, Europa Publications, London, 1980, p. 7.
28. R. J. Overy, op. cit., p. 120. In 1940 the tonnage of bombs dropped on the United Kingdom was under 37 000 and in 1941 under 22 000. It was not until 1943 that the weight of bombs dropped on Europe was much above 50 000 tons.
29. Suchenwirth, op. cit., p. 54.
30. Overy, op. cit., p. 101–2.
31. Overy, op. cit., p. 116.
32. It is difficult for a non-specialist to follow the changes in industrial structure from 1933 to 1945. Rings go well back into the development of German industry and the significance and pervasiveness of the changes from Junkers' 'complexes' to Milch's 'rings' and Speer's 'commissions' is not very clear. What does stand out is the greater freedom of the 'commissions' to make their own arrangements.
33. Manpower increased by 70 per cent between the spring of 1940 and the beginning of 1942 while between those two years the increase in the number of aircraft produced was 44 per cent.
34. Ibid., p. 138n.
35. USBSS, *The Effects of Strategic Bombing on the German War Economy*, October 1945, p. 154.
36. The figures given by Wagenführ (*Rise and Fall of German War Economy 1939–1945*) show an increase by structure weight from 11.9 in July 1943 to 18.5 in July 1944. Whereas in 1942 and 1943 there was little or no increase above the figure for March (inflated no doubt by seasonal factors) there was a rise of 40 per cent in 1944 between March and July.
37. USSBS, 'The Effects of Strategic Bombing on the Germany War Economy'.
38. The original specification of the Me 262 was for an all-up weight of 4½ tons but in the course of development of the aircraft, this increased to 8 tons, so that extra engine thrust was required. The BMW 003 engine, designed for a 600 kg thrust had not proved satisfactory on the early model and although it proved capable of development to provide up to 1000 kg Messerschmitt switched to the Ju 004 which became available in the middle of 1942. Five different firms were at work on jet development before the war – in striking contrast to the limited development effort in the United Kingdom.
39. Suchenwirth, op. cit., p. 123.
40. A full account of Hitler's part in the development of the Me 262 is given in R. Suchenwirth, op. cit., pp. 119–26.
41. The total number of man hours expended in the designing departments, including the preparation of the production drawings, was about 200 000, the design staff (including jig and tool design) amounting to 370, or more than double normal practice.
42. In view of the importance attached by the Germans to the example of

the He 162 a fuller note is appended based on what I learned on the Farren Mission and drafted in August 1945. (*Appendix*, page 149).

43. Homze, op. cit., p. 228.

44. I prepared this note in August 1945 on the basis of information collected in July as a member of the Farren Mission.

45. I have accepted the dates given to us by Heinkel rather than those given by Schelp of the RLM. Schelp told us that the Heinkel 178 first flew early in 1939 and the Heinkel 280 late in 1939 or at the beginning of 1940.

46. This means that, as we were told by Dr Vogt of Blohm and Voss, the decision to order the Volksjäger from Heinkel *had already been taken* when the leading firms were invited, at five days' notice, to meet the specification. The meeting presided over by Göring on 23 September to decide between the candidates was pure rubber-stamping.

It may be worth pointing out that the planning of aircraft production was the responsibility of Herr Frydag, and that the Chairman of the Entwicklungskommission was Herr Lucht. Herr Frydag was also the Managing Director of Heinkel, the 'winning' firm, and at loggerheads with Messerschmitt, who not only did not compete but actively opposed the whole idea. Herr Lucht had been sacked by Messerschmitt about the beginning of 1944.

CHAPTER 8: PLANNING AIRCRAFT PRODUCTION IN THE UNITED STATES

1. Rae (*Climb to Greatness*, MIT Press, 1968, p. 149) gives a monthly average figure for 1939 of 63 200 for airframes and aero-engines.

2. Craven and Cate, *The Army Air Force in World War II*, vol. VI, Chicago University Press, 1955, p. 263.

3. Rae, op. cit., p. 103.

4. Ibid., p. 122.

5. Ibid., p. 104.

6. F. Walton, *Miracle of World War II*, Macmillan, New York, 1956, p. 355.

7. Rae, op. cit., p. 142; Craven and Cate, *op. cit.*, p. 289.

8. Craven and Cate, op. cit., vol. 6, p. 288.

9. I. B. Holley, *Buying Aircraft: Matériel Procurement for the Army Air Forces*, Office of the Chief of Military History, U.S. Army, Washington, DC, 1964, p. 264.

10. Ibid., p. 266.

11. Holley, op. cit., p. 270.

12. Col. W. S. Lowe, 'British History of the Aircraft Scheduling Unit', Exhibit 17 in PRO CAB 102/36.

13. 'Report by Professor Jewkes on Lyttleton Mission', PRO AVIA 9/40.

14. The peak rate in any month of the war was just over 9000 in March 1944.

15. Report by Professor Jewkes on Lyttelton Mission, PRO AVIA 9/40.

16. Craven and Cate, *op. cit.*, pp. 189, 353.

17. Jewkes, *loc. cit.*

18. Ibid.
19. H. G. Vatter, *The U.S. War Economy in World War II*, Columbia University Press, 1985, p. 62.
20. Donald Nelson, *Arsenal of Democracy*, (Harcourt, Brace, New York, 1946), p. 384.
21. Holley, op. cit., p. 272.
22. PRO CAB 102/36, Exhibits 7, 13 and 17.
23. Ibid., Exhibit 13.
24. Ibid.
25. Ibid., Exhibit 17.
26. British representation on the JAC and ASU reflected the large British stake in American production. In 1941, 68 per cent of all aircraft produced were sent in the months before Pearl Harbor to powers engaged in war with the Axis powers; of the 68 per cent, three-quarters went to the United Kingdom, i.e. over half US output of military aircraft (R. J. Overy, *The Air War*, p. 60). Even when Britain's share of American output had become tiny, the arrangement continued. The United States went to great pains to meet British requirements throughout the war.
27. Col. W. S. Lowe, op. cit., p. 2 of Introduction, May 1945.
28. Craven and Cate, op. cit., p. 341.
29. Ibid., p. 344
30. Walton, op. cit., p. 524.
31. PRO CAB 102/36, Exhibit 13.
32. Holley, op. cit., p. 271
33. PRO CAB 102/36 Exhibit 24.
34. Report on Mission to the USA in July–August 1943 in PRO AVIA 9/40.
35. Jewkes in PRO AVIA 9/40.
36. Craven and Cate, p. 317.
37. Ibid., p. 314.
38. Rae, op. cit., p. 140.
39. Vatter, op. cit., p. 72.
40. Rae, op. cit., p. 122.
41. Vatter, op. cit., p. 60.
42. Ibid., p. 61.
43. As Walton points out, 'the true accomplishment of the industry is the production of 15 000 parts of the automobile, properly scheduled to arrive at the right stations on the moving workbench at the right time' (Walton, op. cit., p. 523).
44. Overy, op. cit., p. 615.
45. Ibid.
46. Craven and Cate, op. cit., p. 330; Overy, loc cit.
47. Rae, op. cit., p. 133.
48. An indication of the difference was that, while a pound of airframe weight cost $5–8, a pound of automobile averaged 20–25 cents (Holley op. cit., p. 523).
49. T. Lilley, 'Conversion to War-time production technique' in *Problems of Accelerating Aircraft Production during World War II*, pp. 119–29 (Boston: Harvard Business School, 1947).

50.   Rae, op. cit., pp. 145–6
51.   Rae, op. cit., p. 135.
52.   There is a good short account of Ford's experience in Holley, op. cit., pp. 518–28.
53.   Craven and Cate, op. cit., p. 345n.
54.   'Almost every American plane used in combat during the Second World War was at least on the drawing boards before the war began' (Rae, op. cit., p. 103).
55.   Cripps to Churchill, November 1943, in PRO AVIA 9/51.
56.   Rae, op. cit., p. 159.
57.   Craven and Cate, op. cit., p. 361. The average weight of American aircraft, excluding spares, rose during the war from 3500 to 11 000 lb, while in the United Kingdom the rise was from 4300 to 8000 lb, and in Germany there was a fall from 7000 lb in 1941 to about 4000 lb in 1944.
58.   Ibid.
59.   Craven and Cate's figures show structure weight of airframes in 1944 as nearly 1½ billion lb and a rise from 21 lb per man-year in 1941 to 96 lb in 1944, while others show only 952 million lb in 1944 and a rise from 1.42 lb per man-*day* in 1941 to 2.76 lb in 1944.
60.   This account is based on Craven and Cate, op. cit., pp. 347ff.

Bibliography

PUBLISHED SOURCES

F. R. Banks, *I Kept no Diary*, Airlife Publications, London, 1978.

D. N. Chester (ed.), *Lessons of the British War Economy*, Cambridge University Press for NIESR, 1951.

W. F. Craven and J. L. Cate, *The Army Airforce in World War II*, Vol VI, Chicago University Press, 1955.

W. Deist, *The Wehrmacht and German Rearmament*, Macmillan for St Antony's College Oxford, 1981.

E. Devons, *Planning in Practice*, Cambridge University Press, 1950.

—— *Planning and Economic Management*, Manchester University Press, 1970.

K. Hancock and M. M. Gowing, *British War Economy*, HMSO and Longmans Green, 1953.

HMSO, *Statistical Digest of the War*.

I. B. Holley, *Buying Aircraft: Matériel Procurement for the Army Airforce*, Office of the Chief of Military History, U.S. Army, Washington, DC, 1964.

E. L. Homze, *Arming the Luftwaffe*, University of Nebraska Press, 1976.

P. Inman, *Labour in the Munitions Industries*, HMSO and Longmans Green, 1957.

T. Lilley, 'Conversion to War-time Production Technique' in *Problems of Accelerating Production during World War II*, Boston: Harvard Business School, 1947.

I. S. Lloyd, *Rolls Royce: The Merlin at War*, Macmillan, 1978.

D. Nelson, *Arsenal of Democracy*, Harcourt Brace, New York, 1946.

R. Overy, *The Air War*, Europa Publications, London, 1980.

R. Overy, *Goering: The 'Iron Man'*, Routledge and Kegan Paul, London, 1984.

H. M. D. Parker, *Manpower*, HMSO and Longmans Green, 1957.

M. M. Postan, *British War Production*, HMSO and Longmans Green, 1952.

M. M. Postan, D. Hay and J. D. Scott, *Design and Development of Weapons*, HMSO and Longmans Green, 1964.

J. B. Roe, *Climb to Greatness: The American Aircraft Industry 1920–1960*, MIT Press, Cambridge, Mass., 1968.

J. D. Scott and R. Hughes, *The Administration of War Production*, HMSO and Longmans Green, 1955.

R. Suchenwirth, *Historical Turning Points in the German Airforce Effort*, U.S.A.F. Historical Division, Air University, 1959.

United States Strategic Bombing Survey, *The Effects of Strategic Bombing on the German War Economy*, 1945.

United States Strategic Bombing Survey, Aircraft Division Report.

H. G. Vatter, *The U.S. War Economy in World War II*, Columbia University Press, 1985.

F. Walton, *Miracle of World War II*, Macmillan, New York, 1956.

C. Webster and N. Frankland, *The Strategic Air Offensive against Germany, 1939–1945*, 4 vols., HMSO, 1961.

UNPUBLISHED SOURCES

E. Devons, Interrogations of Speer, Frydag and Heinkel, June 4–7 1945.
E. Heinkel, 'Jet Fighter Heinkel 162', June 1945.
R. J. Overy, 'German Aircraft Production 1939–42', Cambridge PhD thesis, 1978.
R. Wagenfuhr 'Rise and Fall of German War Economy 1939–1945', 1945.

Papers in the Public Record Office, Kew

1. Ministry of Aircraft Production (AVIA series)
    AVIA 9/40, Reports by Professor Jewkes on visits to the United States.
    AVIA 10/269 Labour Statistics 1942–44.
    AVIA 10/311 MAP Statistical Review
    AVIA 10/375–411 A. K. Cairncross papers.
2. Cabinet Office Historical Series (CAB 102)
    CAB 102/36 W. S. Lowe, The British History of the Aircraft Scheduling Unit.
    CAB 102/47 D. McKenna, Development and Production of Propellers.
    CAB 102/51 D. Parry, Reciprocating Aero-Engines and Engine Accessories: Production and Programmes 1935–45.
    CAB 102/52 Aircraft – the Spares Problem.
    CAB 102/93 Germany's War Effort.

Index